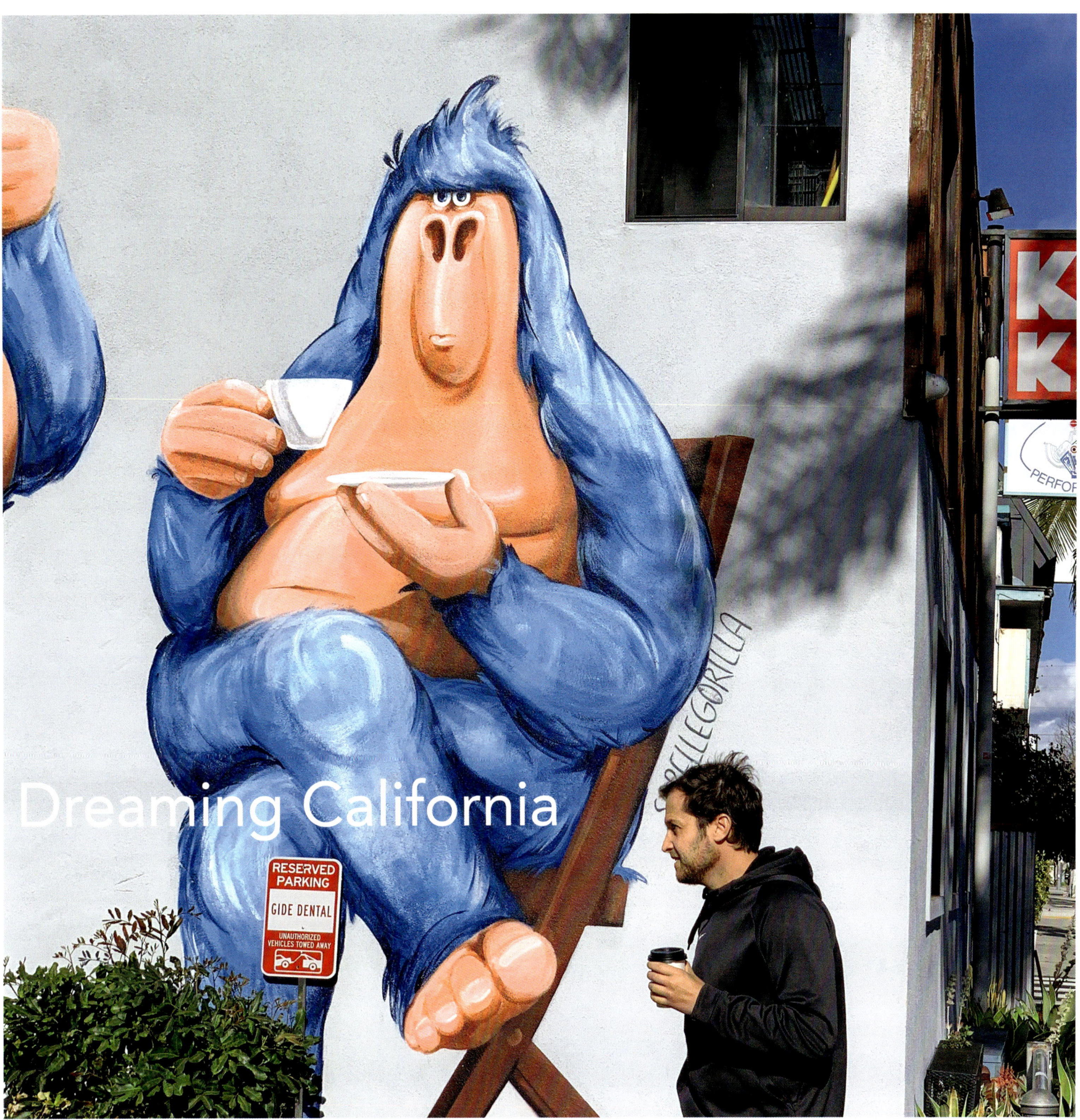
Dreaming California
RESERVED PARKING
GIDE DENTAL
UNAUTHORIZED
VEHICLES TOWED AWAY
SUBTLEGORILLA
K
K
PERFOR

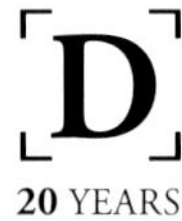

20 YEARS

Cofounders: Taj Forer and Michael Itkoff
Creative Director: Ursula Damm
Copy Editor: Gabrielle Fastman

ISBN: 978-1-954119-20-8

Printed by Ofset Yapimevi, Turkey

Daylight Books
E-mail: info@daylightbooks.org
Web: www.daylightbooks.org

Susan Ressler

Dreaming California

High End, Low End, No End in Sight

*Essays by Larry Lytle
and Mark Rice*

Daylight

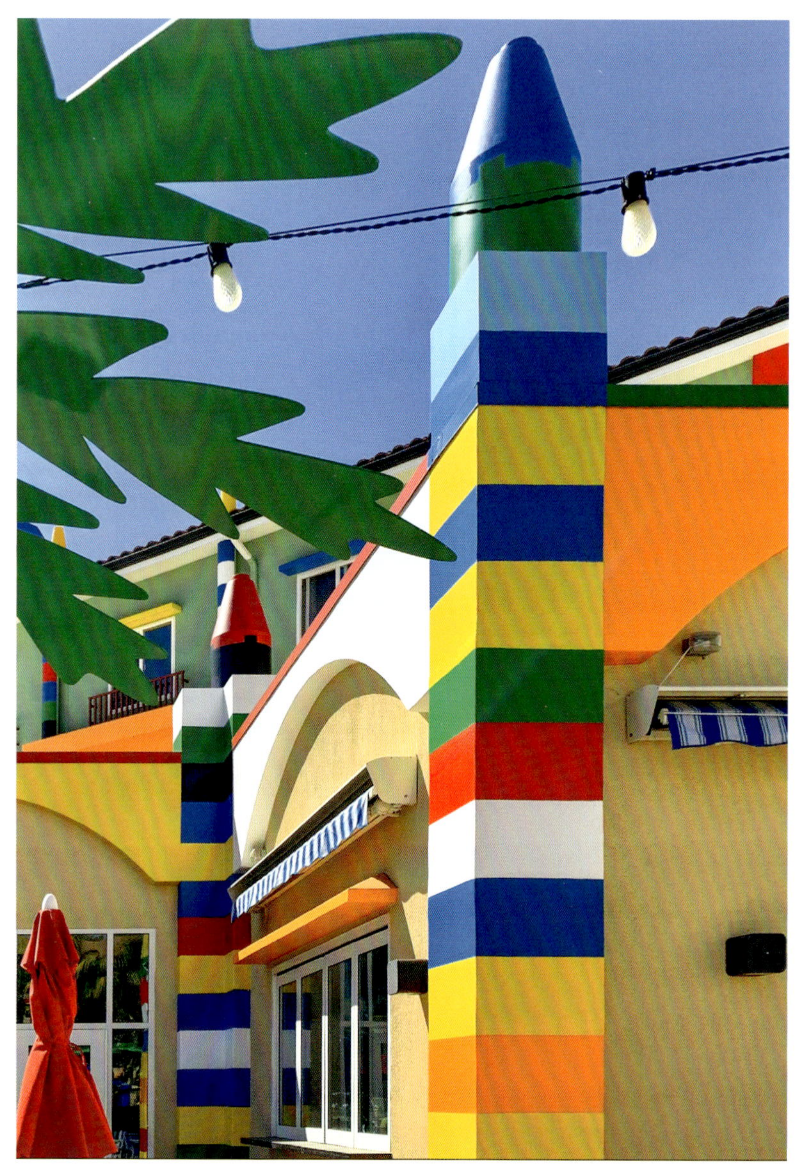

Legoland, Carlsbad

Pizza Parlor, Carson

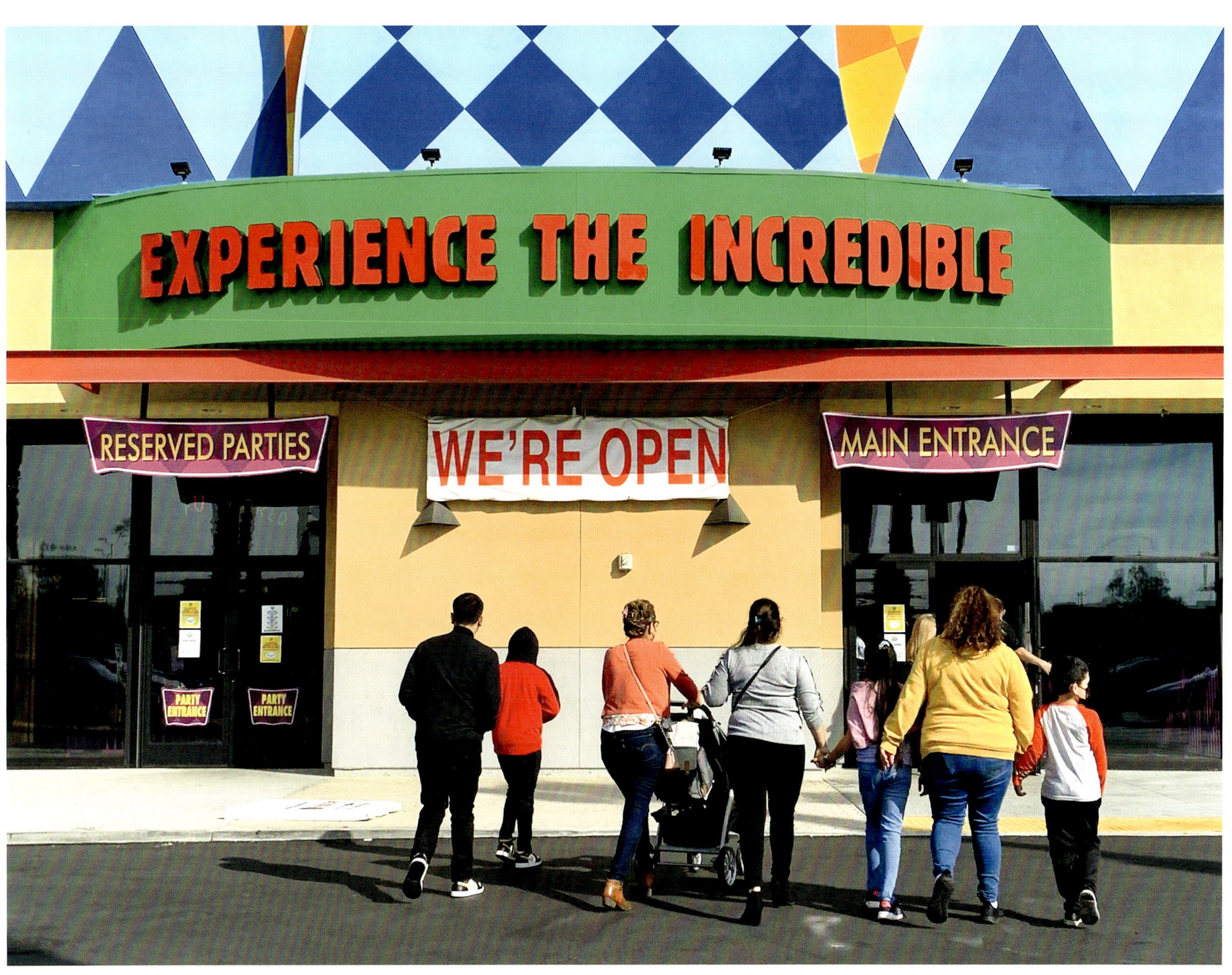

EXPERIENCE THE INCREDIBLE
RESERVED PARTIES
WE'RE OPEN
MAIN ENTRANCE
PARTY ENTRANCE
PARTY ENTRANCE

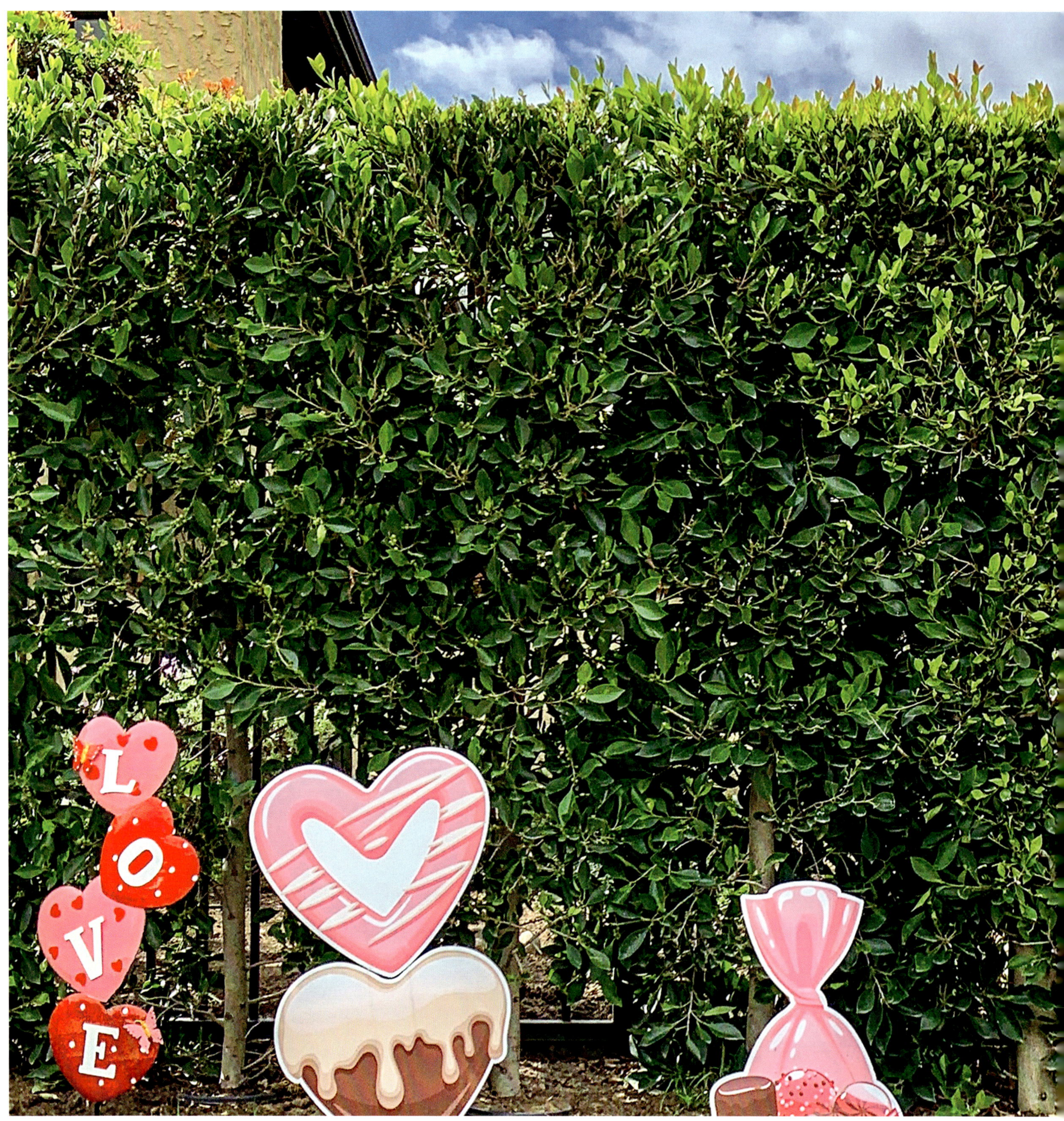
L
O
V
E

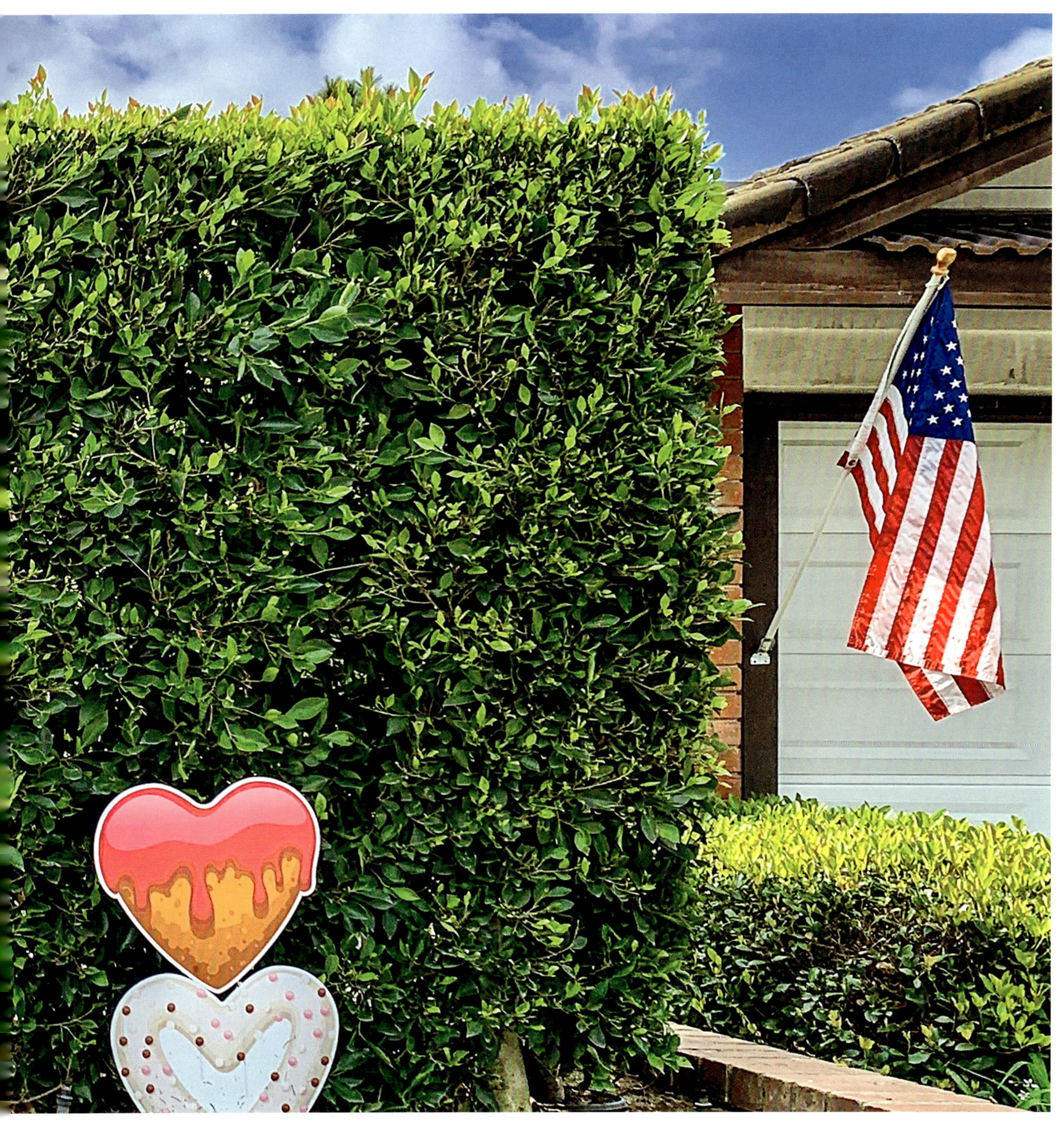

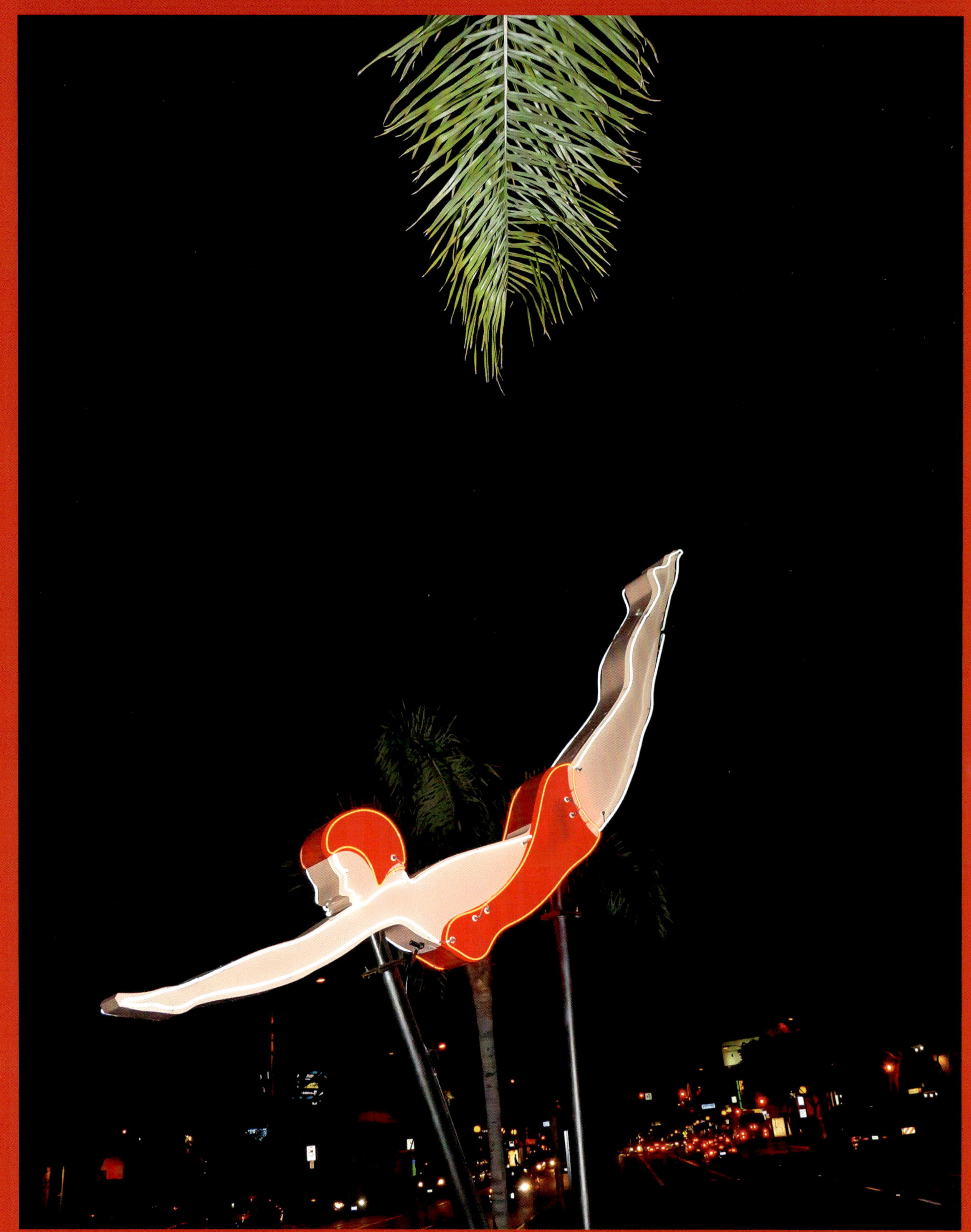

Foreword

In *Dreaming California*, photographed between 2010 and 2022, Susan Ressler returns to Southern California—Los Angeles in particular—this time to examine its architectural landscape and focus on social disparities that extend well beyond the Golden State.

These photographs comprise a meditative series that, in her words, focuses on "wealth, power, privilege, and social inequity." She examines and reimagines outdoor spaces where public and private collide. Ressler views Southern California, and especially Los Angeles, as a bellwether for the rest of the country, noting insightfully that what happens here often presages trends throughout the United States and beyond. California's influence on America has been historically documented in accounts dating back to the mid-nineteenth-century gold rush. The Golden State has typically been lauded as a locus of opportunity and new beginnings, a.k.a. "The California Dream." Ressler makes astute and colorful use of this mythology-cum-reality.

I personally agree with Ressler's assessment. As a native Angeleno (and San Fernando Valley boy), I've witnessed the slide into wealth disparity as post–World War II tract homes, which once were affordable housing for new families, now typically sell for upwards of one million dollars. I've experienced the small-town feel of unique areas in Los Angeles gradually vanish as they fall victim to new development. Zoning has allowed for large destination shopping malls inhabited by national chain retailers and restaurants to displace the diverse, colorful mom-and-pop stores and coffee shops that lined and enlivened local downtown areas. And I've watched the architecture of these new malls transmogrify into something of a cross between a movie set and the Magic Kingdom, a bastard child, if you will, of Hollywood and Disneyland—two industries (and states of mind) that have permeated and come to represent the zeitgeist of the greater Los Angeles area and Southern California. The photographs in *Dreaming California* cleverly show us the culmination of these mutations.

What I find fascinating about Ressler's process is how she goes about documenting the hyperreality that has overrun public space. Her photographs depict a ramped-up shift in consumerism that's spilled over from the malls, where she first began to photograph in 2010, into suburban, "high-end," and "low-end" neighborhoods up to the present: the gushy, brightly colored yard displays that stay up long after the holiday has passed; the two-story expansion of houses built on small lots that overshadow the rest of the neighborhood; the areas of the city where destination malls and shopping areas compete with amusement parks for our dollars—all of it made possible by Southern California's love affair with the automobile, which represents yet another

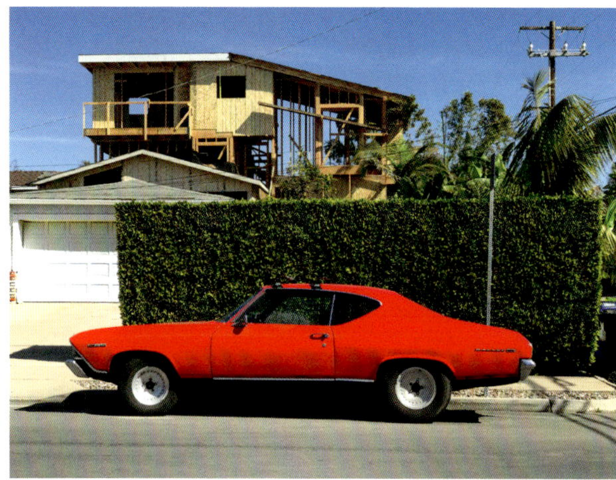

Chevy Malibu and New Construction, Pacific Beach

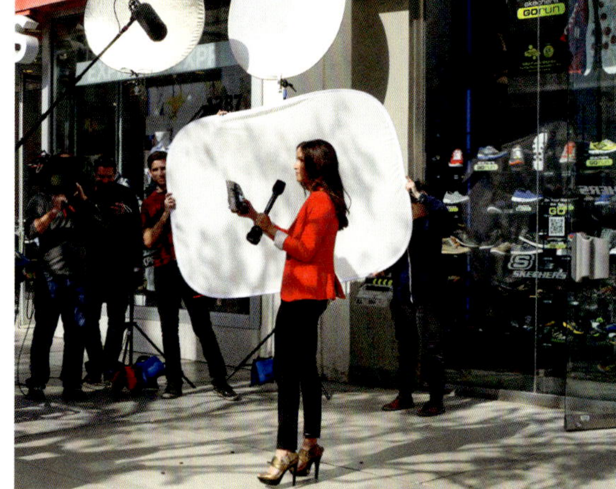

Skechers TV Commercial Shoot, Hollywood

egregious display of consumerism. To live in certain parts of Los Angeles, an expensive car *is* an obligatory symbol of wealth and social status.

Throughout this book we also see the omnipotent presence and influence of the film industry. It's not unusual to come across a street closed off for the making of a movie or TV show, or to watch a crew film a commercial on a sidewalk in a tony neighborhood. Such scenes are woven into the fabric of what Los Angeles has become and how it's perceived, and they are among the reasons why so many tourists visit. The film industry has long played a part in Los Angeles's economy and architecture; it has helped mold the neighborhoods surrounding Hollywood and Beverly Hills, where one can drive through enclaves of fifty-million-dollar homes that butt up against streets lined with tents of the homeless. Just as important, this filmic sensibility inflects many of Ressler's images, where an aura of unreality imbues them with an uncanny and on-point incisive commentary.

One of the many things I appreciate about Ressler's work is that in addition to the facades, she also shows us neighborhoods that have rejected this Disneyfication. Her photographs include urban environs adorned with colorful murals that give expression to a specific community, where vintage signs and storefronts remain in use, even if a bit worse for wear over the years. Ressler commemorates the places in the City of Angels that stubbornly retain their character, areas that somehow manage to evolve holistically, and where comity and hope exist.

Adding to the impact is the amount of detail that Ressler integrates into each photograph. Careful study rewards the attentive viewer—the juxtaposition of signs, banners, window displays, and myriad other background details lend rich visual and thematic context. Multiple themes flow throughout the book—eyes that stare back, solitary figures wandering through film set–like spaces, the ever-present and inescapable advertising that blights most every public arena—symbols of racial and gender inequality, as well as glaring evidence of economic malaise. Ressler's shrewd color palette binds the details and images together. The book leads the viewer through her conceptual narrative, visually linking communities that are exceedingly diverse in a most complex megalopolis, yet cohere in Ressler's lens.

That said, *Dreaming California* is first and foremost an album of stunning photographs. While they conceptually comprise a whole, each image has its own unique point of view. Overall, Ressler's work is inquisitive rather than didactic. Her photographs ask questions rather than proffer polemics. She conveys her own perspective with conviction, but she simultaneously invites viewers to contribute their own assessments regarding what she has deftly rendered in this book.

Though Ressler's scenarios address questions of a sociopolitical nature—consumerism, wealth disparity, racism, sexism, and the like—these photographs are also about the art of photography. Like any artist completely engaged with her medium, she is very aware of how photography functions in the art world. The genres that Ressler is working with are akin to those used by photographers such as Jeff Wall, Cindy Sherman, and even Gregory Crewdson, who all investigate the borderline between reportage and fiction.

As the eminent writer Salman Rushdie observed in *Languages of Truth: Essays 2003–2020* (Random House, 2022), "The truth is not arrived at by purely mimetic means. An image can be captured by a camera or by a paintbrush. A painting of a starry night is no less truthful than a photograph of one: arguably, if the painter is Van Gogh, it's far more truthful, even though less 'realistic.'"

While Ressler doesn't physically stage her photographs, her careful use of composition and color alters and heightens what she records. In her earlier monograph, *Executive Order: Images of 1970s Corporate America* (Daylight, 2018), which utilized black-and-white office interiors (mostly in Los Angeles) to interrogate wealth and power, her geometric compositions generate a sense of sterility. I wrote about this work for *Black & White* magazine when the book was released, noting Ressler's complex compositions, her cool irony and visual puns. The same holds true of *Dreaming California*, where the work often seems staged because it's so clearly seen and finely crafted. The difference is that Ressler now has an empathy for her subjects that's absent in her previous work. Whether it's a homeless person or an African American man with a target on his chest, her photographs enable us to relate in a more compassionate way than when a CEO stands in control behind his desk.

As you consider the photographs in *Dreaming California*, do give them the time they require to fully sink in. Ressler's imagery and concepts are like a mirror; they reflect our contemporary world, revealing the divide between the haves and the have-nots, unabashed consumerism, isolation in the age of easy communication, a constant advertising barrage, and the way in which public spaces have taken cues from movies and amusement parks to entice us to buy more and think less. Susan Ressler has revealed a strange new world, filled with dreams and aspirations. She's asked us to "Experience the Incredible." It's up to us to determine what that means and whether our dreams have spun out of control.

—Larry Lytle

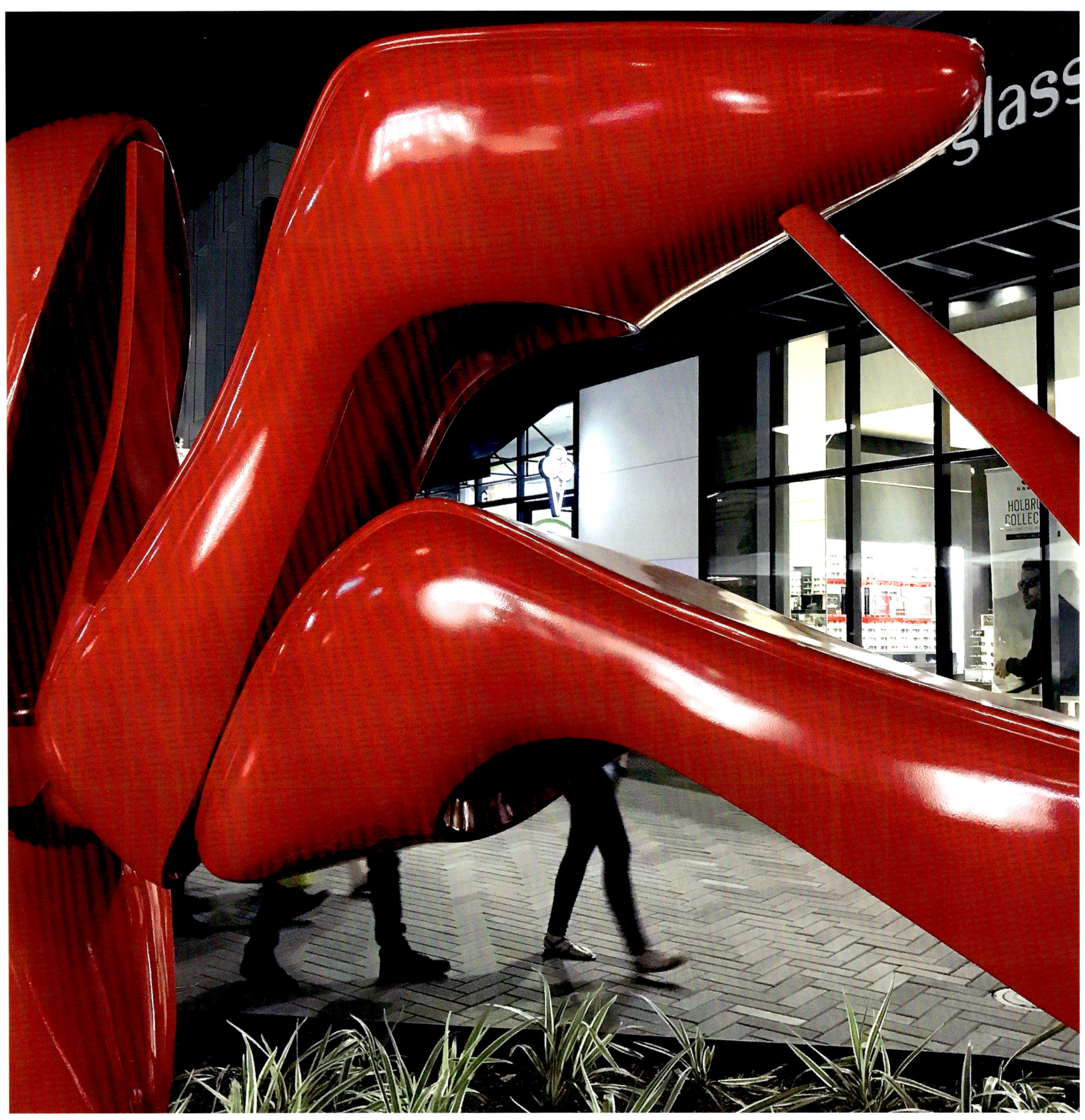

glass
HOLBR
COLLEC

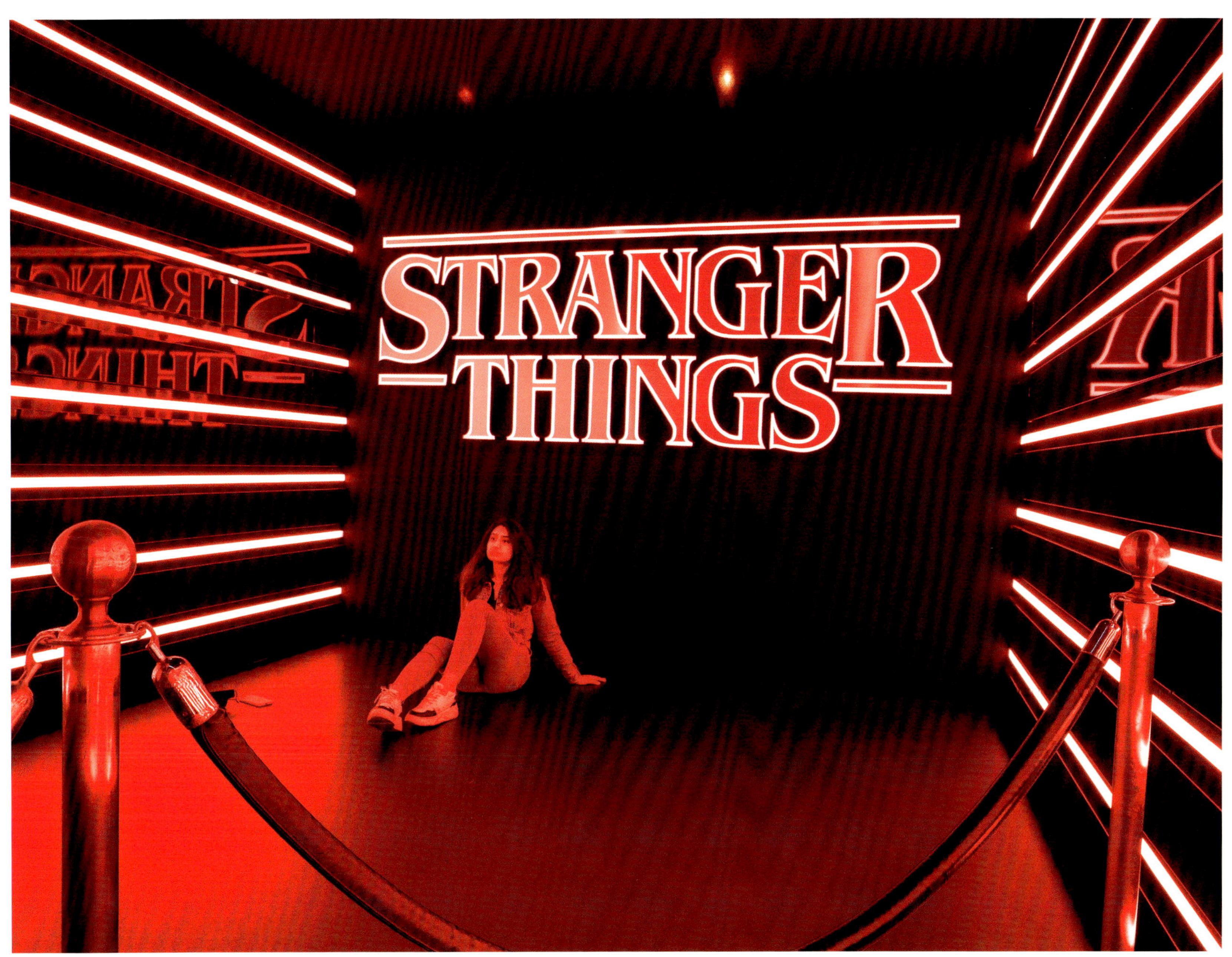
STRANGER
THINGS

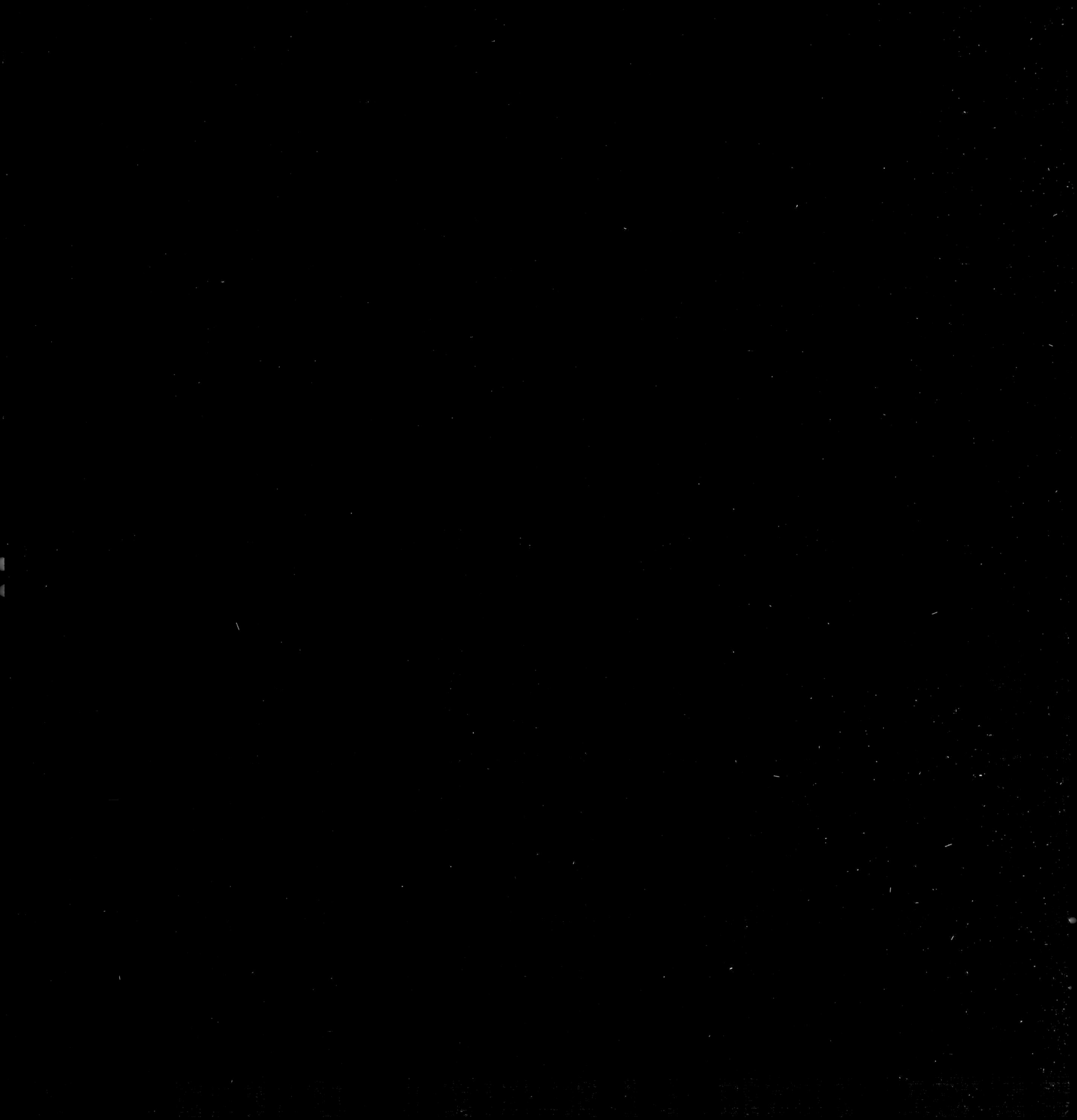

SETS SCENES SIGNS SHOPS

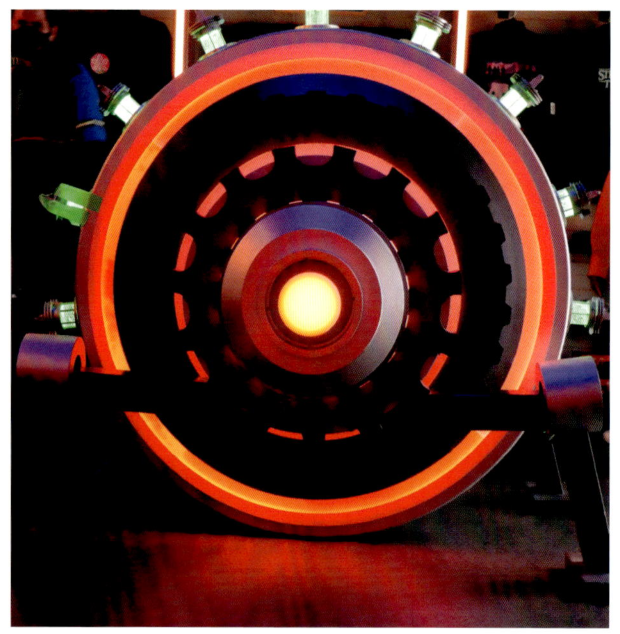

The Americana at Brand is an upscale shopping mall in Glendale that is not unusual, except for one store called Stranger Things. Designed to sell Netflix merchandise, its point-of-purchase displays recreate the Netflix sci-fi horror series in vivid detail. Lights flash, and pop hits from the Talking Heads lend credence to the illusion.

"Burning Down the House," Netflix at the Americana, 2022

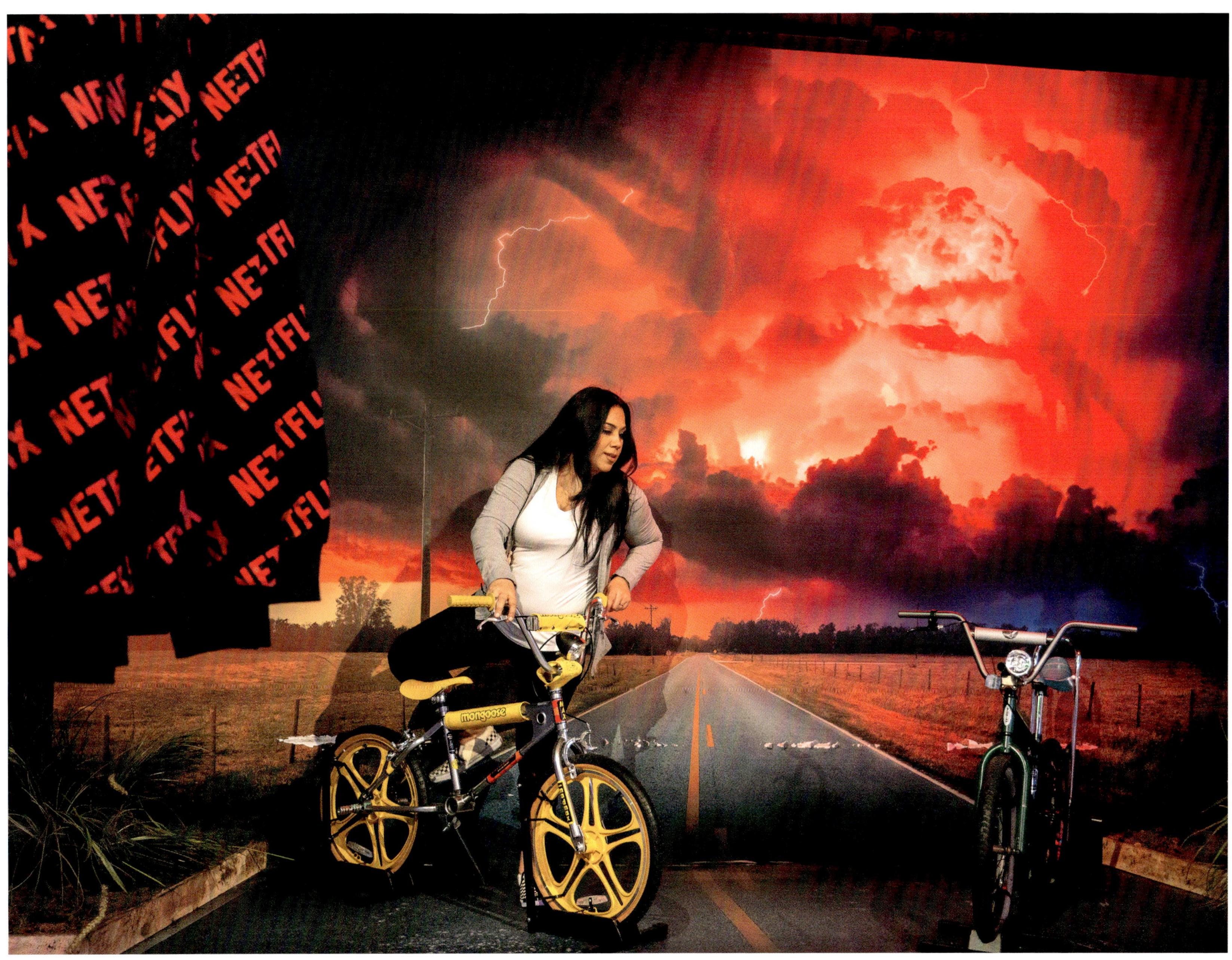
NETFLIX

Like a movie trailer, the next set of images is a prelude. This handful of photos sets the stage. They span 2010 through 2014, from LA to the South Bay, San Diego and back. Made in slick malls and lavish shopping venues, the series is called *High End*. Here, scenes and shops become simulacra.

As the oft-quoted critic Baudrillard noted in *Simulacra and Simulation* (1981), "Disneyland is presented as imaginary in order to make us believe that the rest is real, when in fact all of Los Angeles and the America surrounding it are no longer real, but of the order of the hyperreal and of simulation." As the curtain is pulled back on "The Market," the marquee proclaims, loud and clear: "Now Playing in Theaters Everywhere."

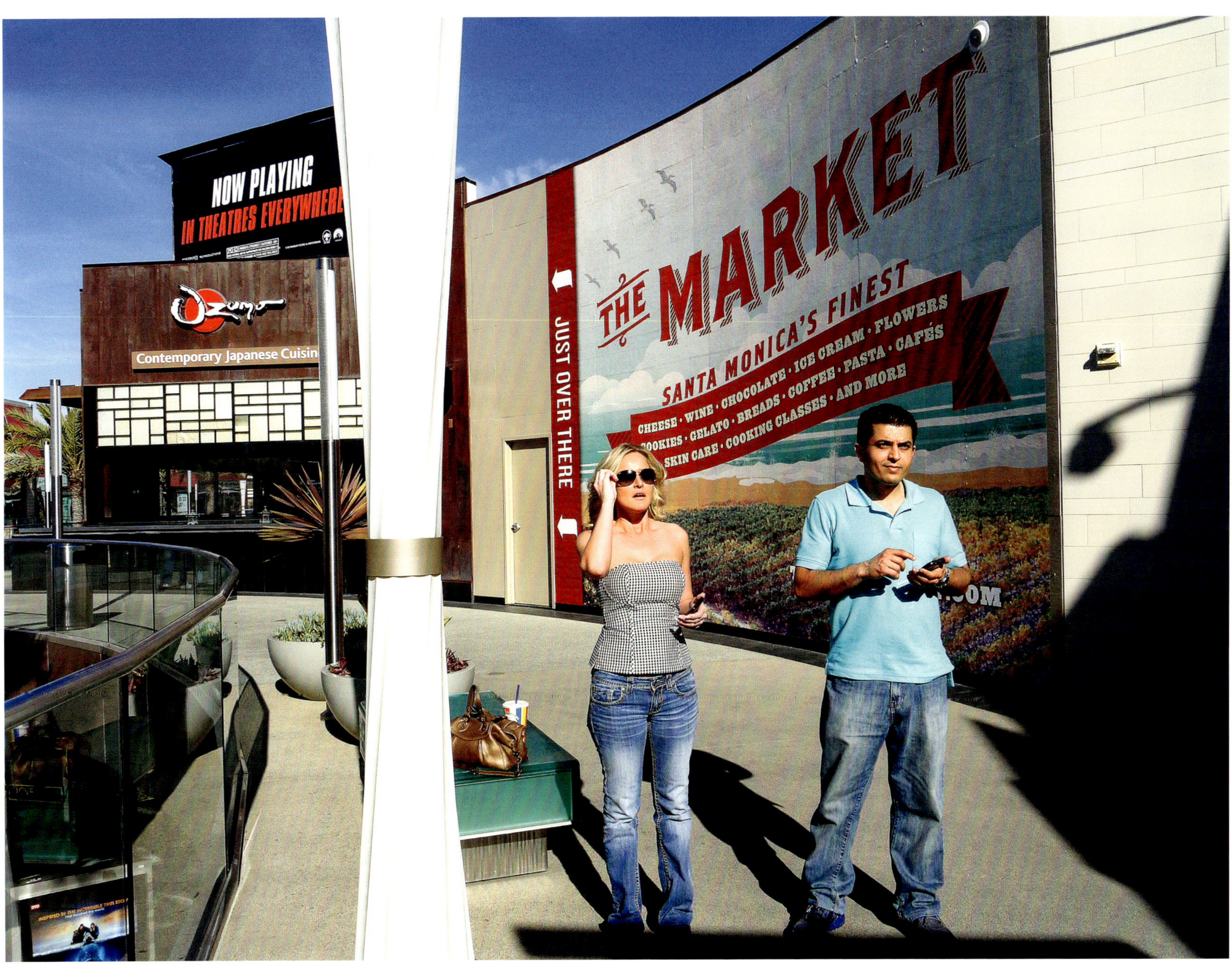
NOW PLAYING
IN THEATRES EVERYWHERE
Ozumo
Contemporary Japanese Cuisine
THE MARKET
SANTA MONICA'S FINEST
CHEESE · WINE · CHOCOLATE · ICE CREAM · FLOWERS
COOKIES · GELATO · BREADS · COFFEE · PASTA · CAFÉS
SKIN CARE · COOKING CLASSES · AND MORE
JUST OVER THERE

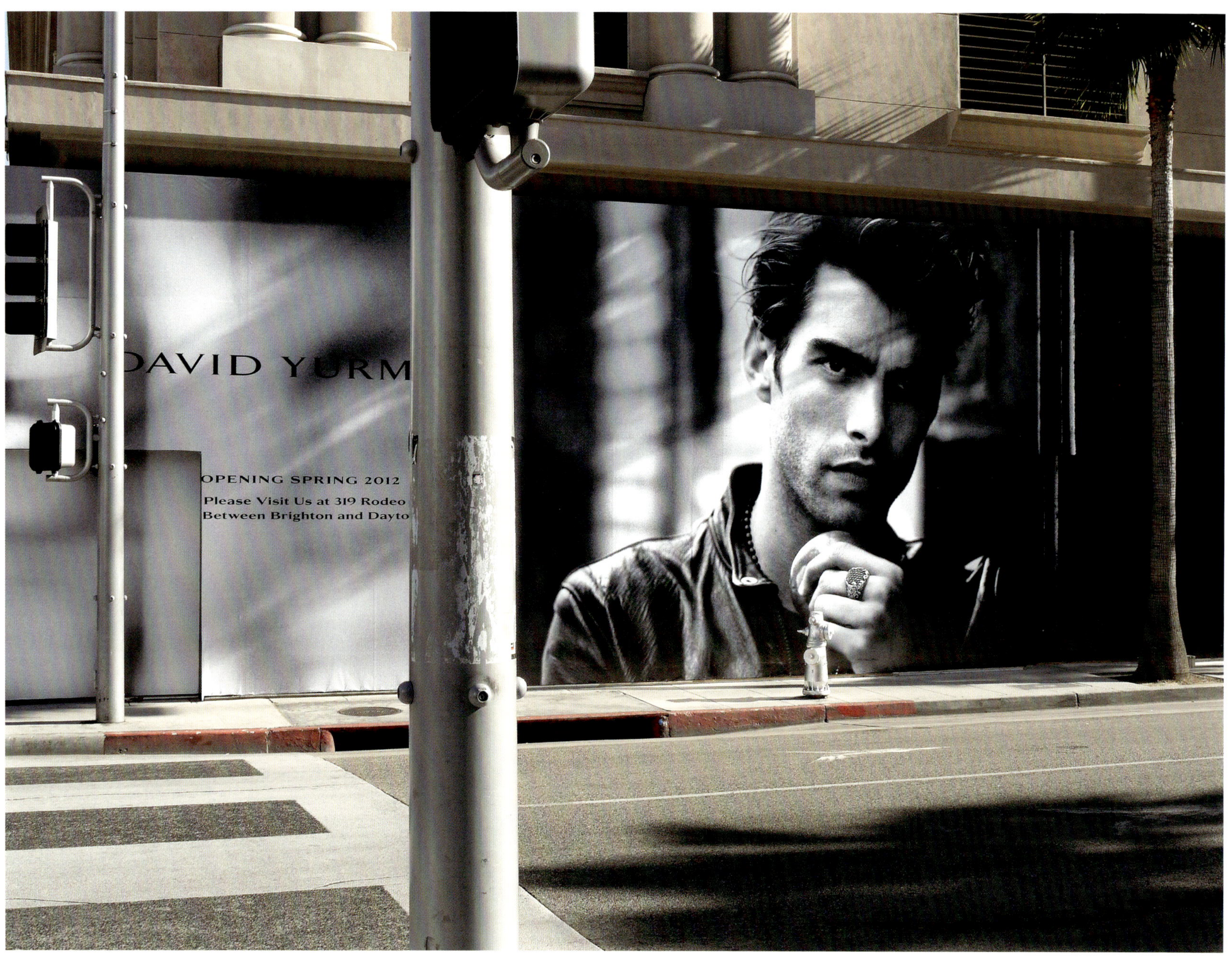

DAVID YURM
OPENING SPRING 2012
Please Visit Us at 319 Rodeo
Between Brighton and Dayto

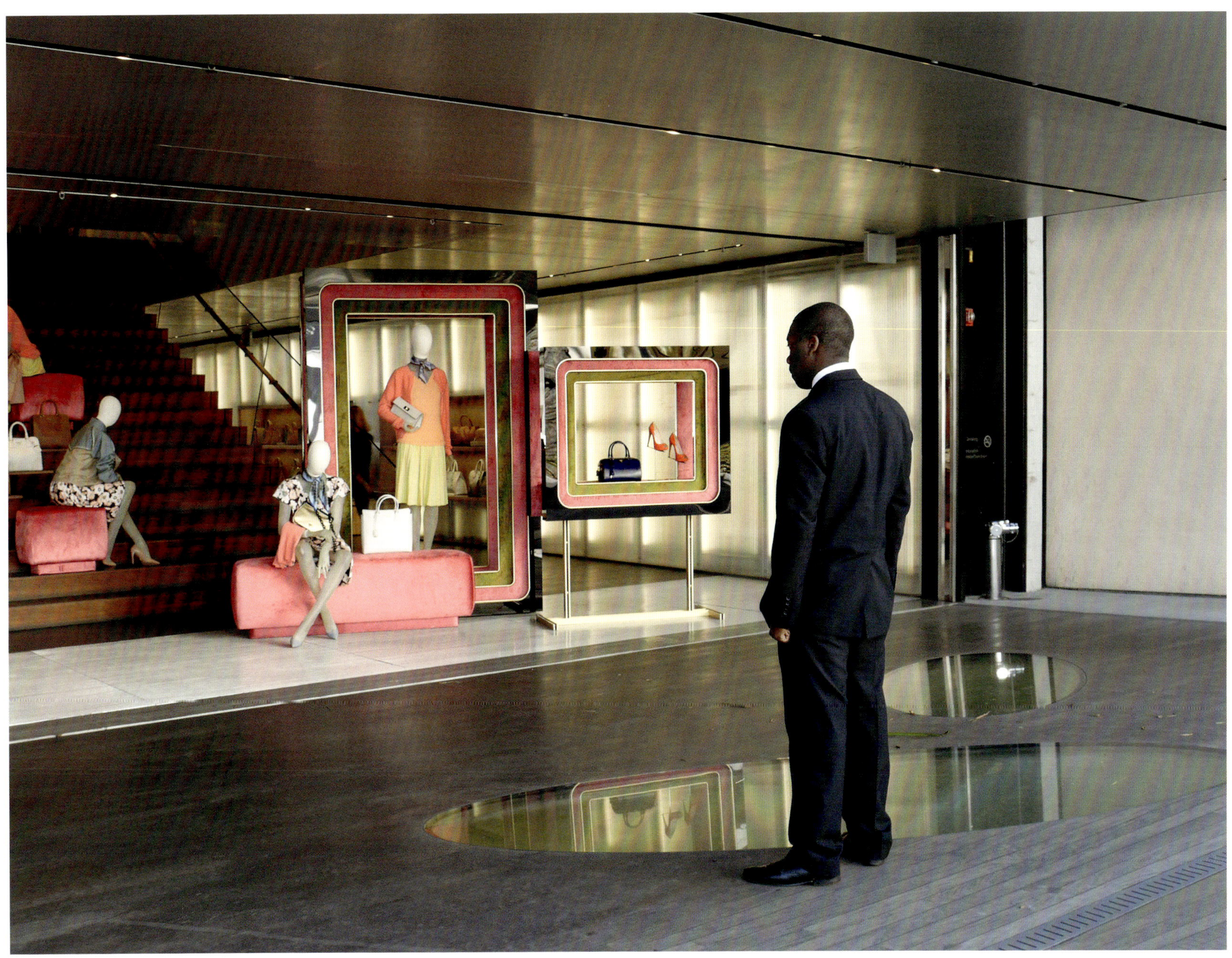

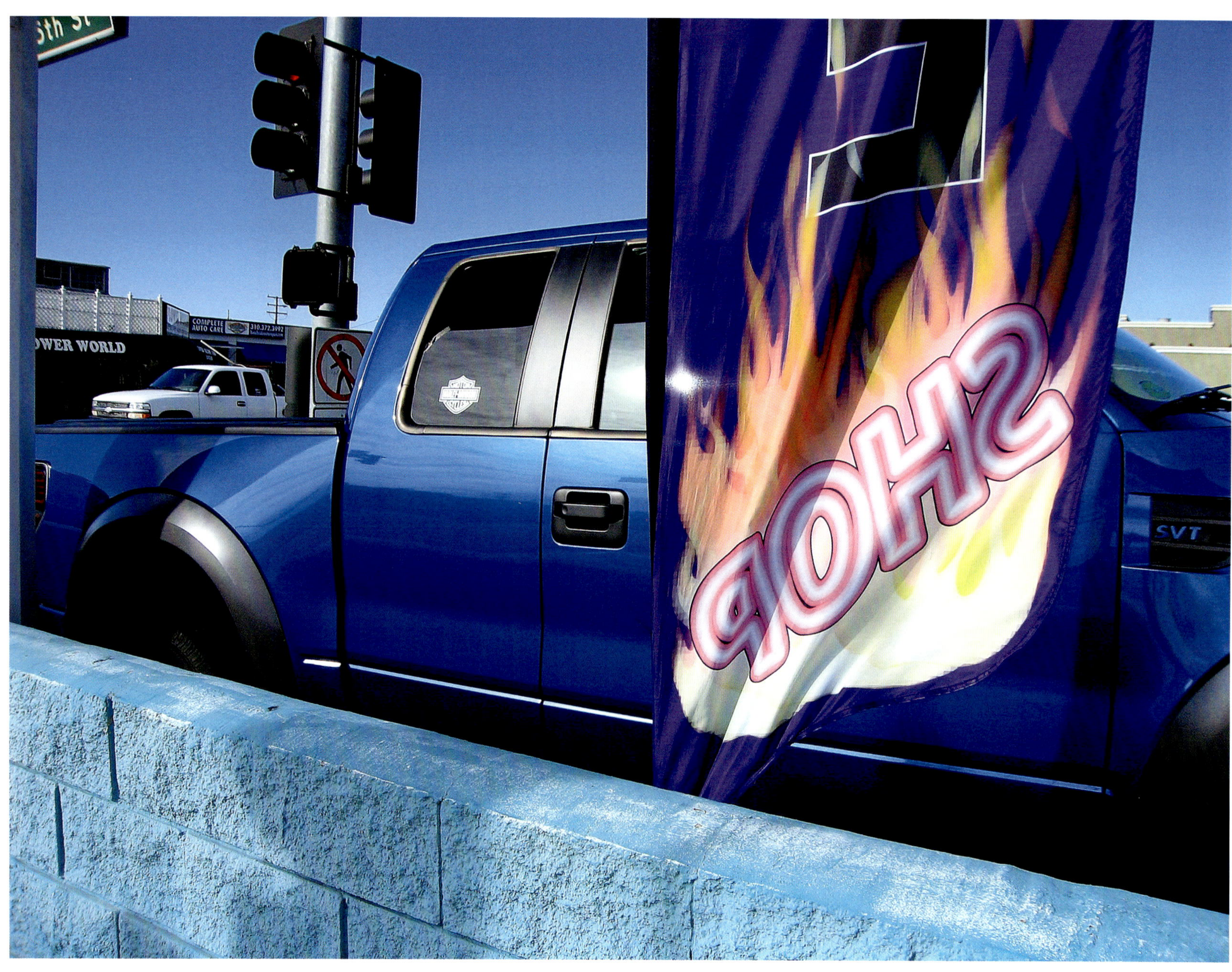
5th St
OWER WORLD
COMPLETE AUTO CARE
310.372.3992
SHOP
SVT

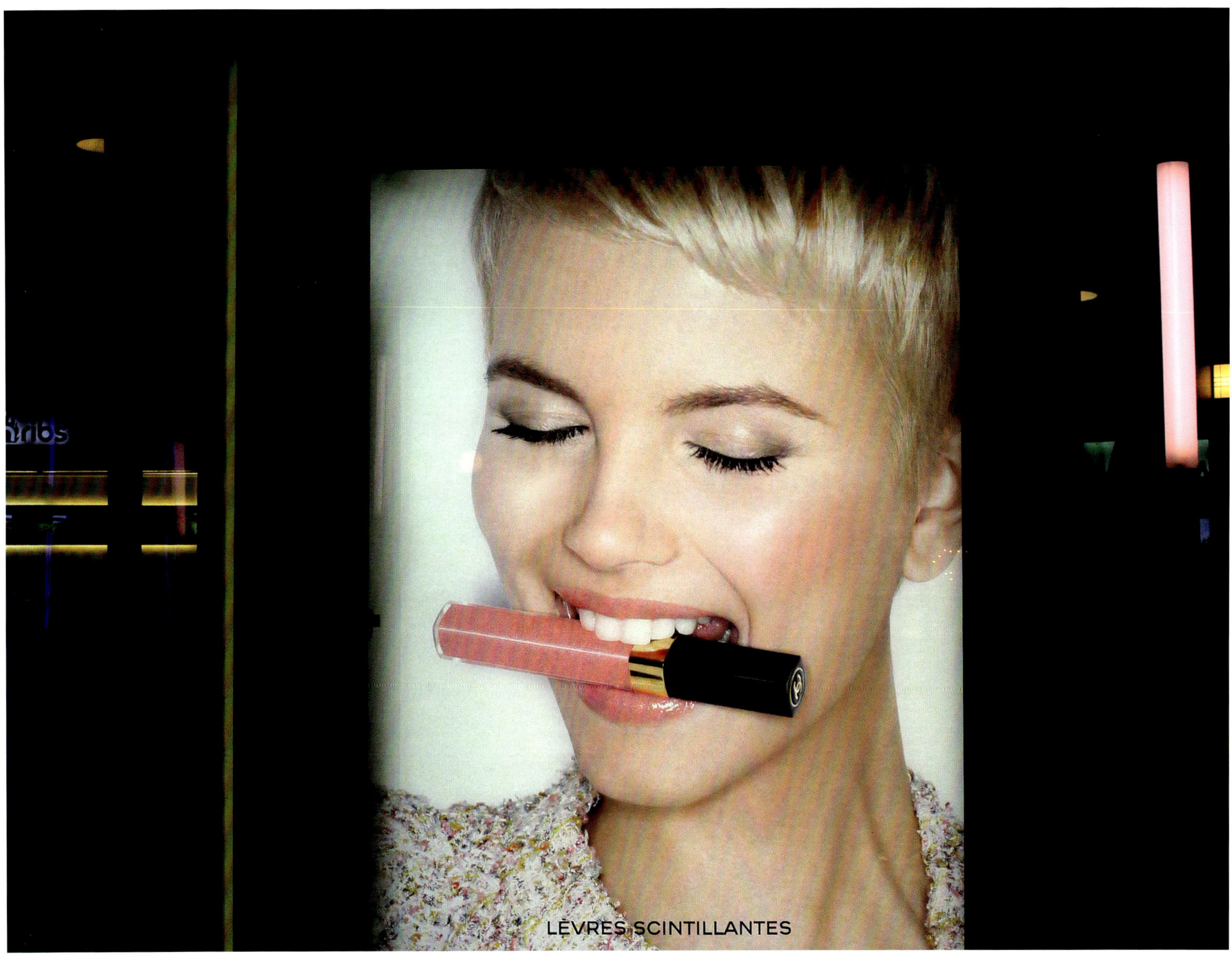

LÈVRES SCINTILLANTES

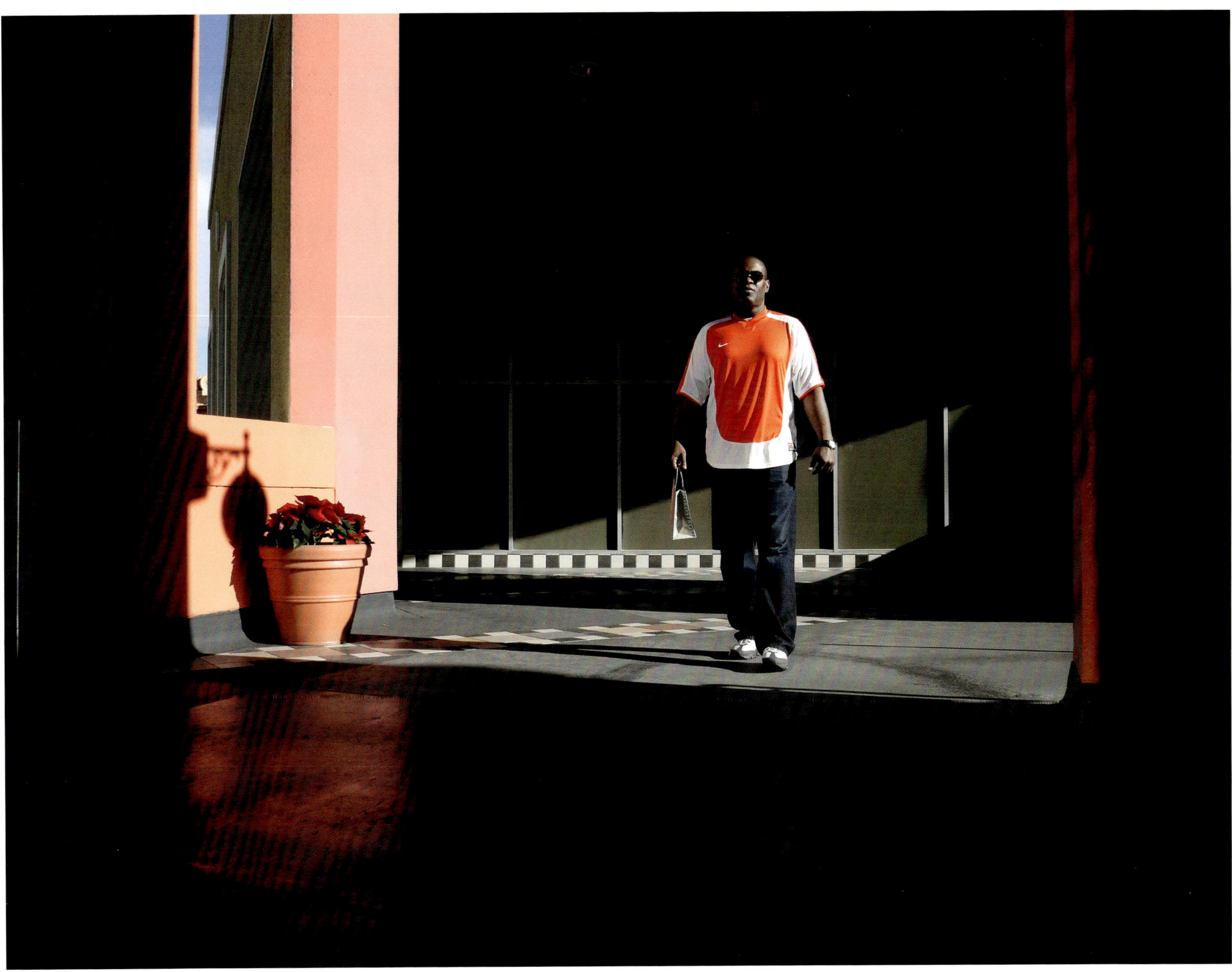

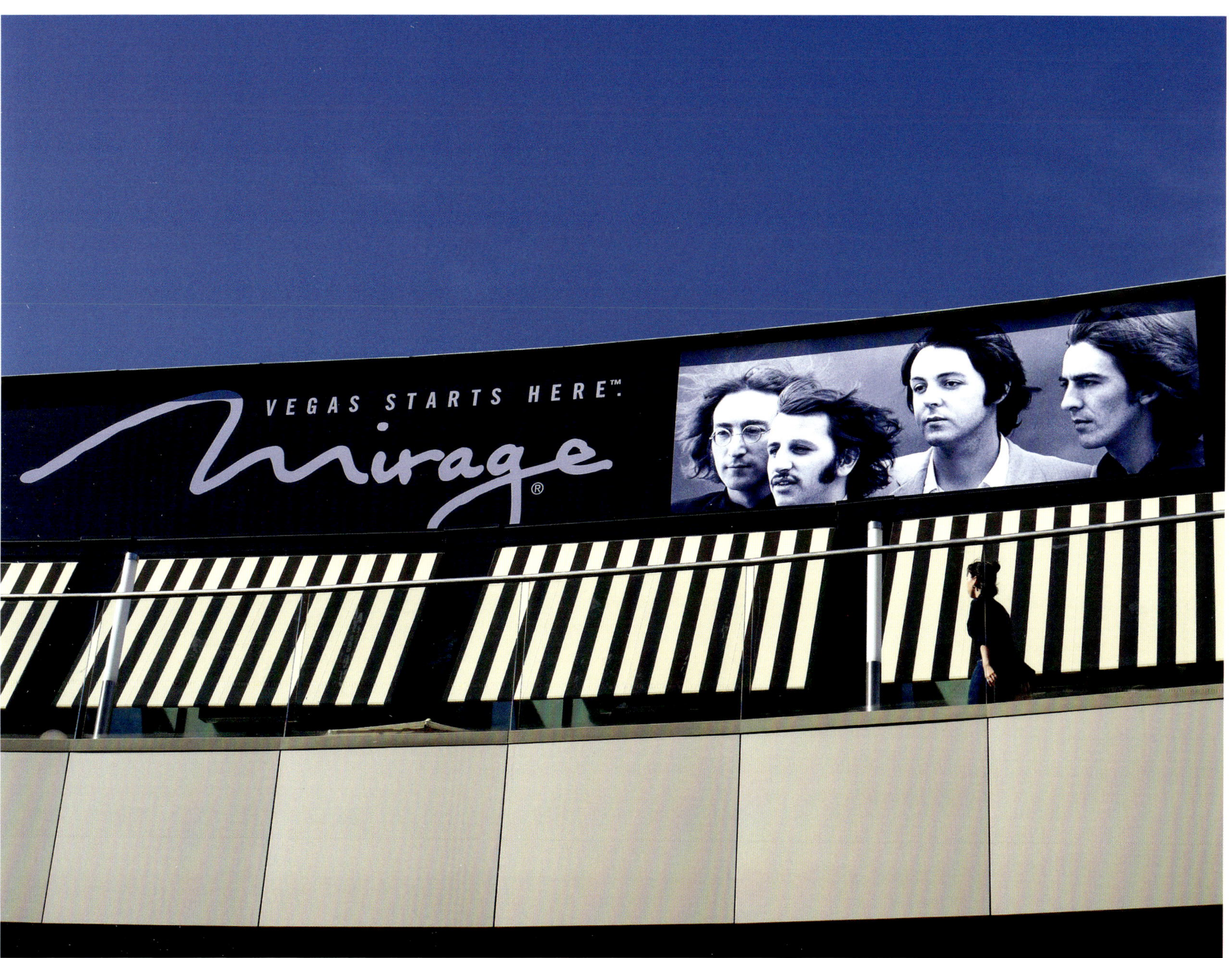

VEGAS STARTS HERE.™
mirage®

Sometimes scenes morph into sets unintentionally. When signs collide with a particular place and time, the resemblance to film can be uncanny. This is Guy Debord's "society of the spectacle," where the authentic is replaced with its representation. But at what human cost?

NUART shows Oscar Shorts next to CineFile Video, Santa Monica, 2022

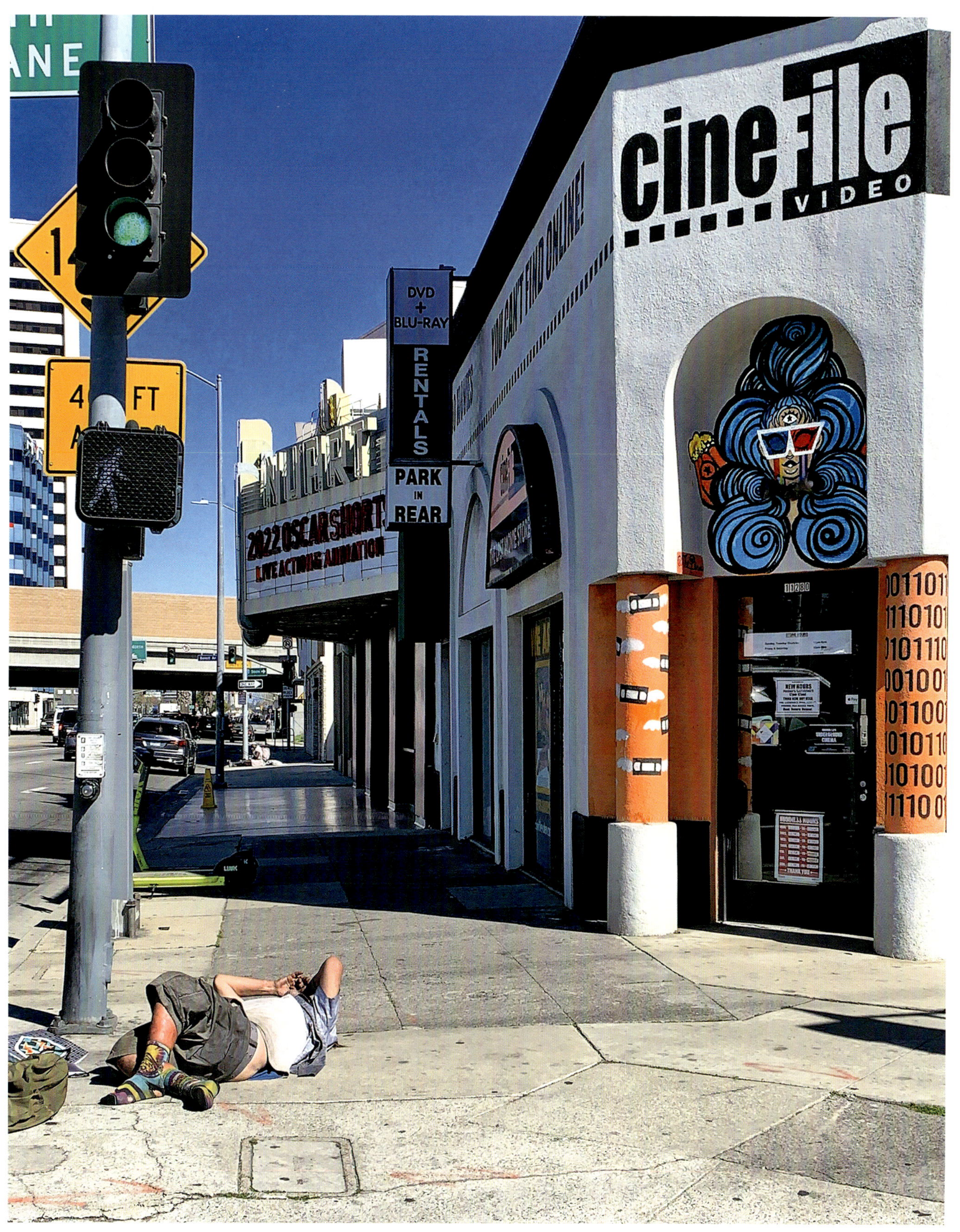

cineFile
VIDEO
YOU CAN'T FIND ONLINE!
DVD
+
BLU-RAY
RENTALS
PARK
IN
REAR
2022 OSCAR SHORTS
LIVE ACTION & ANIMATION
1
40 FT
00110111
11101011
01011101
00100101
01110001
01011001
01001101
11100101

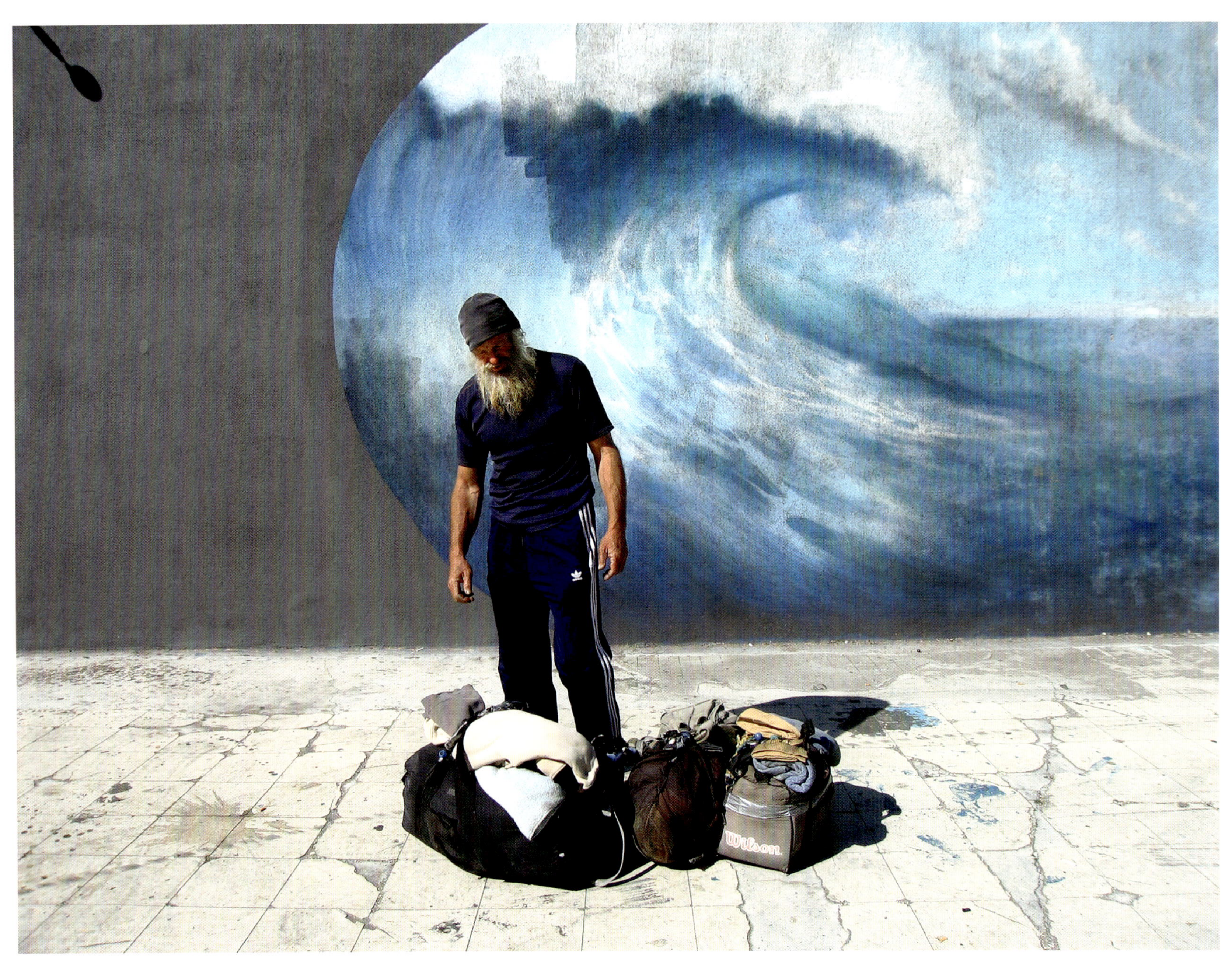

"I'm goin' to Hawaii," Redondo Beach

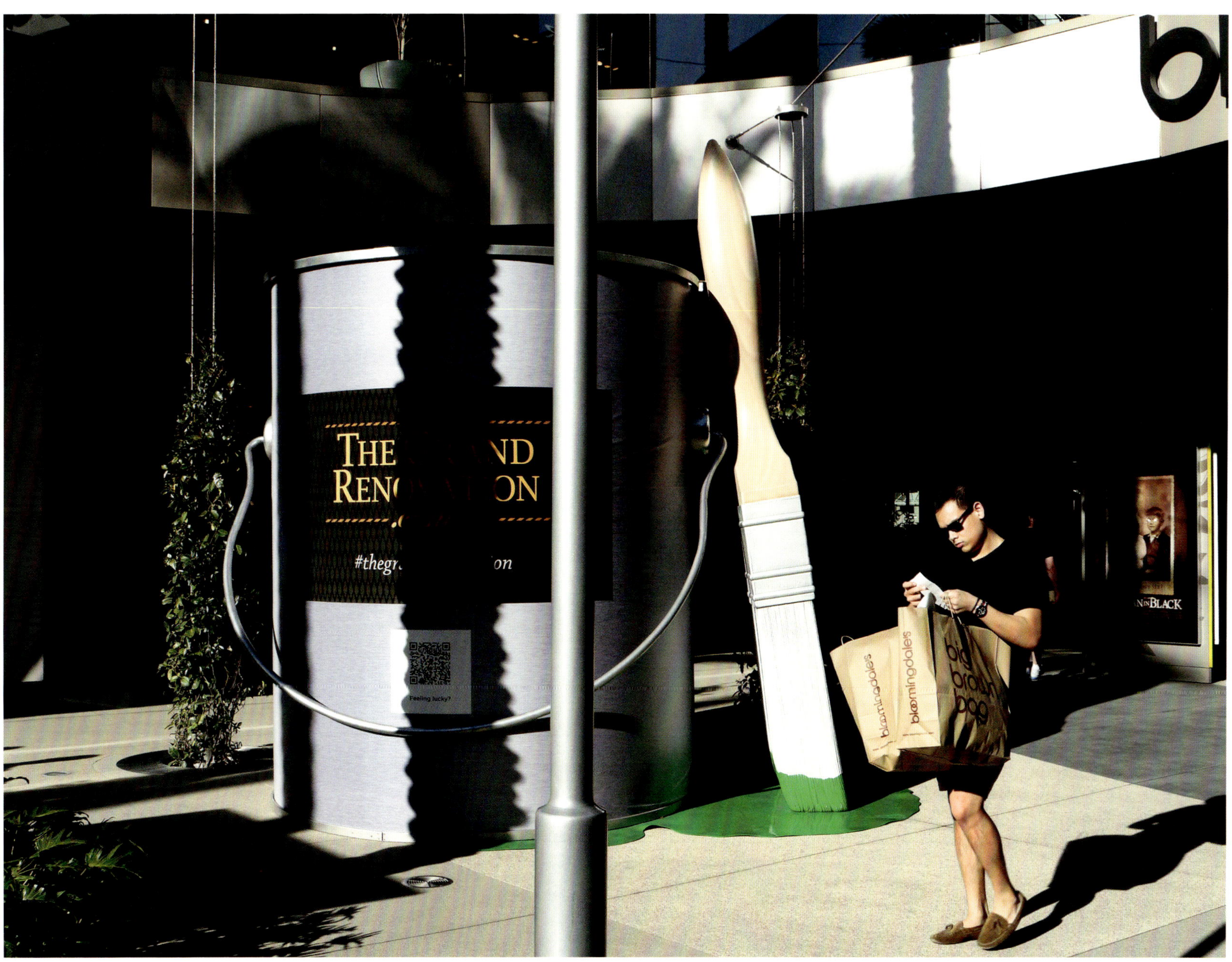

"The Grand Renovation," MGM, Santa Monica

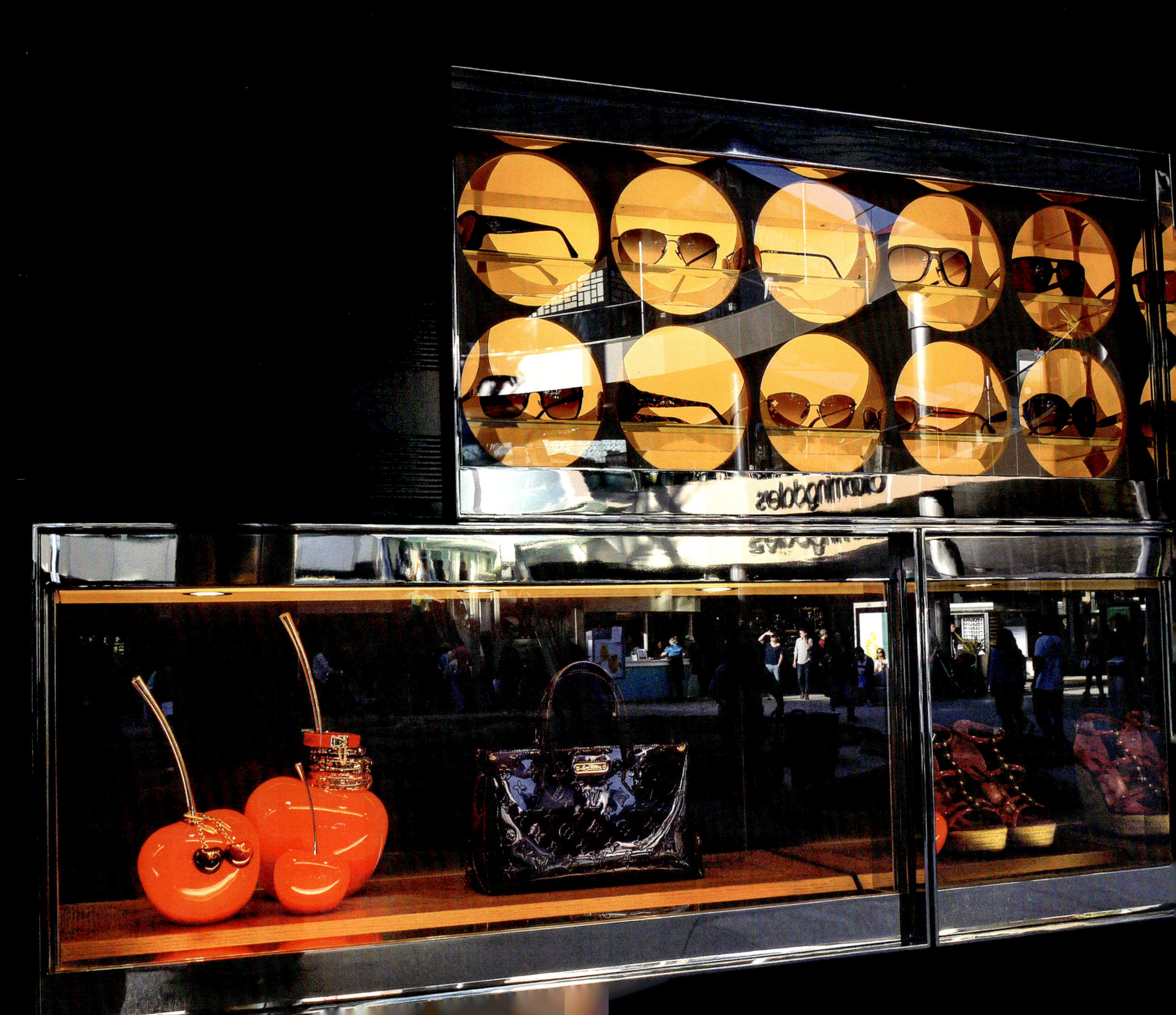

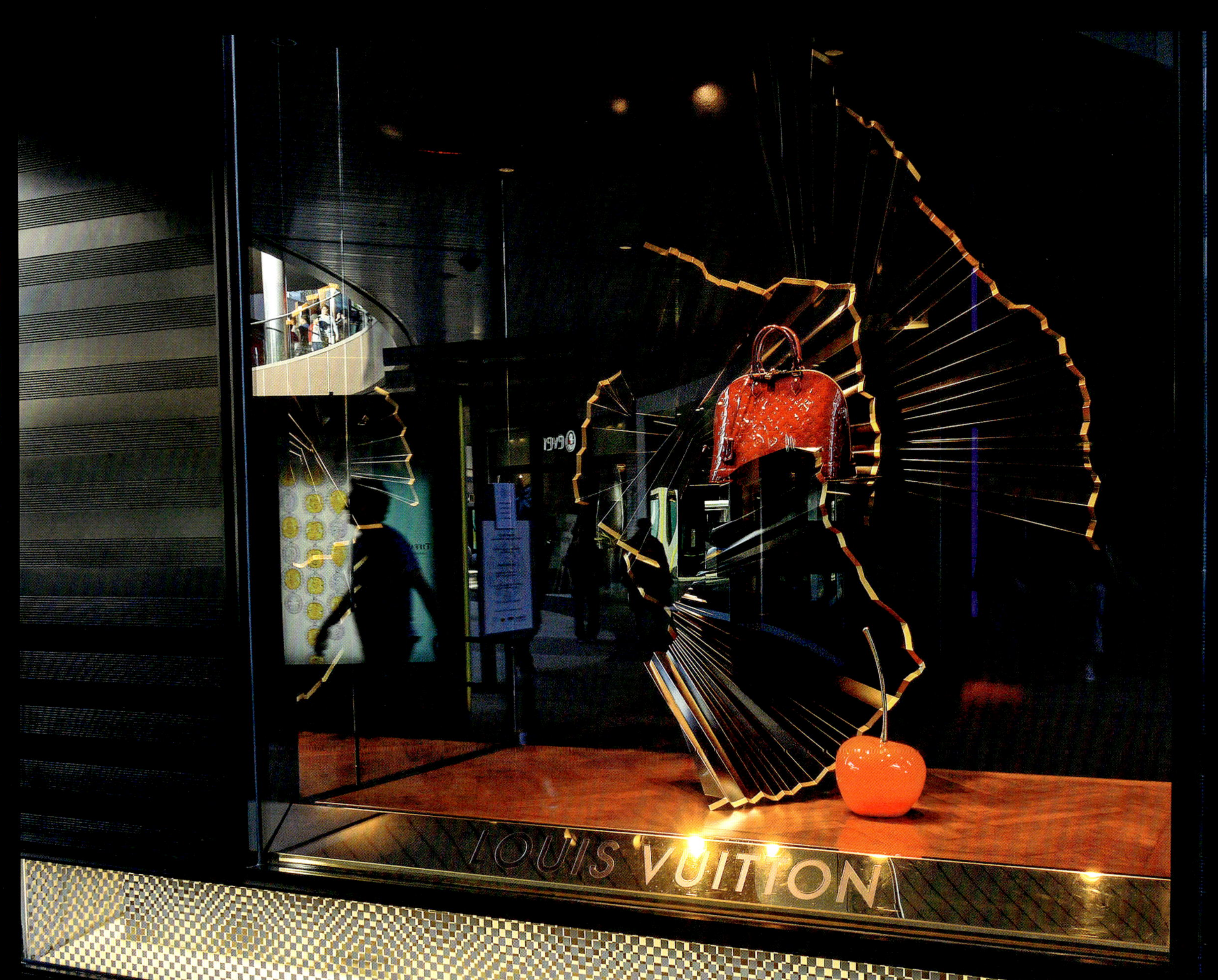
LOUIS VUITTON

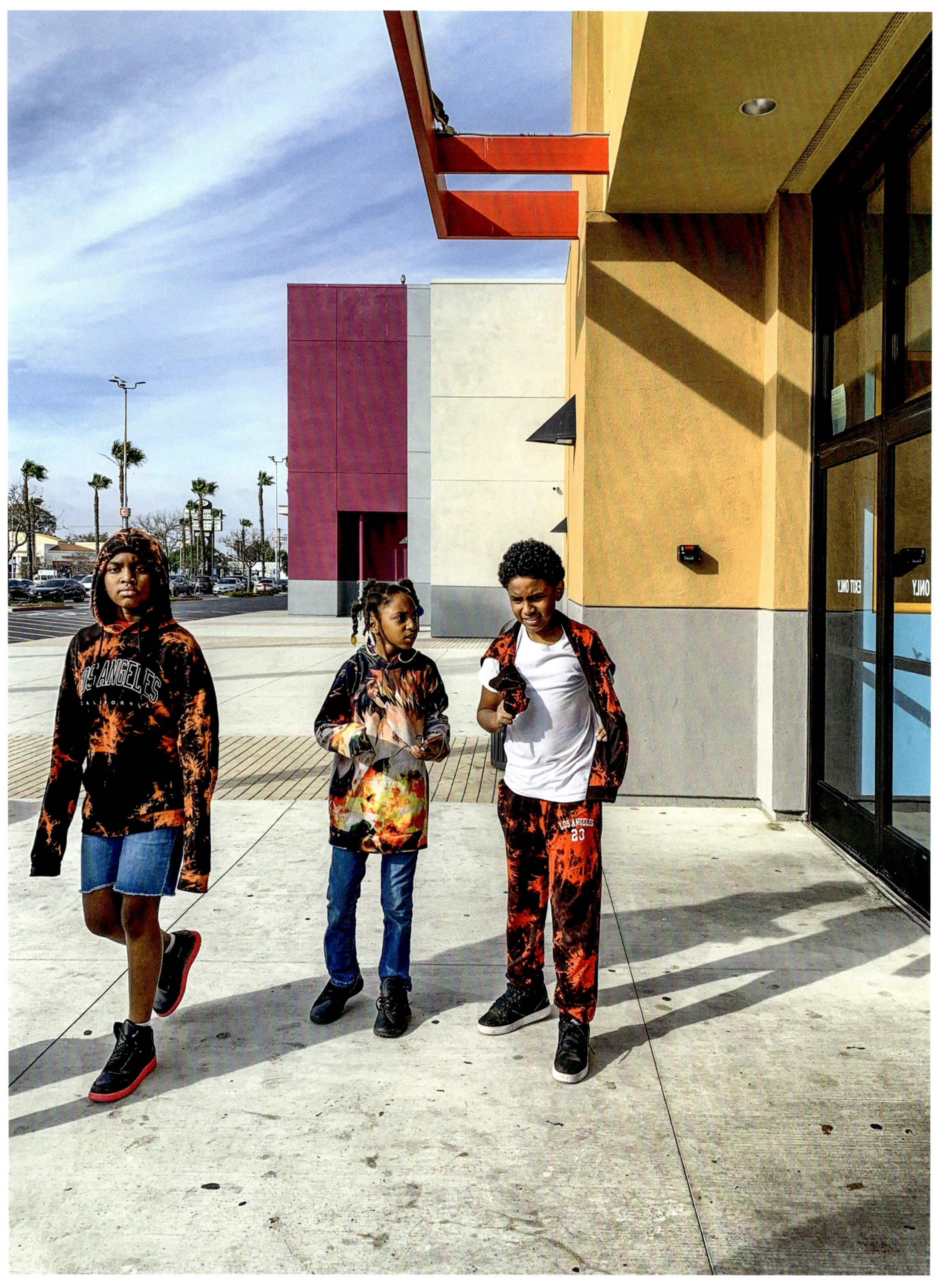

EXIT ONLY
ONLY
LOS ANGELES
23

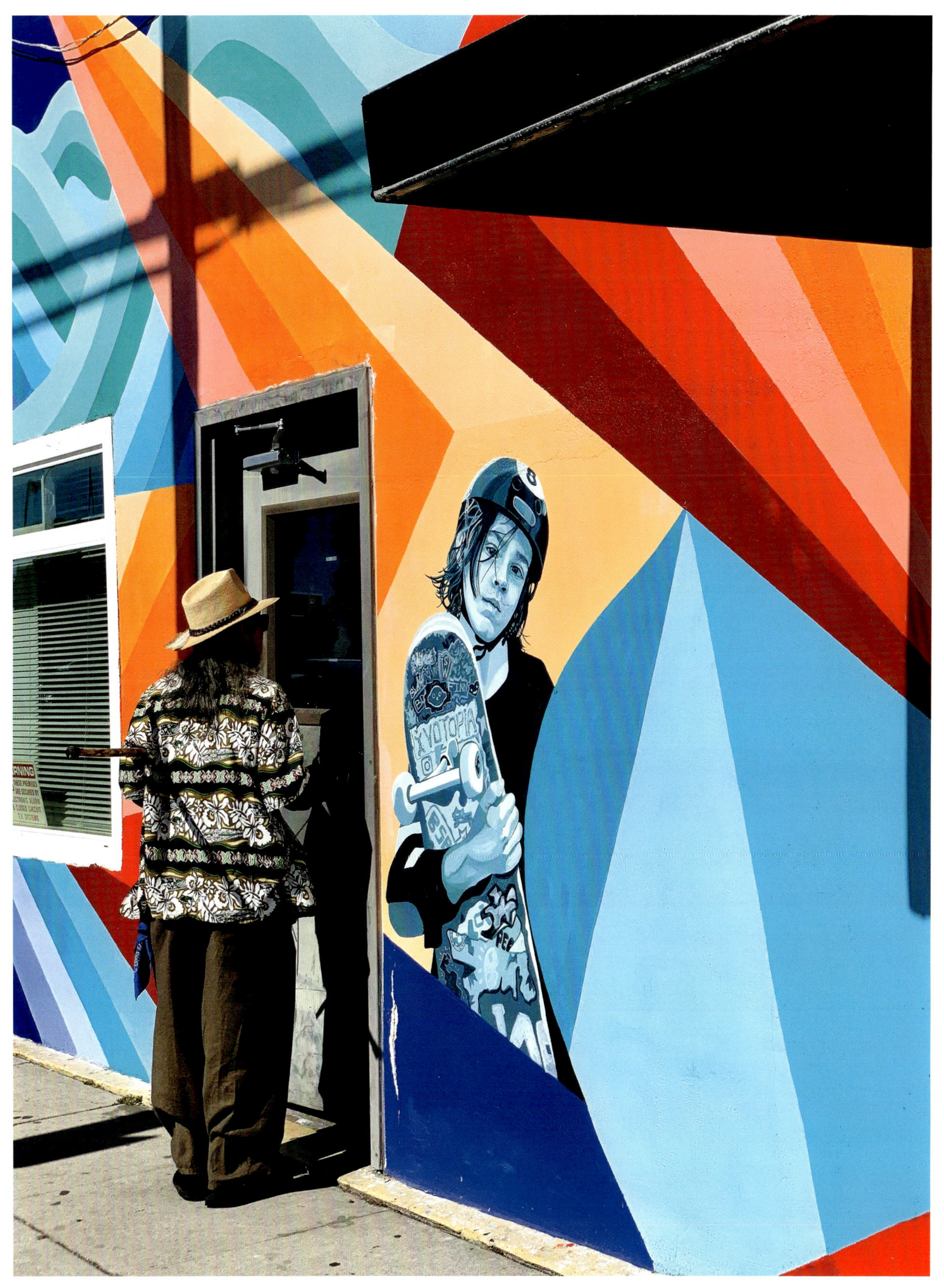

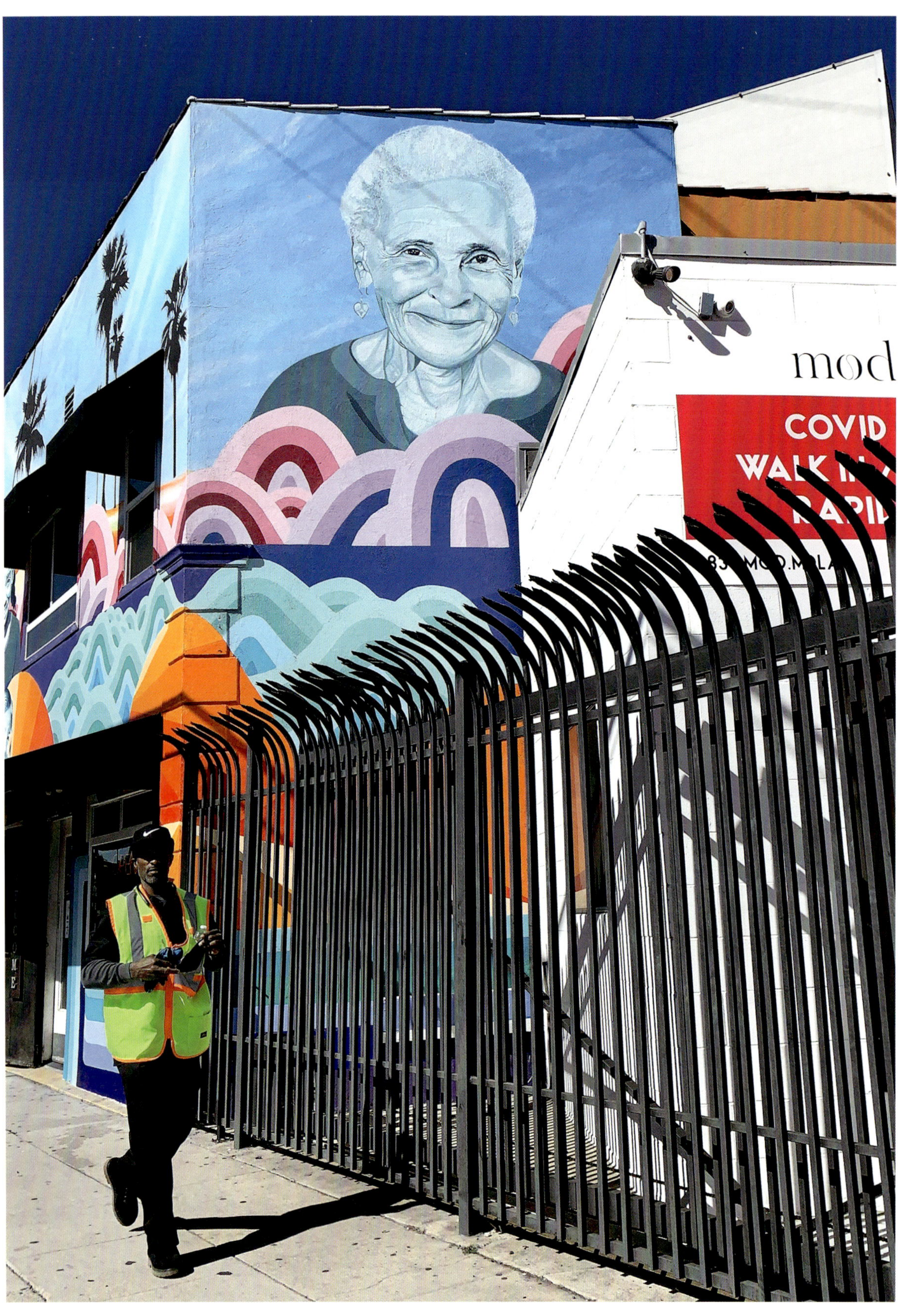

mod
COVID
WALK IN
RAPI
83 MOD.M.LA

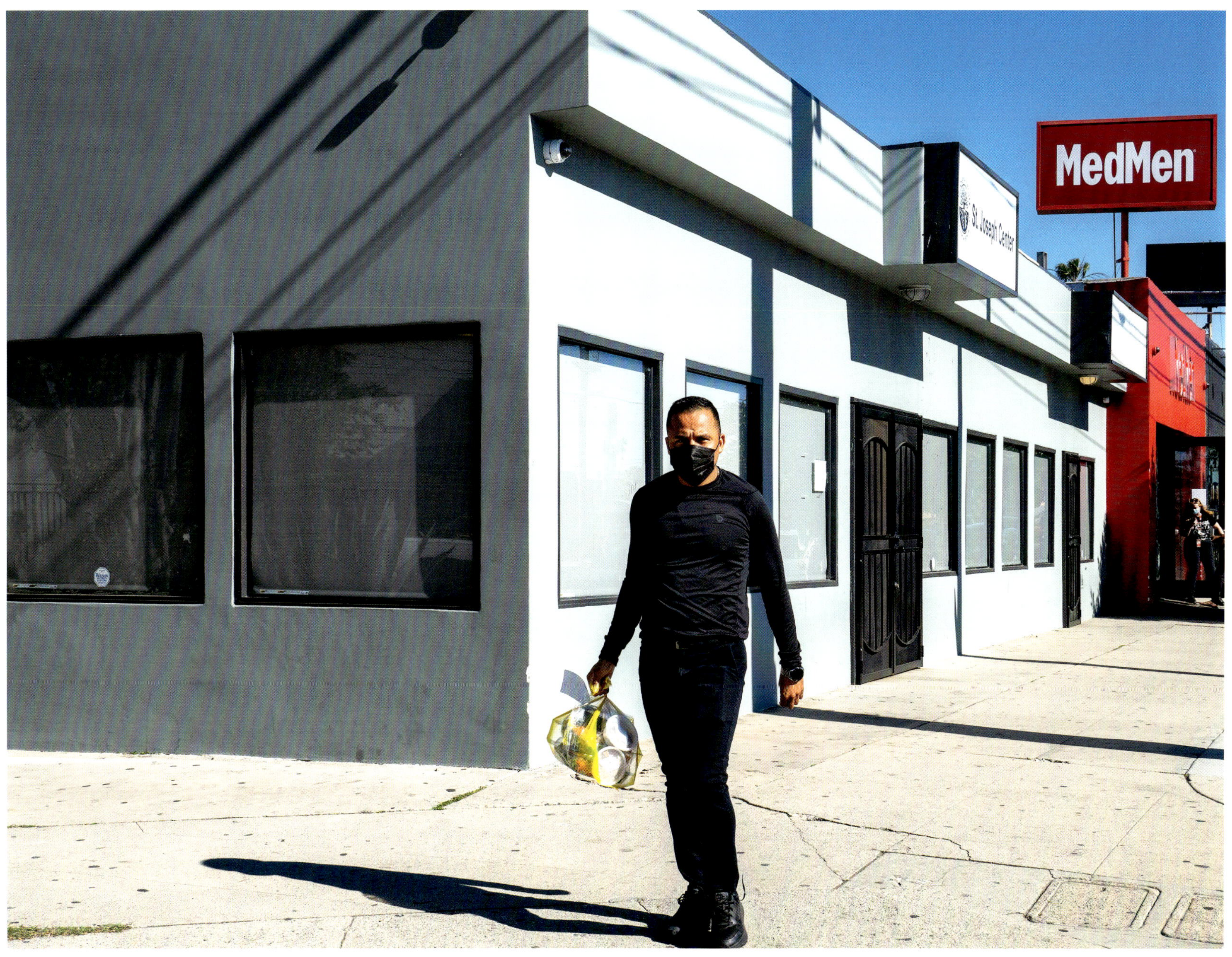

Covid Testing, Venice

Cannabis Shop, Venice

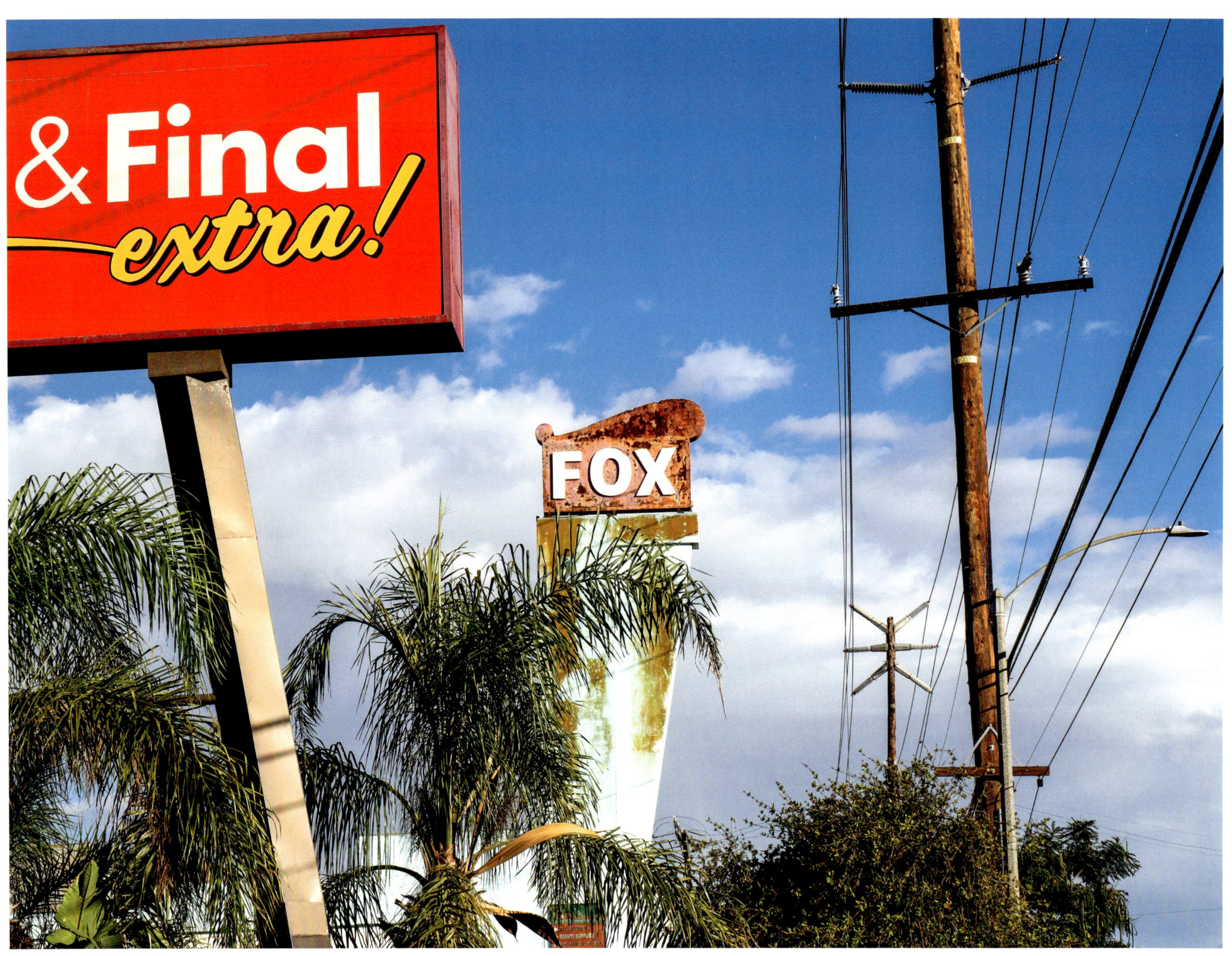

Fox Theater, Venice

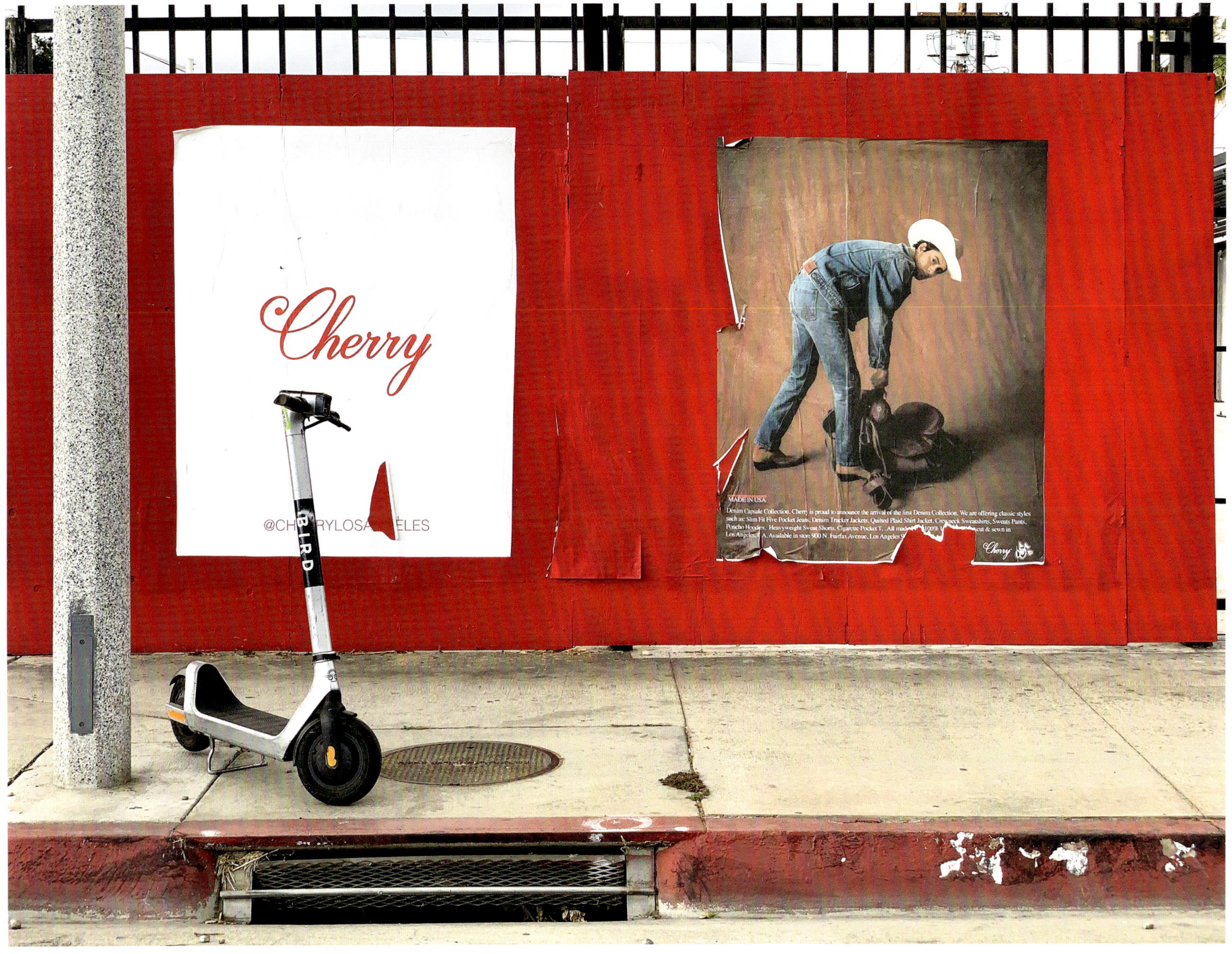

"Cherry," Los Angeles

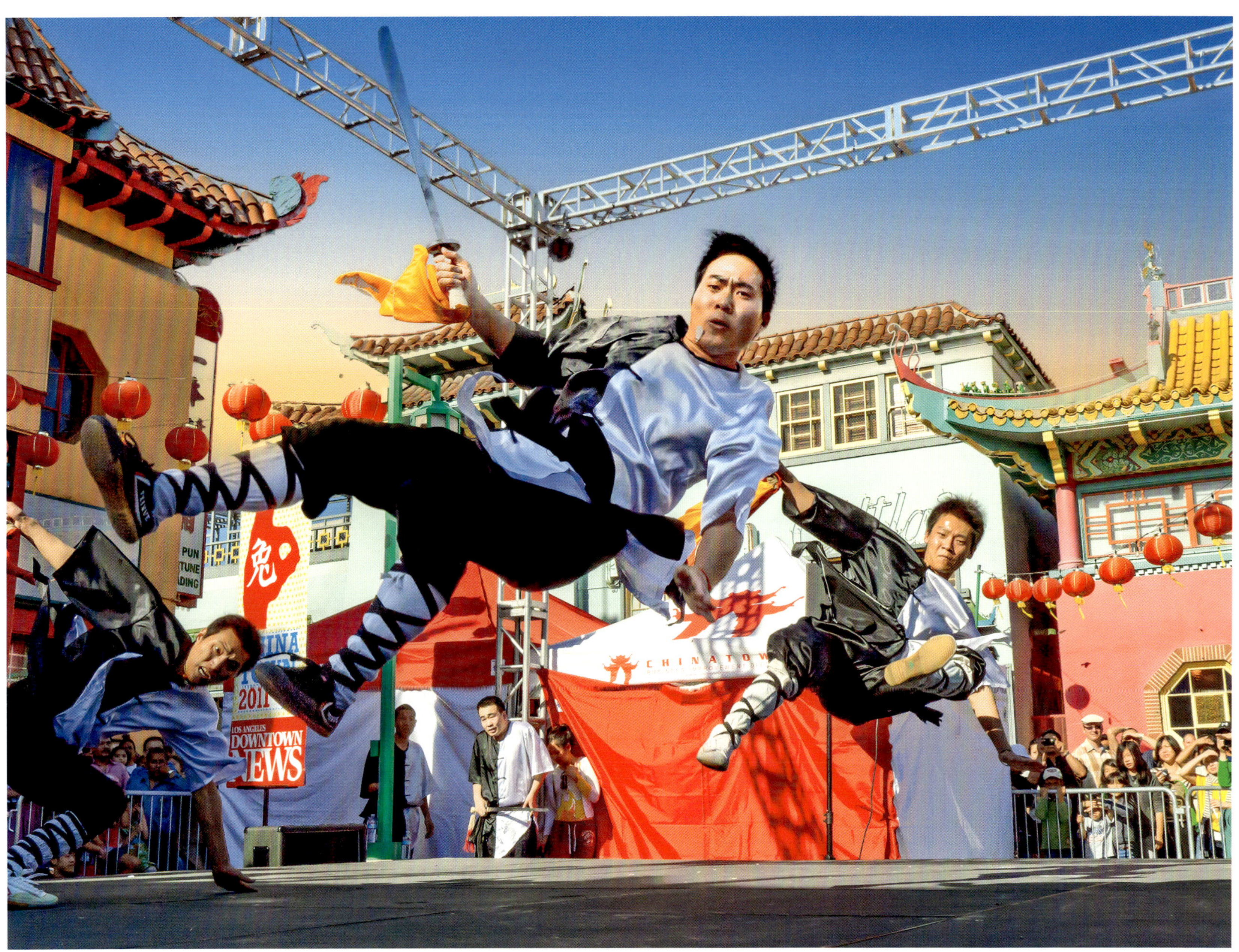

Chinatown Festival, Los Angeles

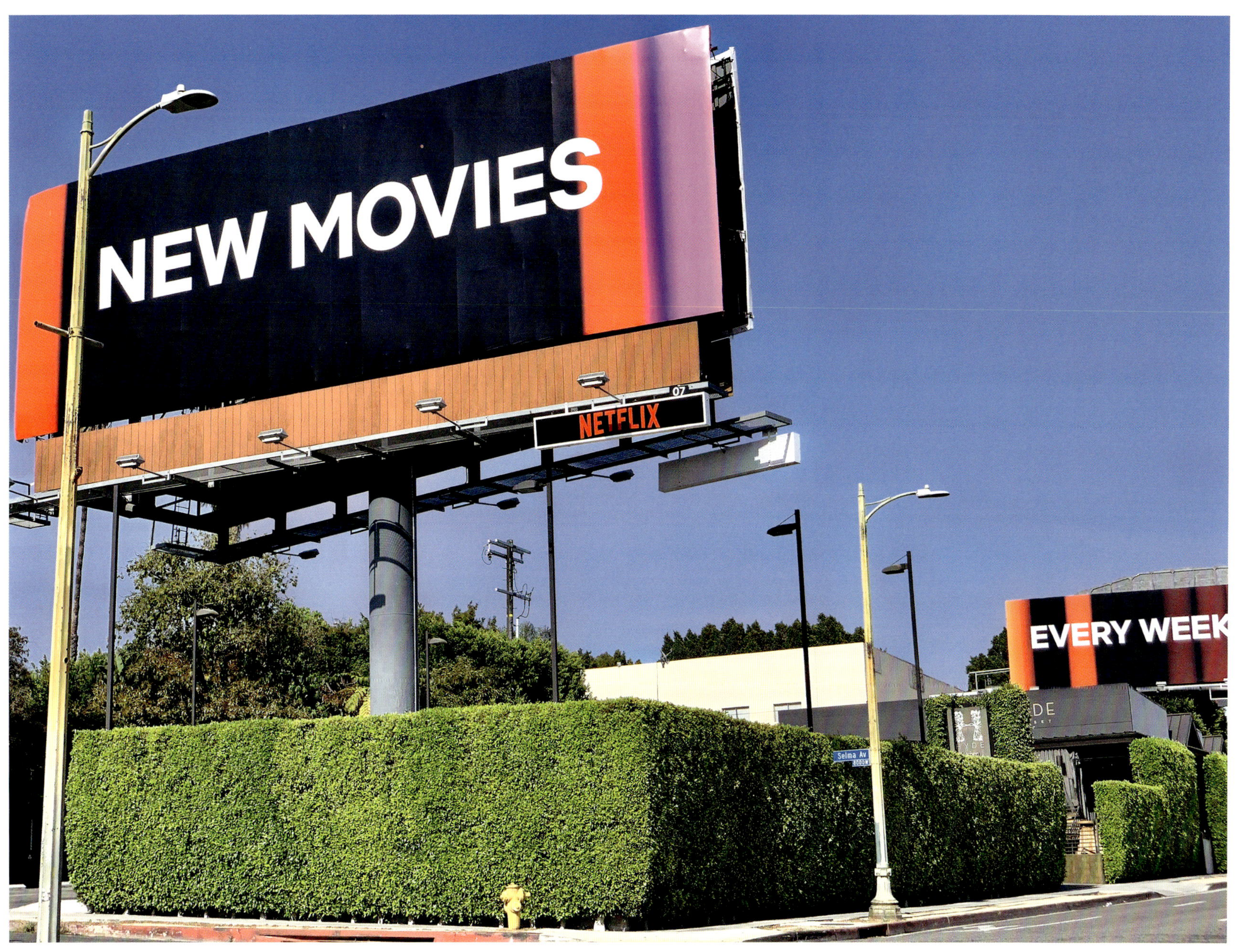

Netflix Billboards, West Hollywood

*R*EAL *E*STATE

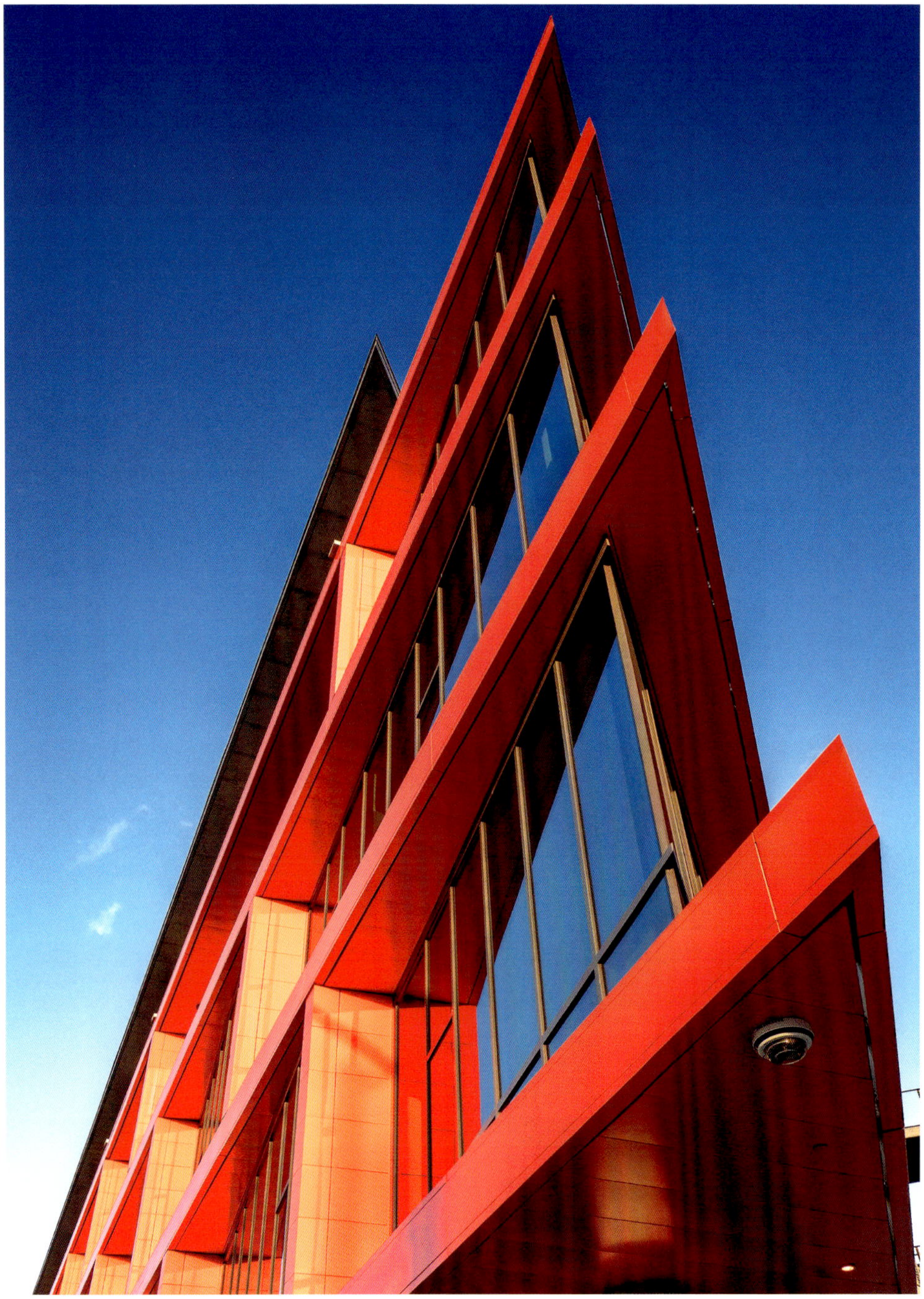

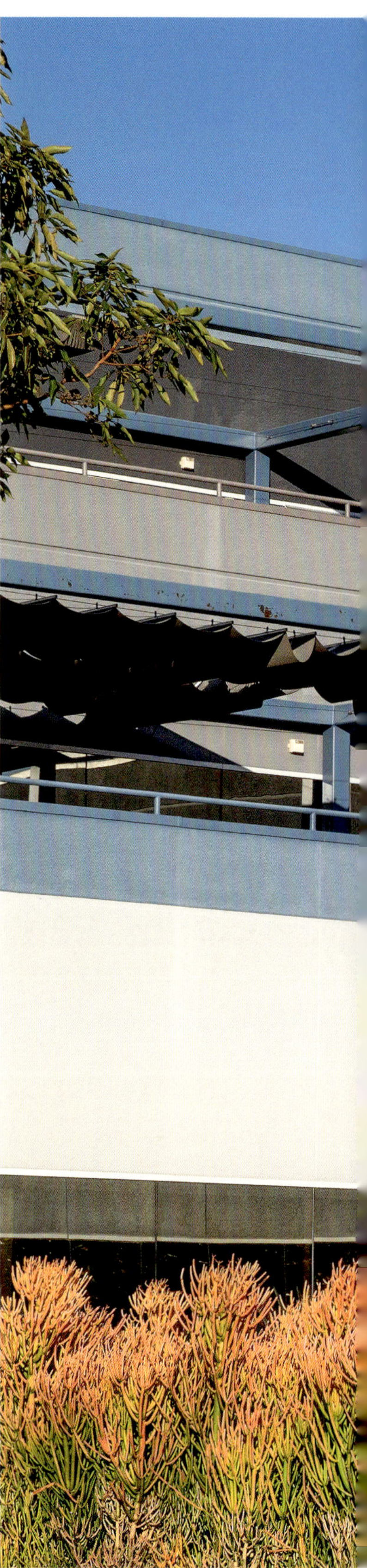

Tech Headquarters, Hayden Tract, Culver City

"17900" Office Park, Irvine

Pacific Coast Development, Malibu (next pages)

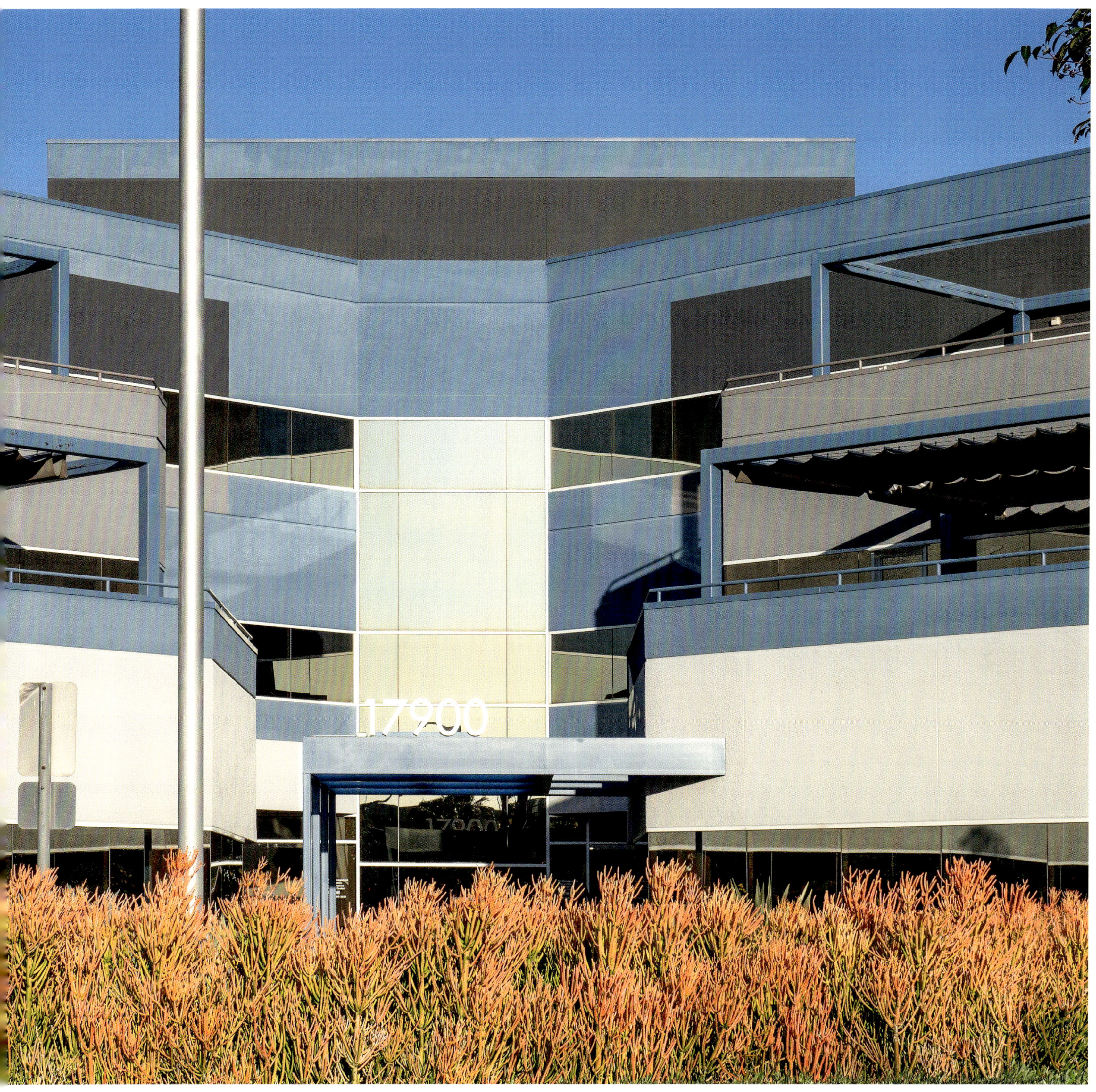
17900

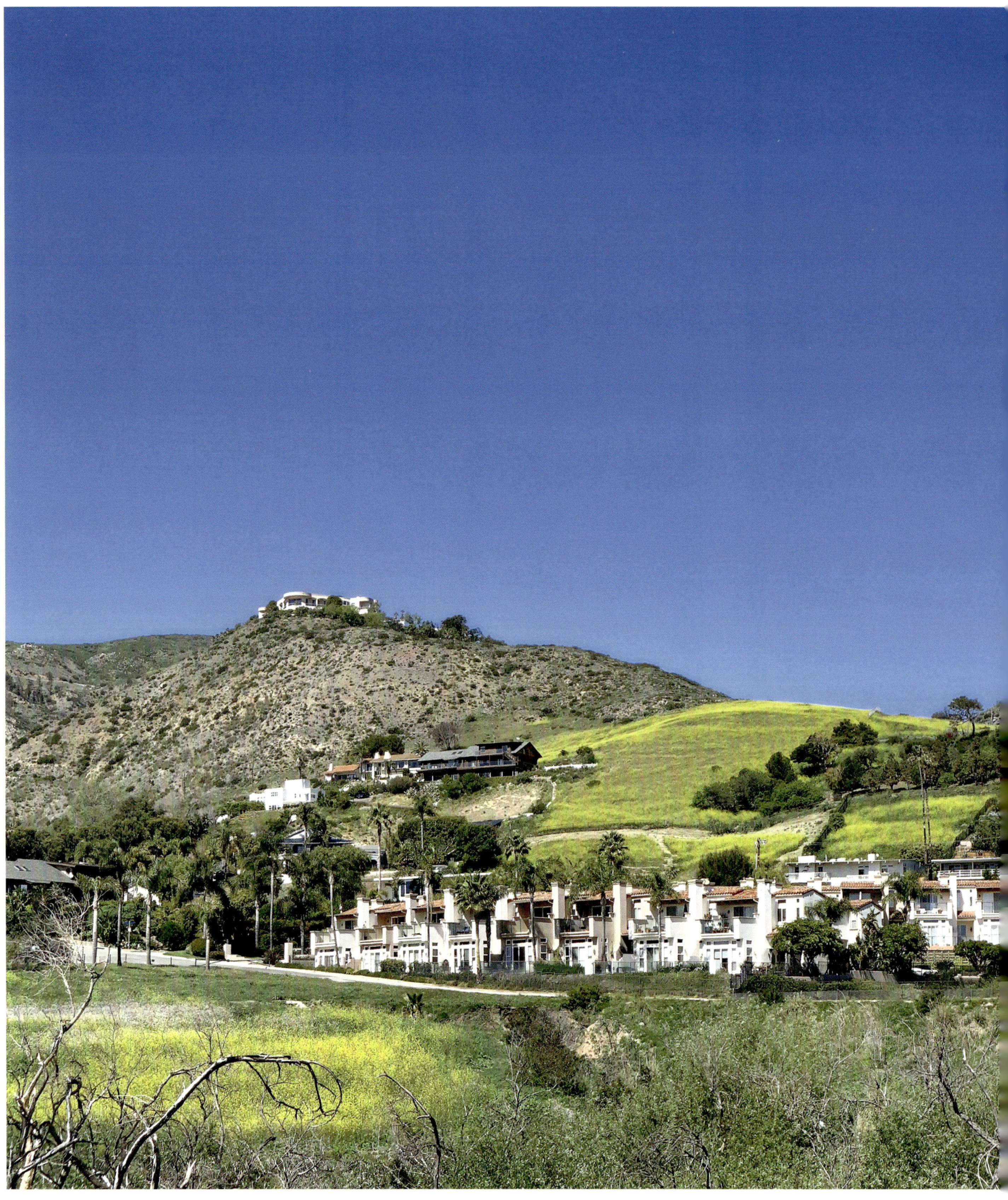

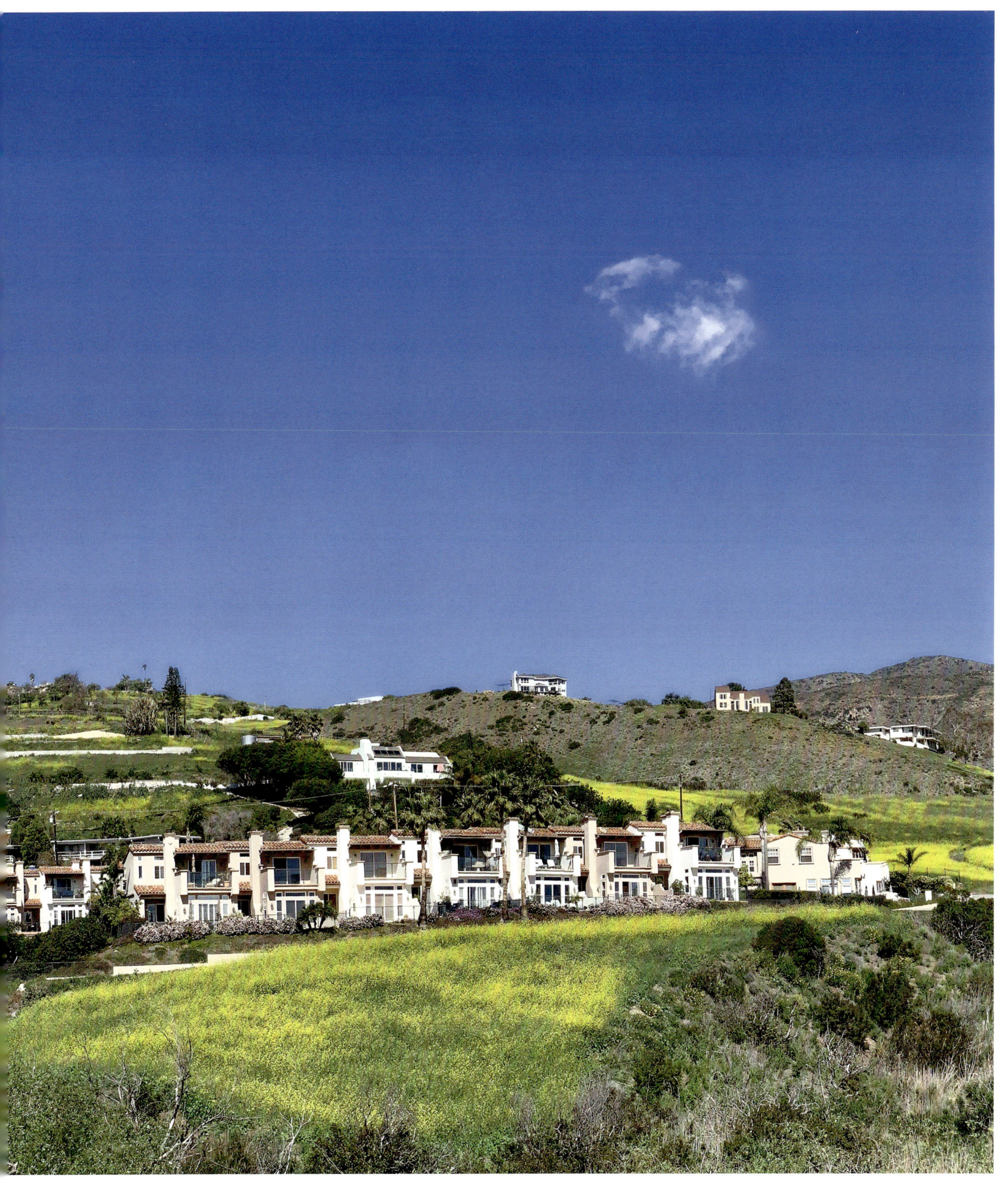

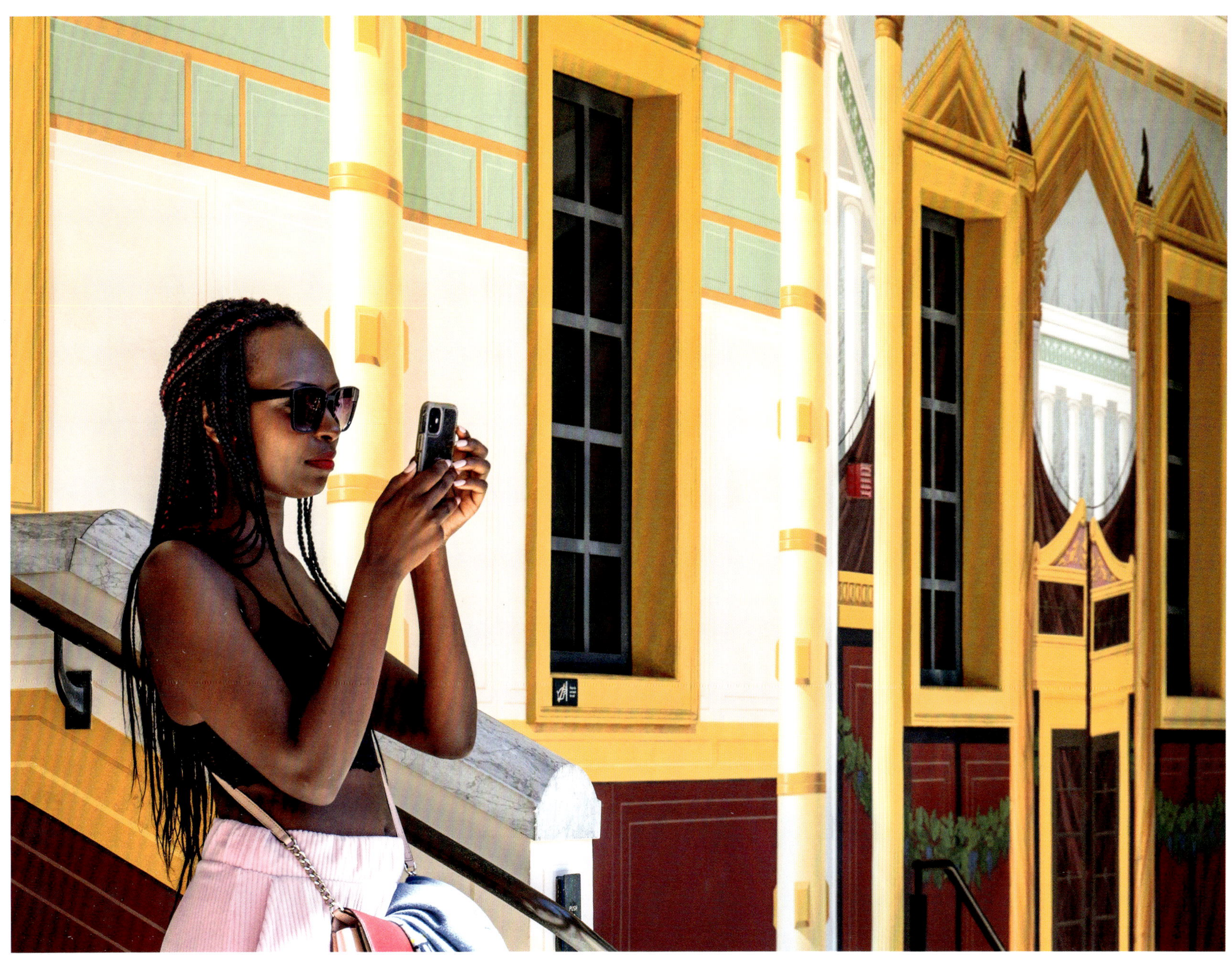

The Getty Villa, Malibu

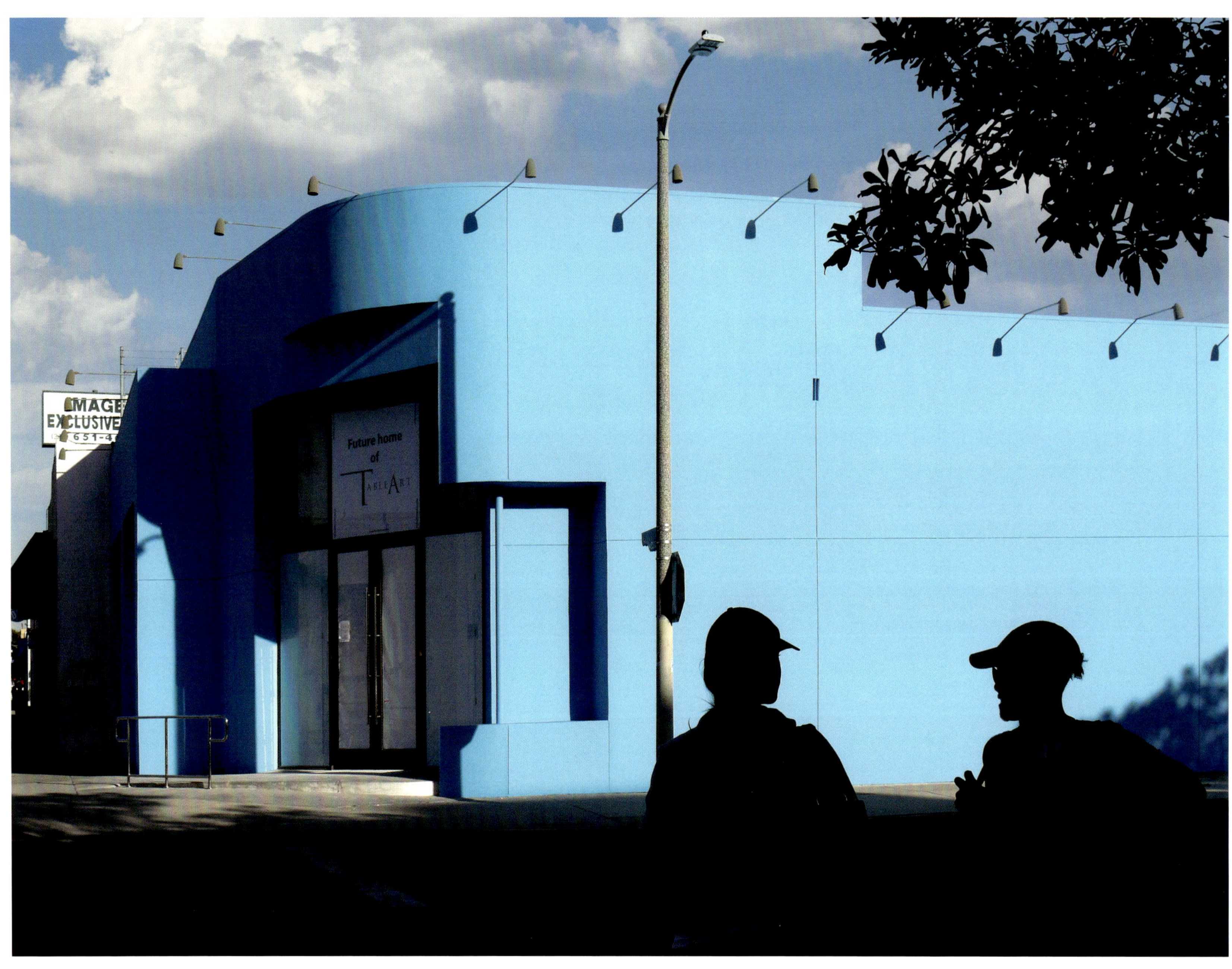

"Future Home of Table Art"
West Hollywood, 2012

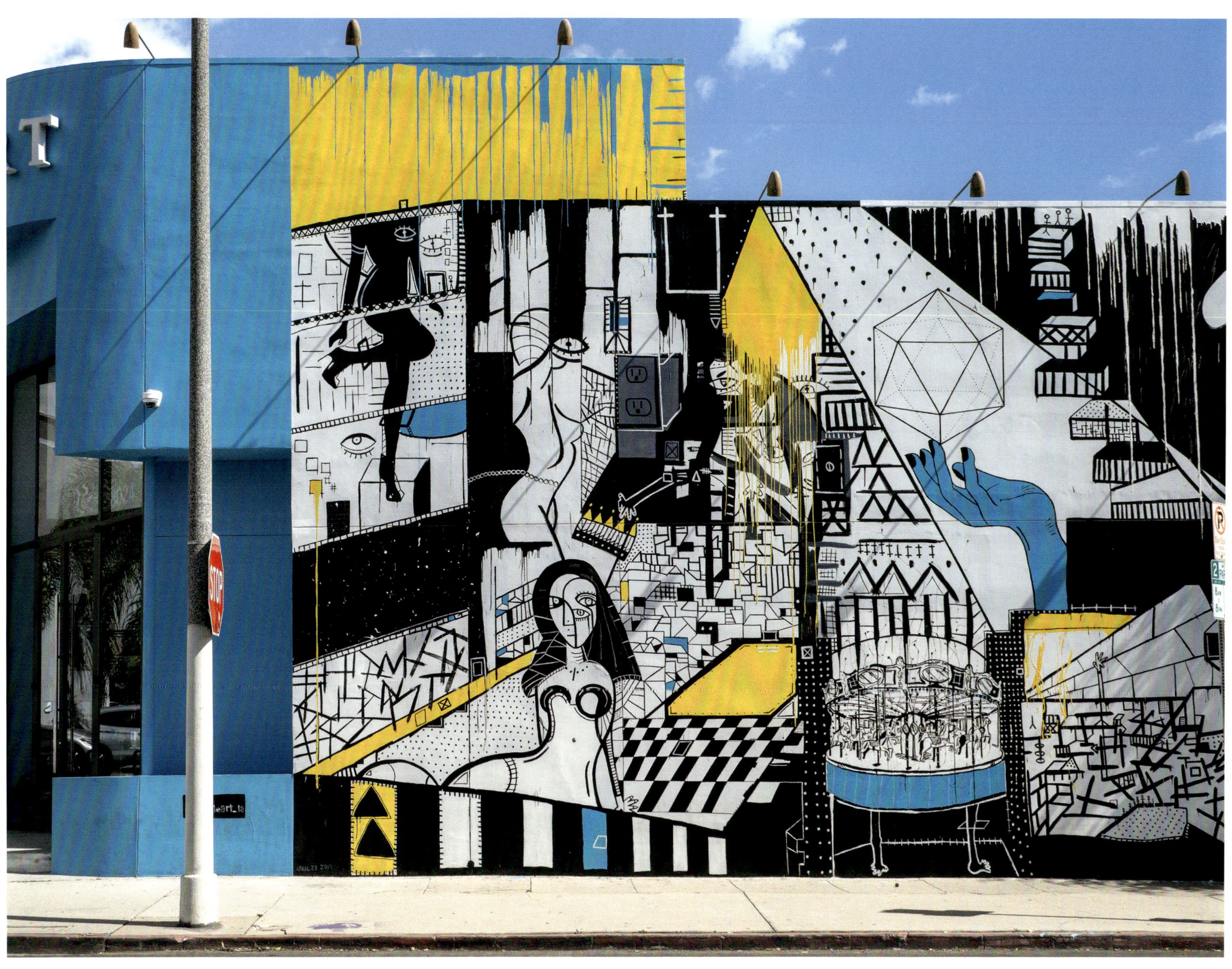

Current home of Table Art
West Hollywood, 2022

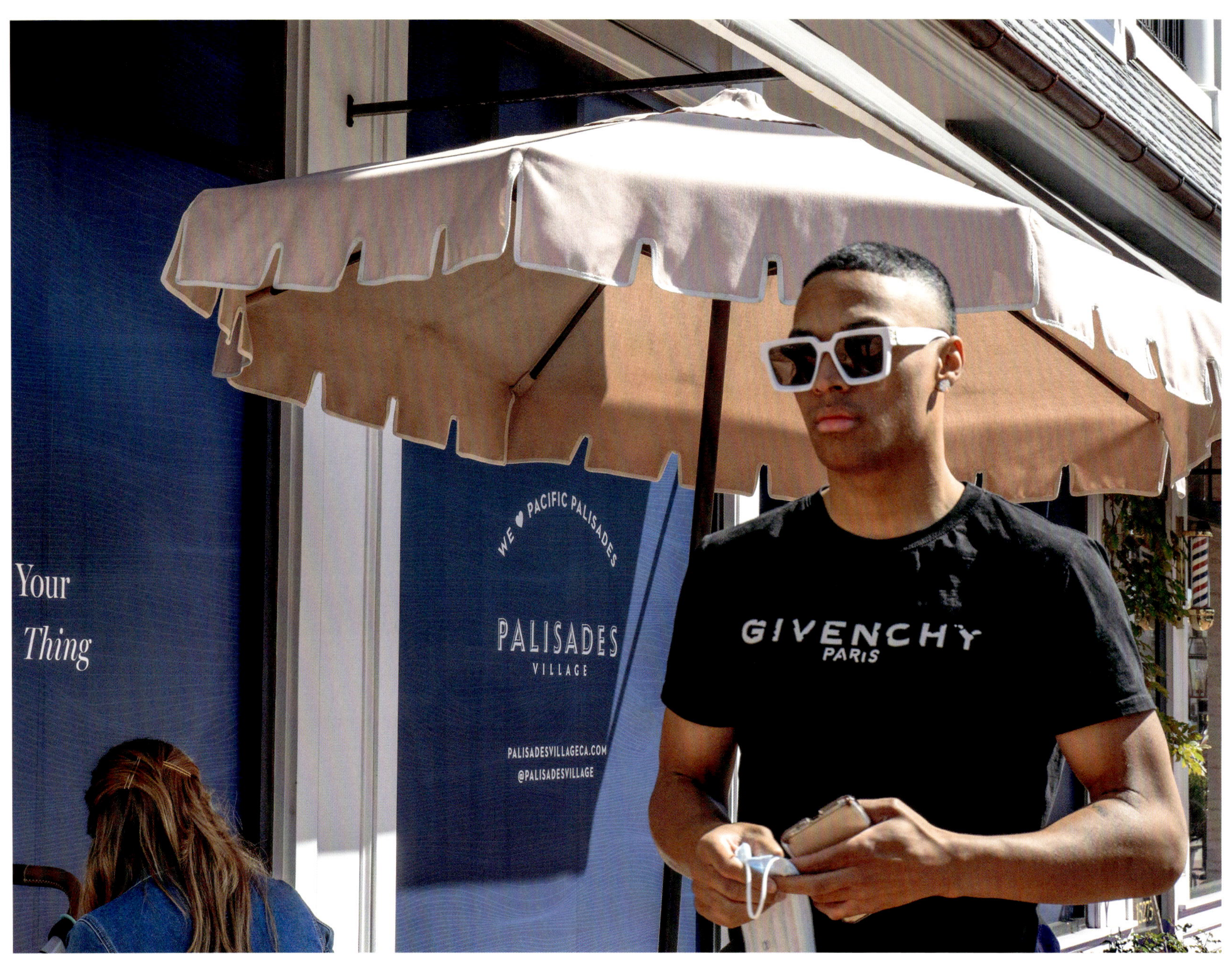

Sunset Blvd., Pacific Palisades

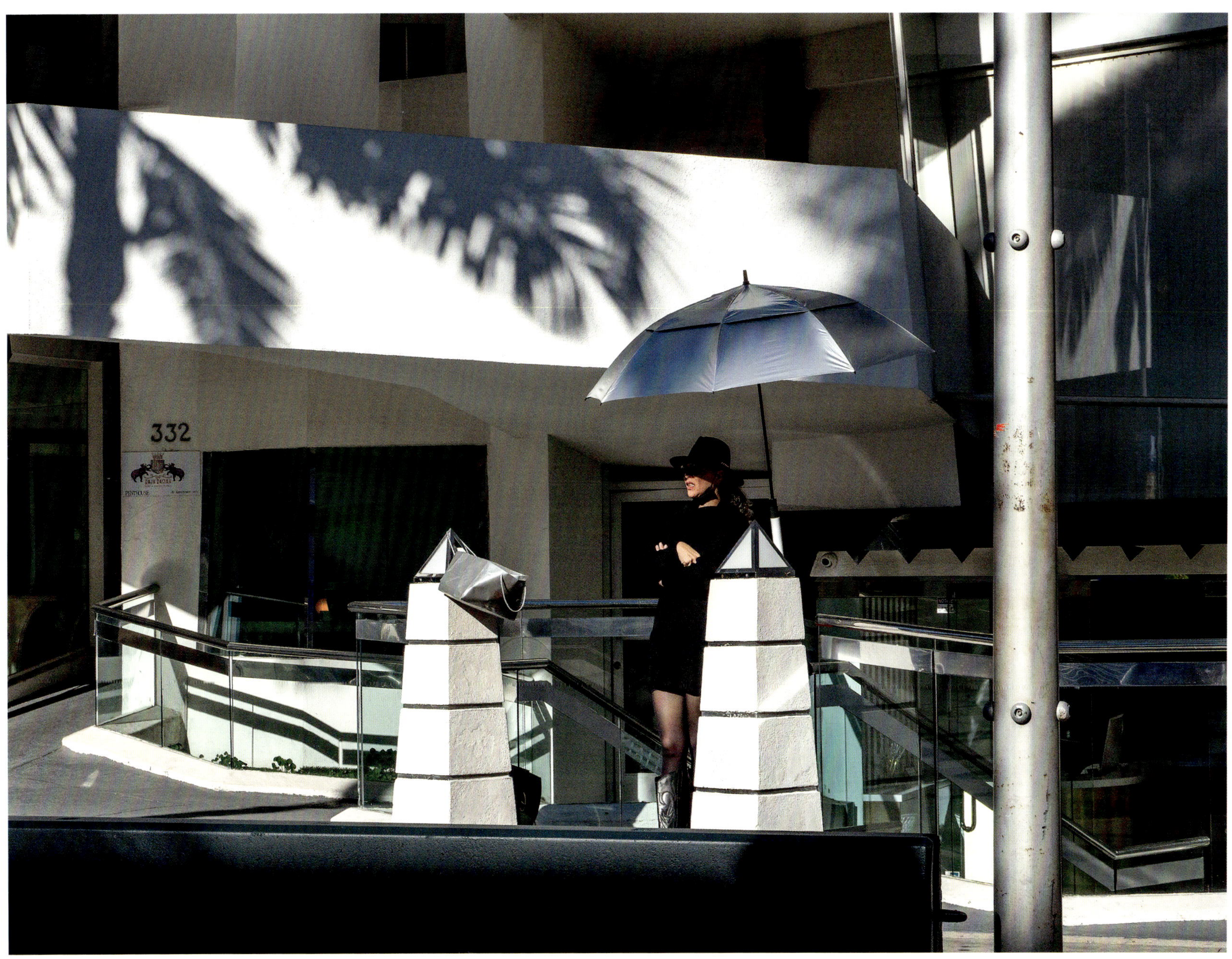

Rodeo Drive, Beverly Hills

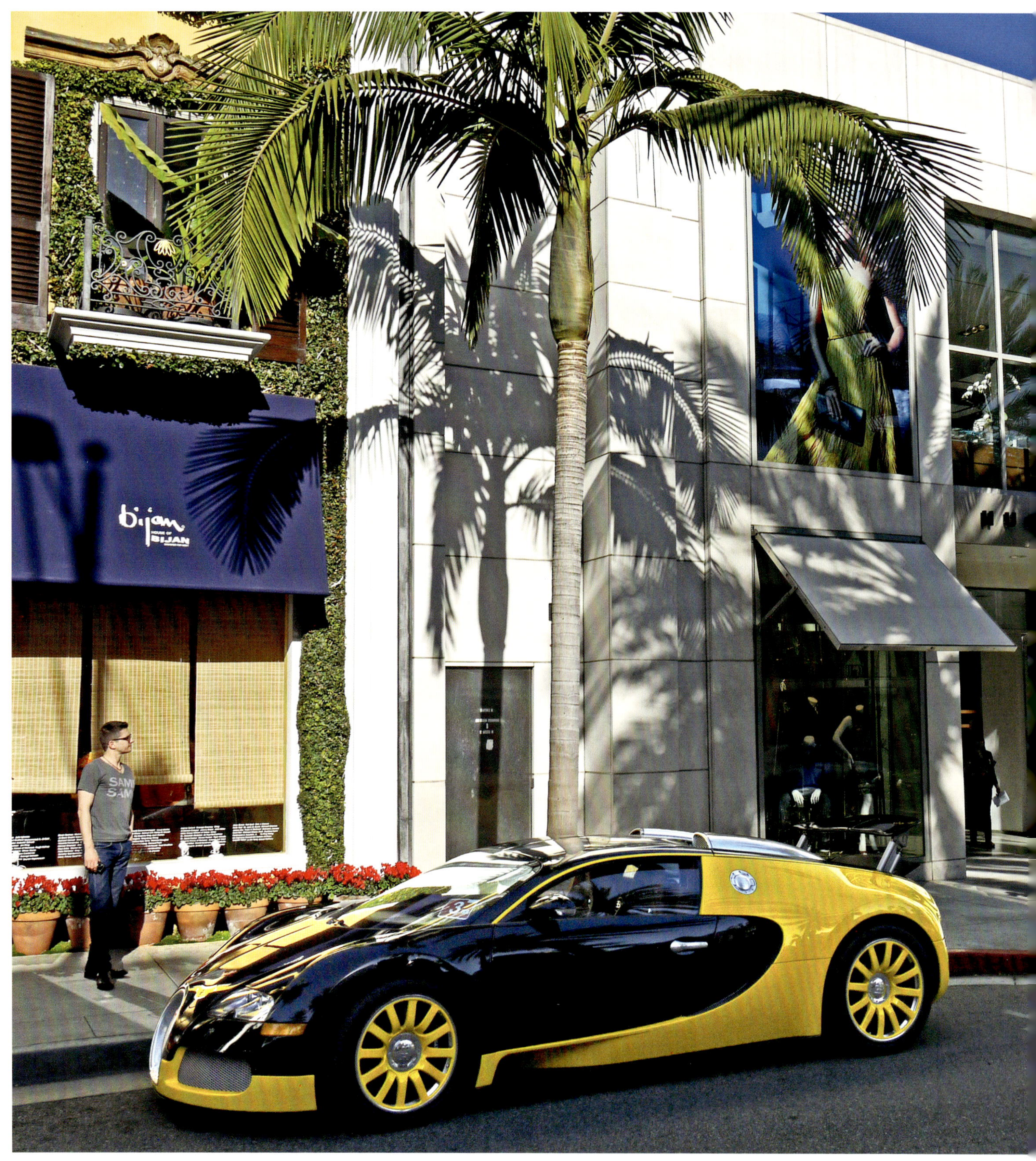

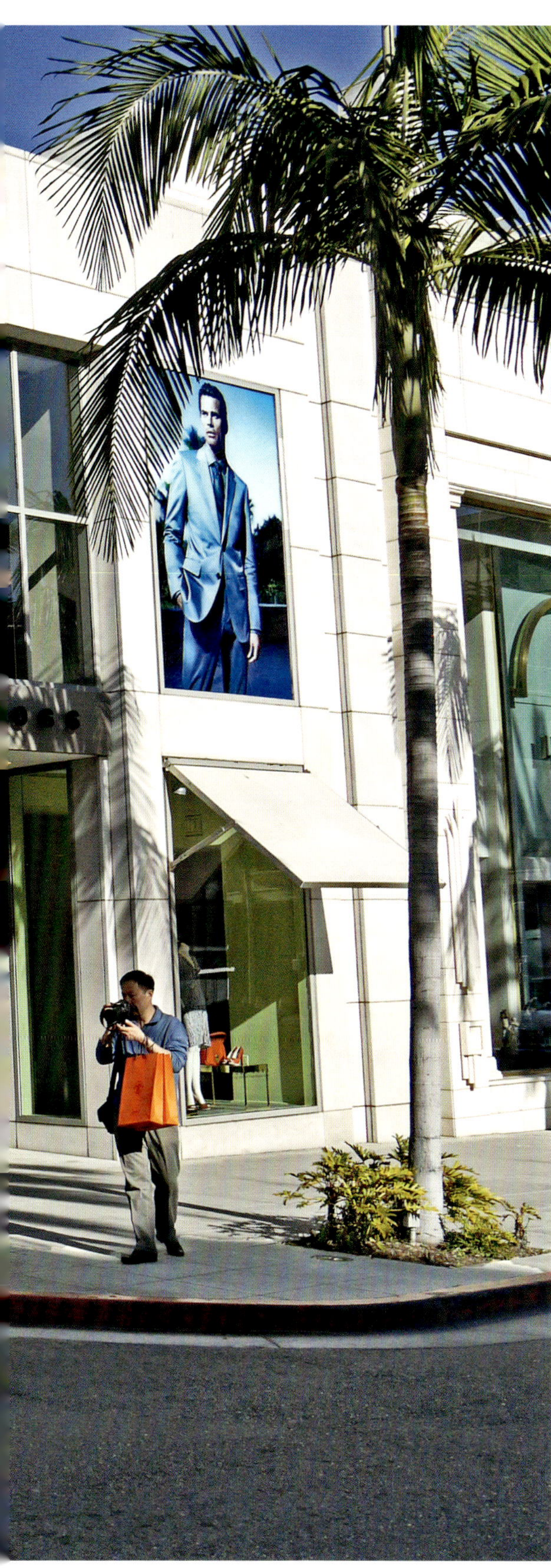

Bugati, Rodeo Drive, Beverly Hills

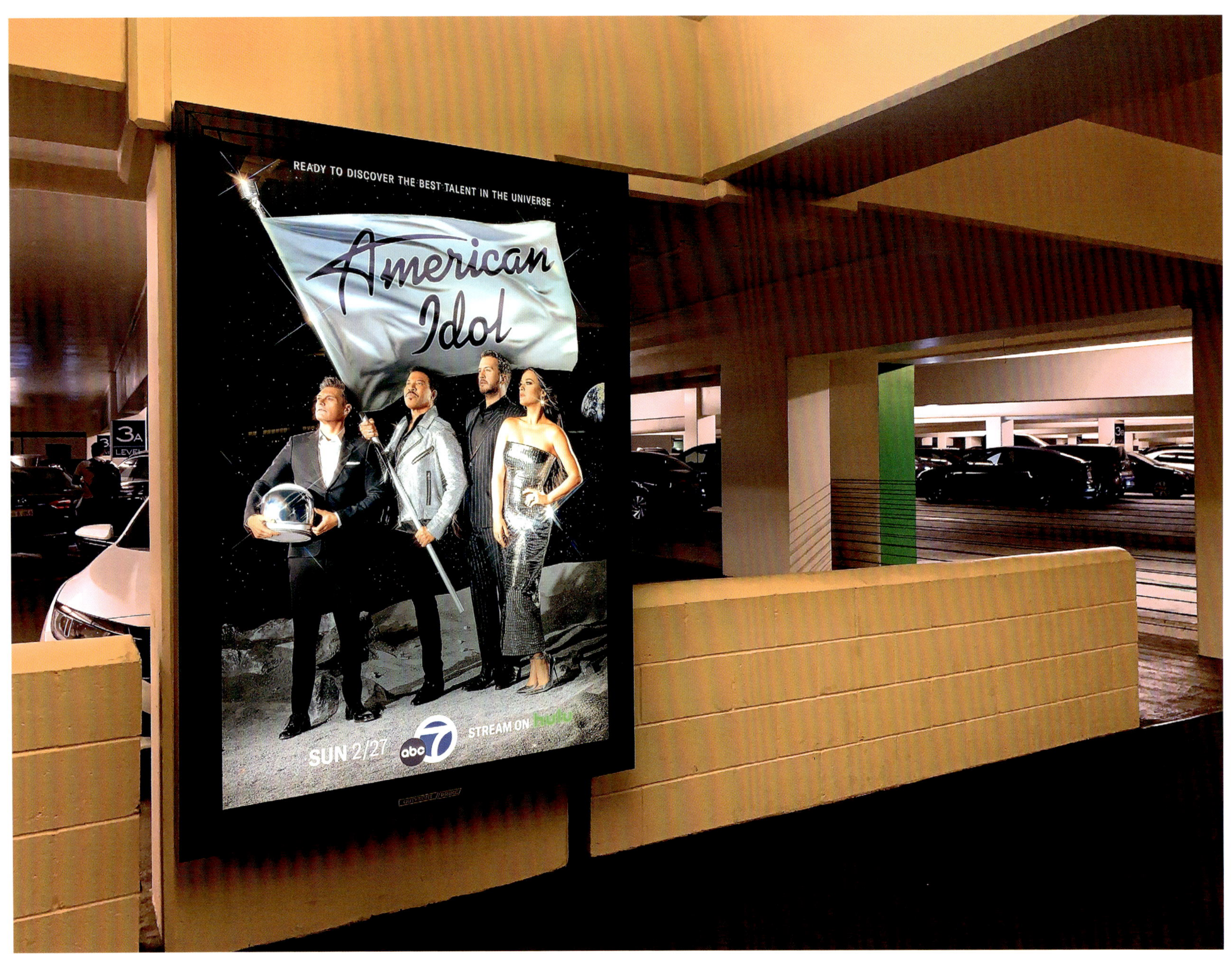

"American Idol," 2022
Americana at Brand Mall, Glendale

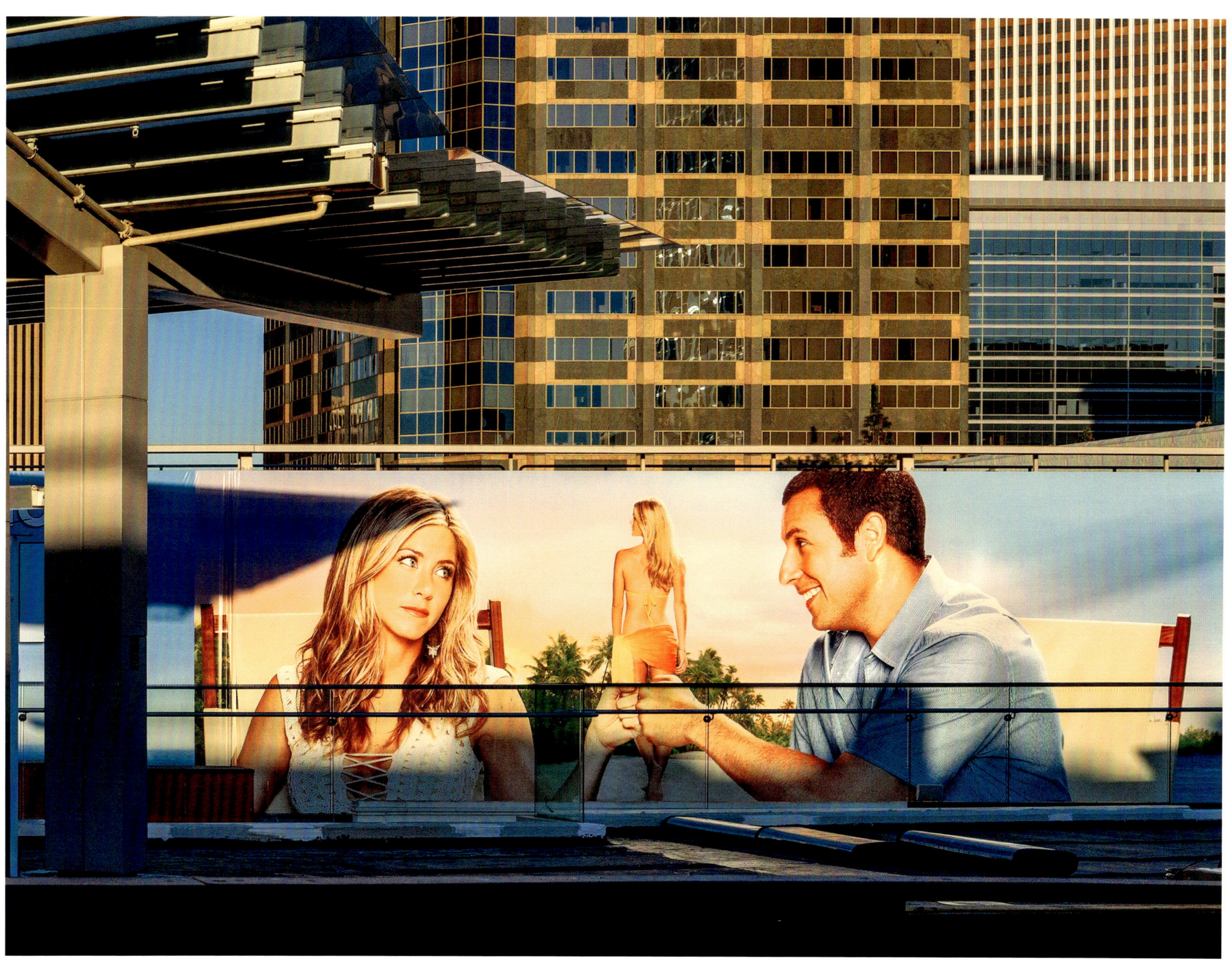

"Just Go With It," 2011
Jennifer Aniston and Adam Sandler, Century City

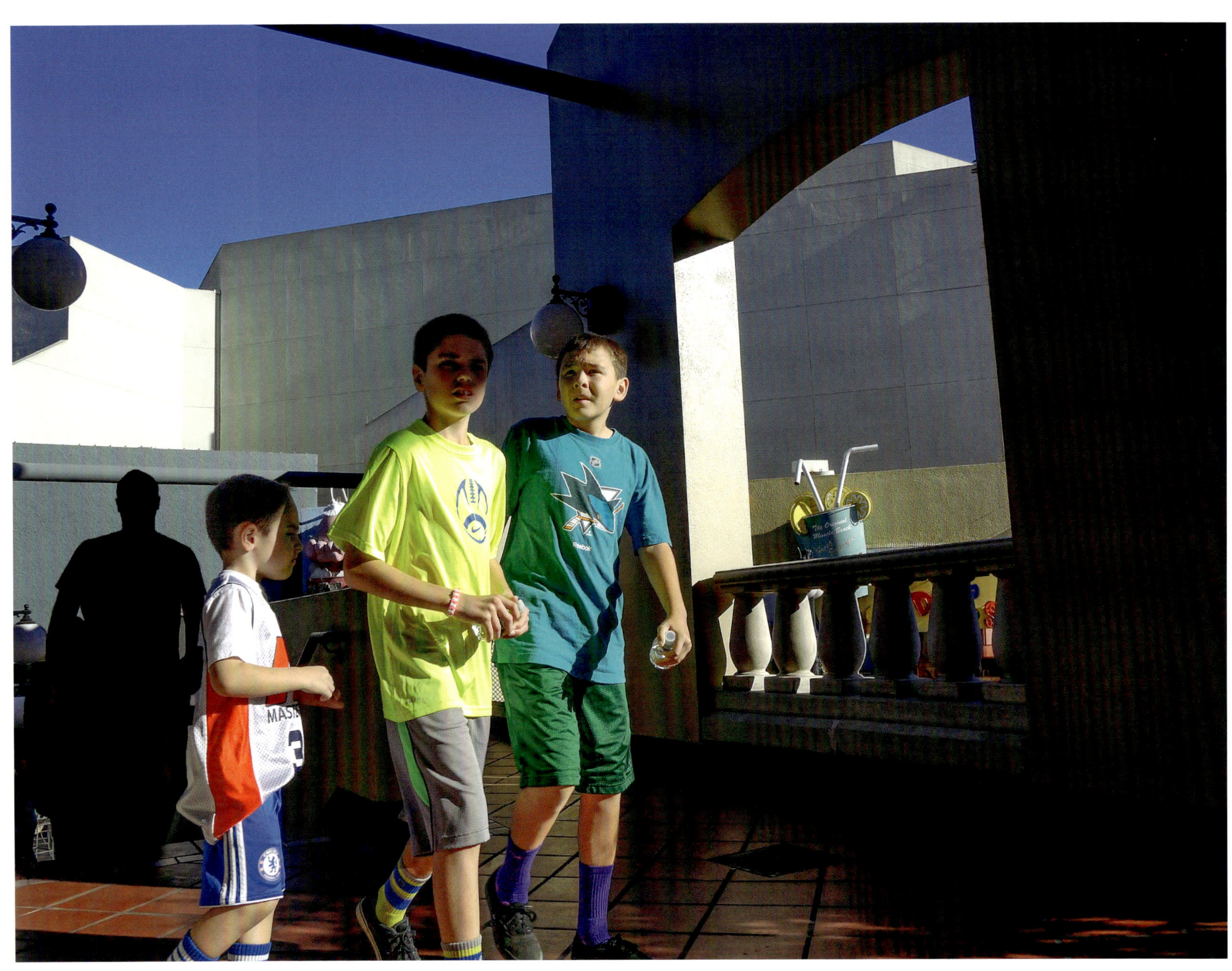

Nike, Horton Plaza Mall, San Diego

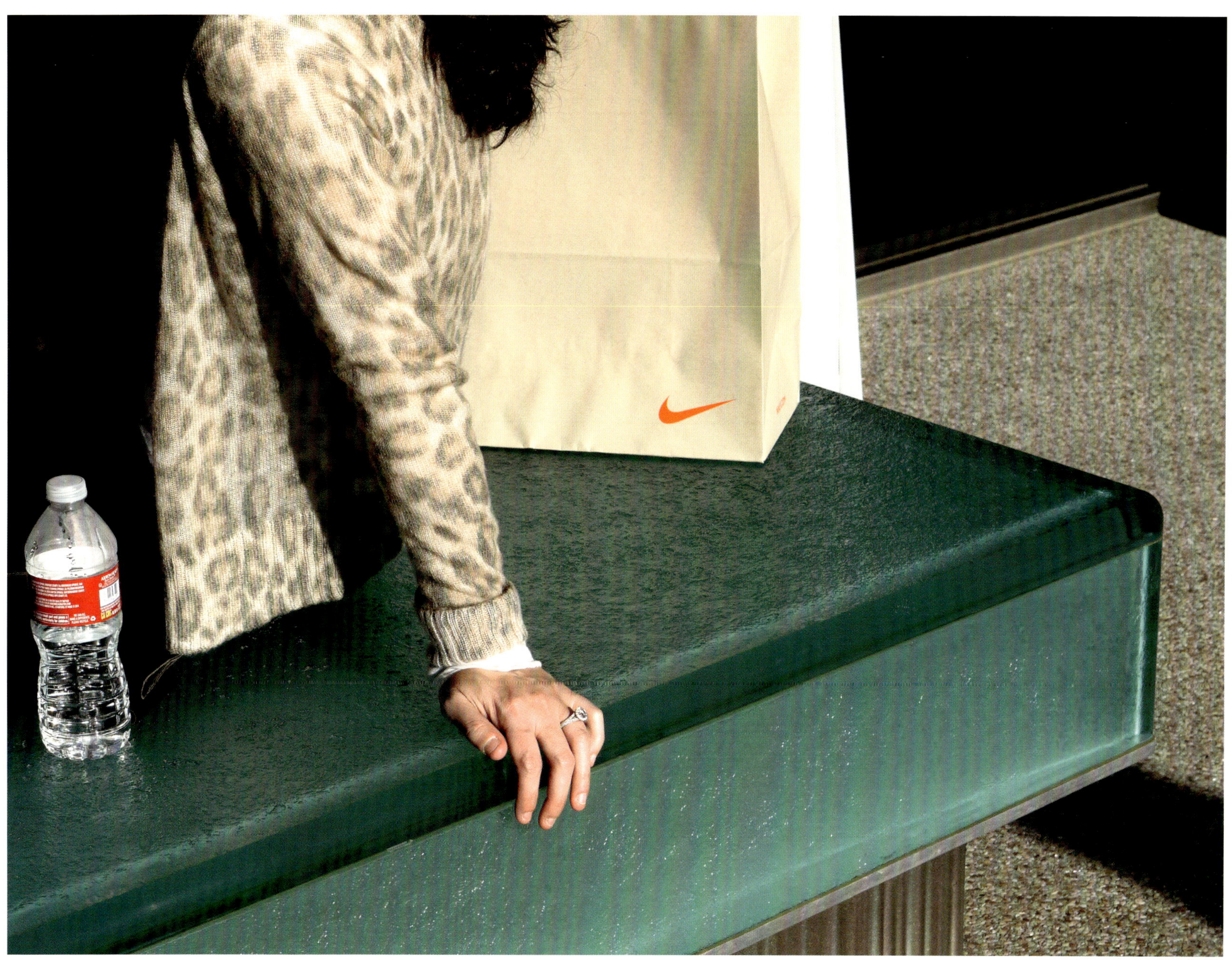

Nike, Santa Monica Mall, Los Angeles

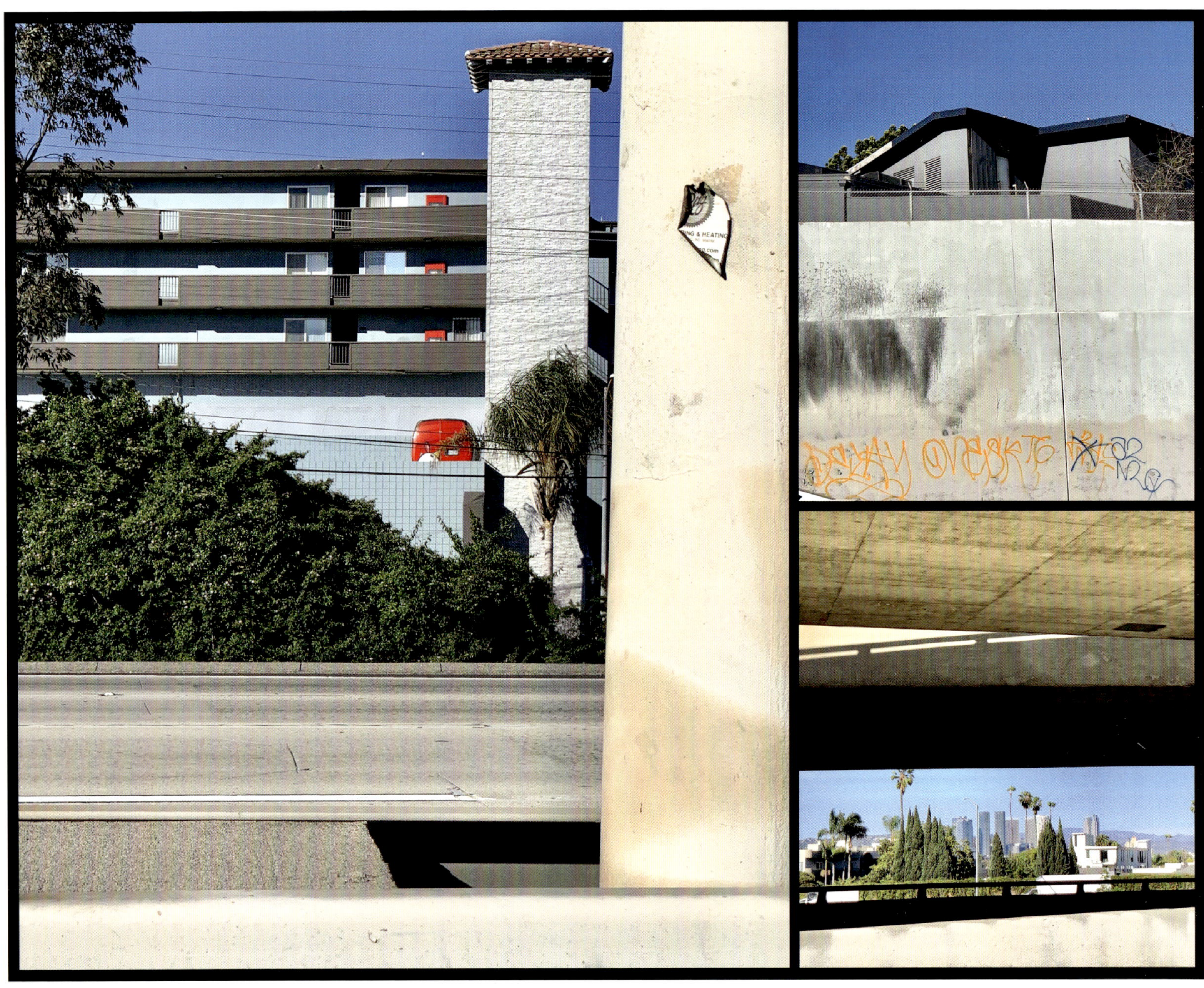

From the I-10 Freeway, Santa Monica to Los Angeles

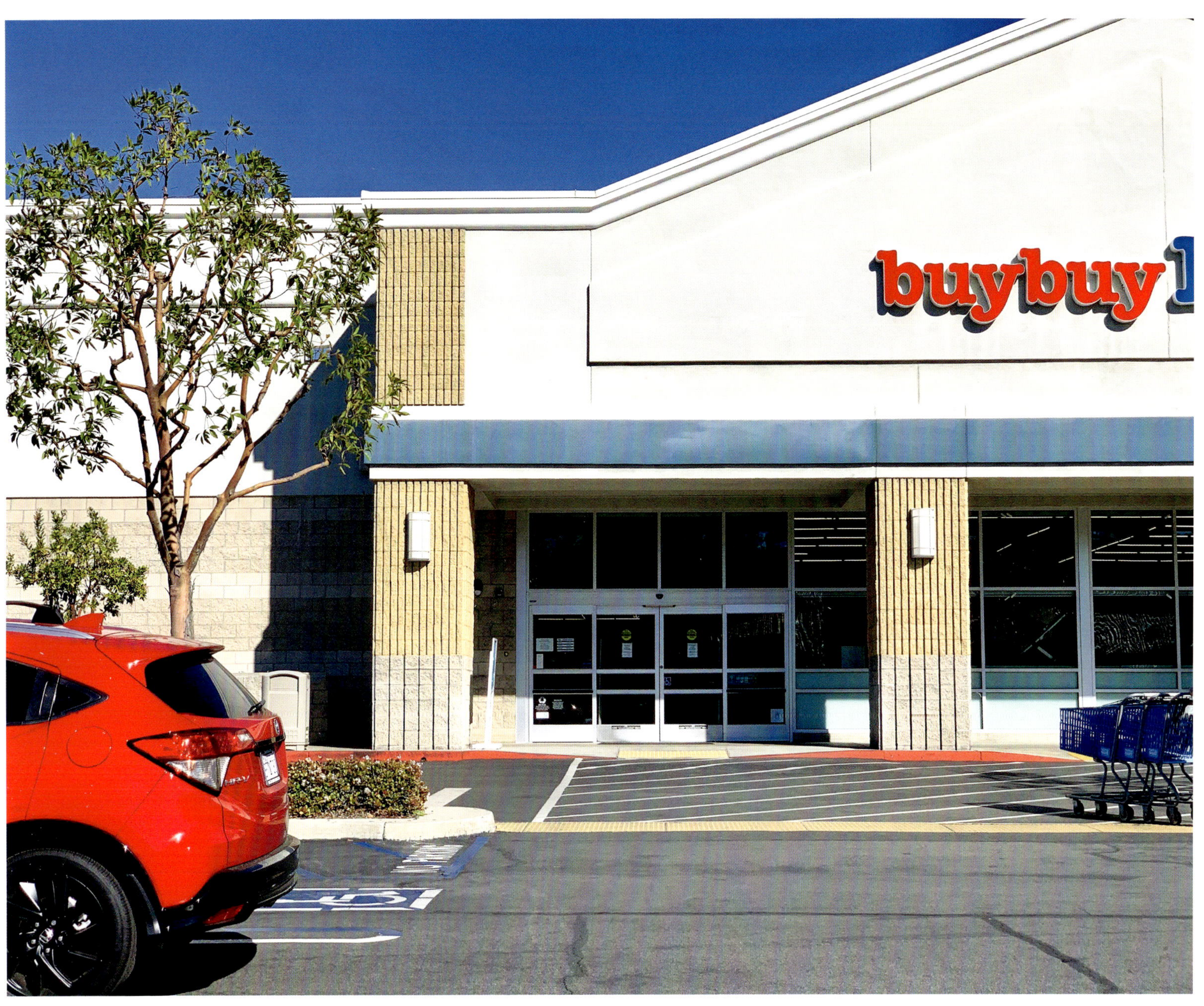

Next to the I-405 Freeway, Los Angeles to San Diego

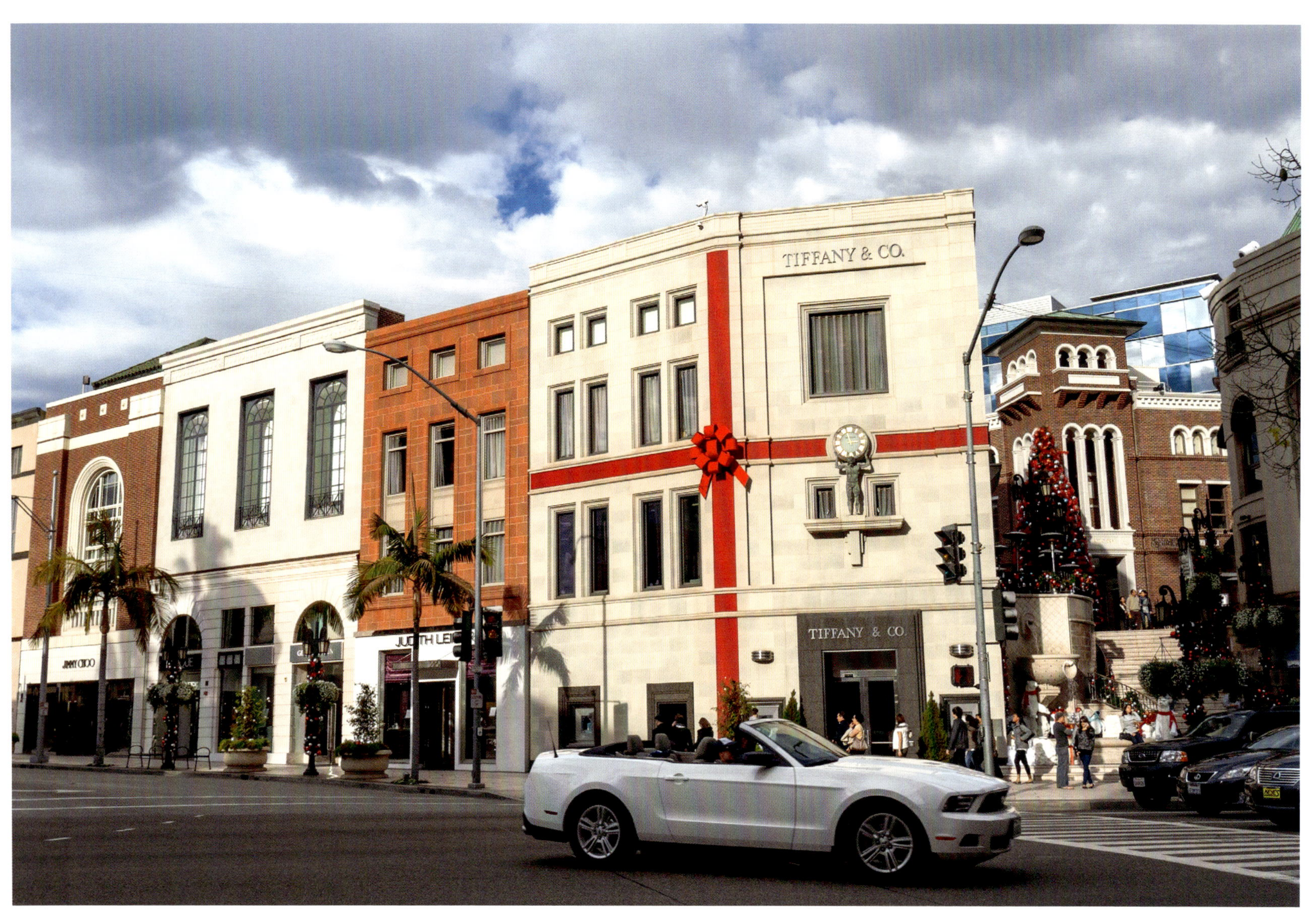

Tiffany & Co. at Christmas
Wilshire @ Rodeo, Beverly Hills

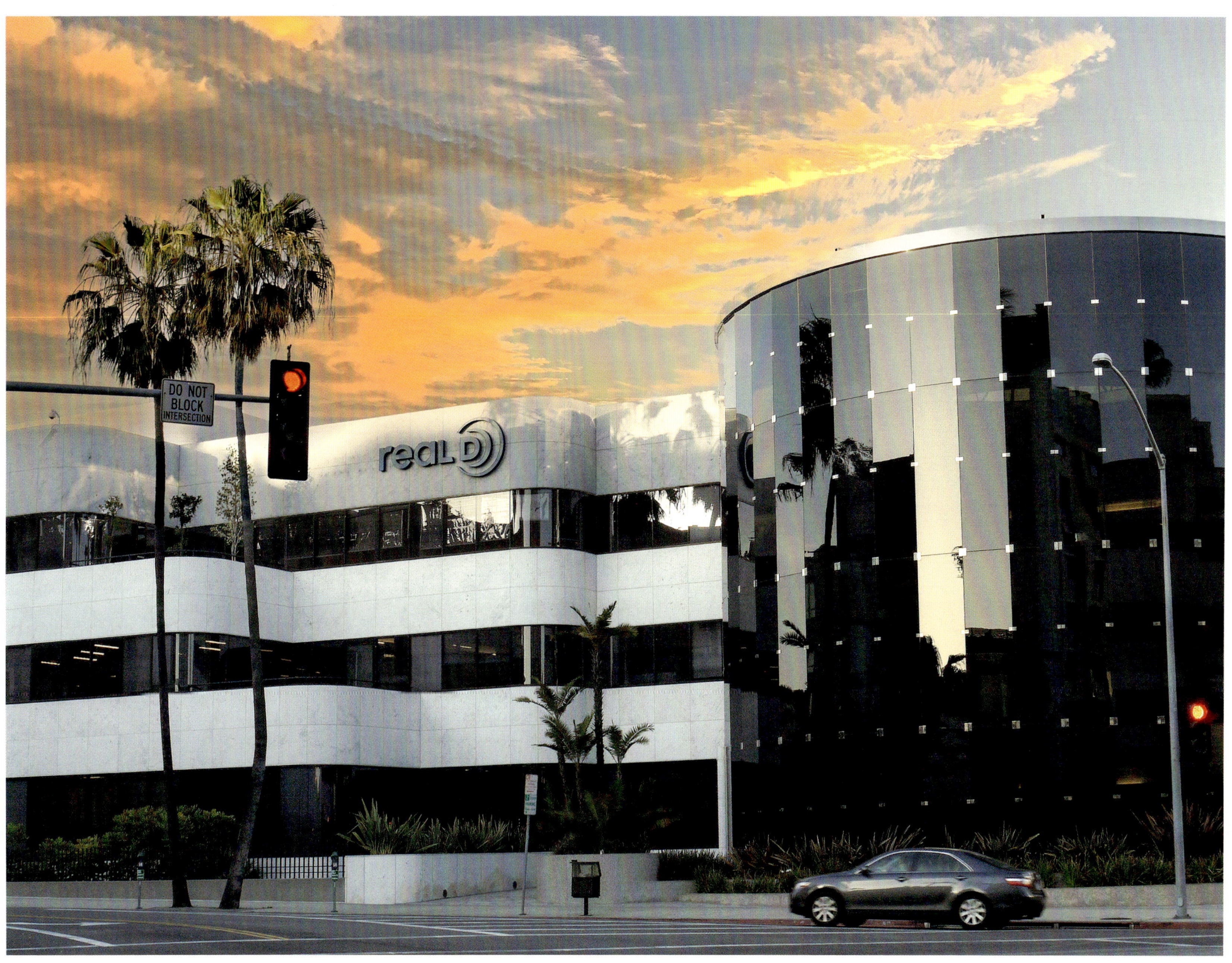

RealD (3D Cinema) Headquarters, Beverly Hills

"advanced technology is indistinguishable from magic"

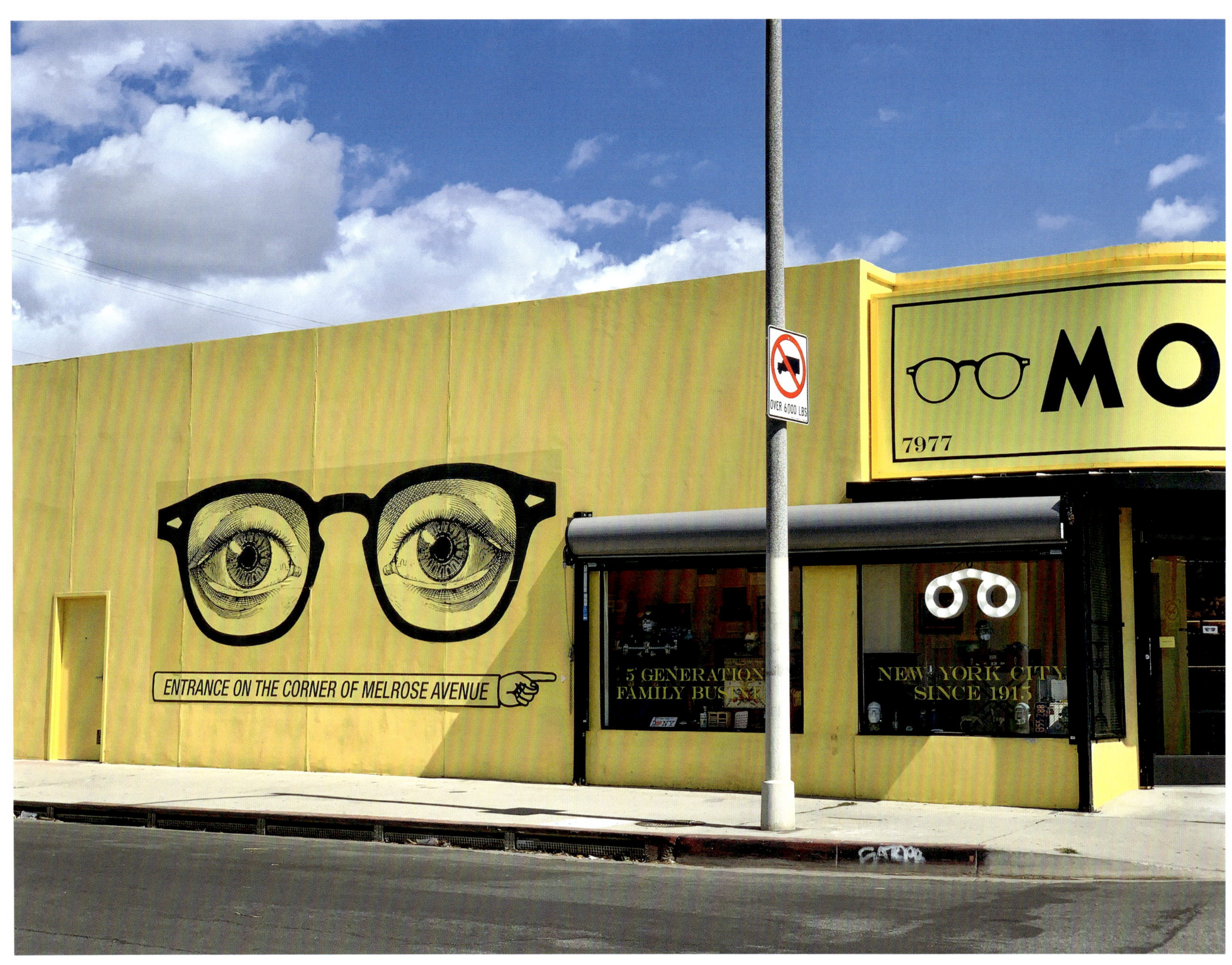

"New York City Since 1915"
West Hollywood

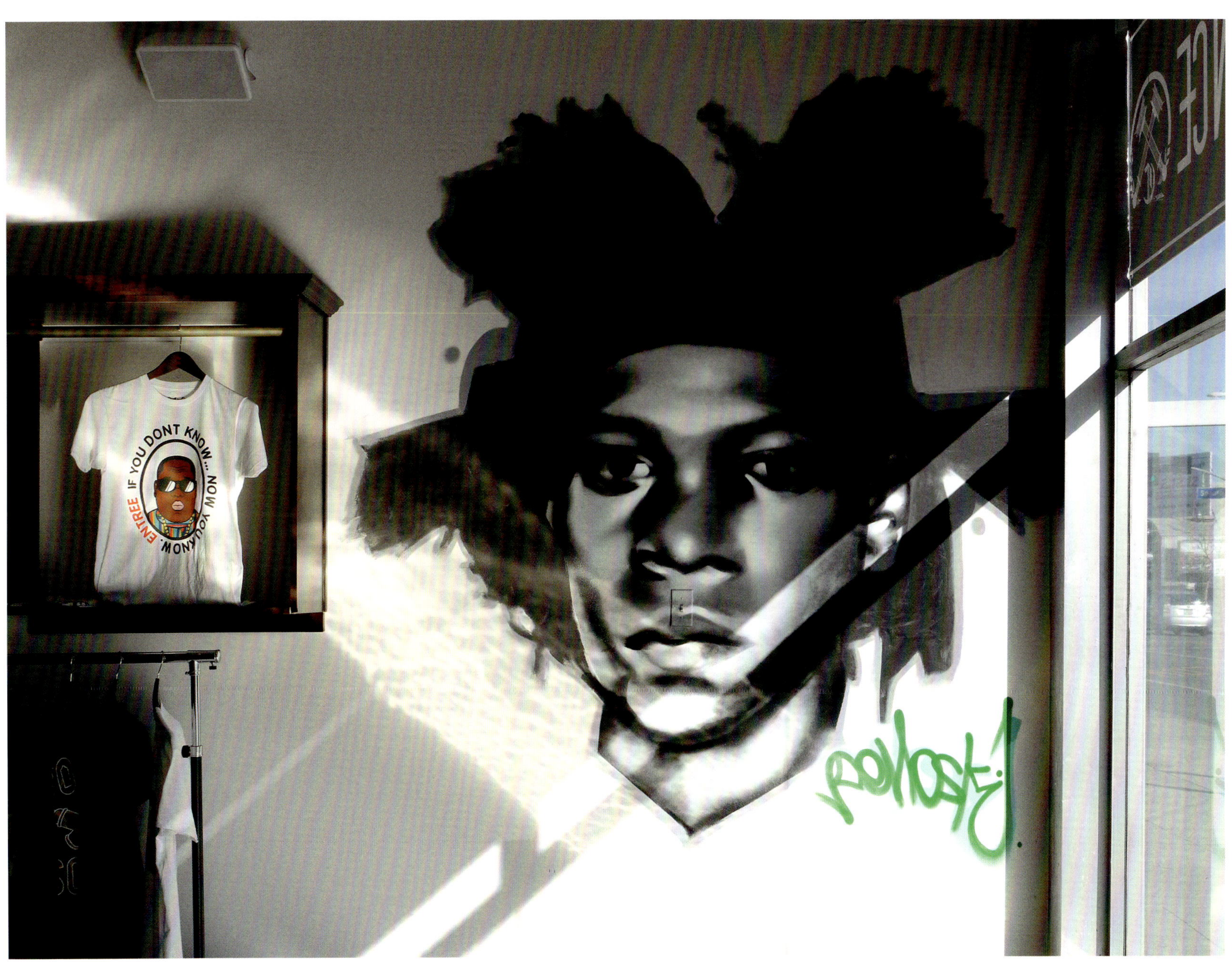

"If You Don't Know, Now You Know"
West Hollywood

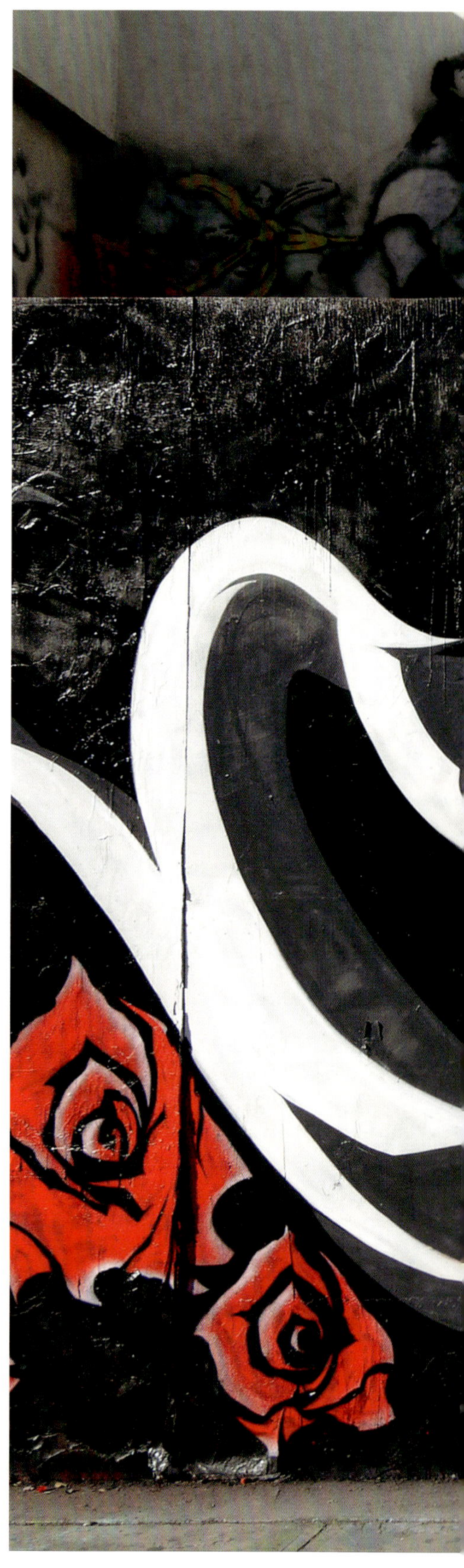

Melrose Moving East, Hollywood

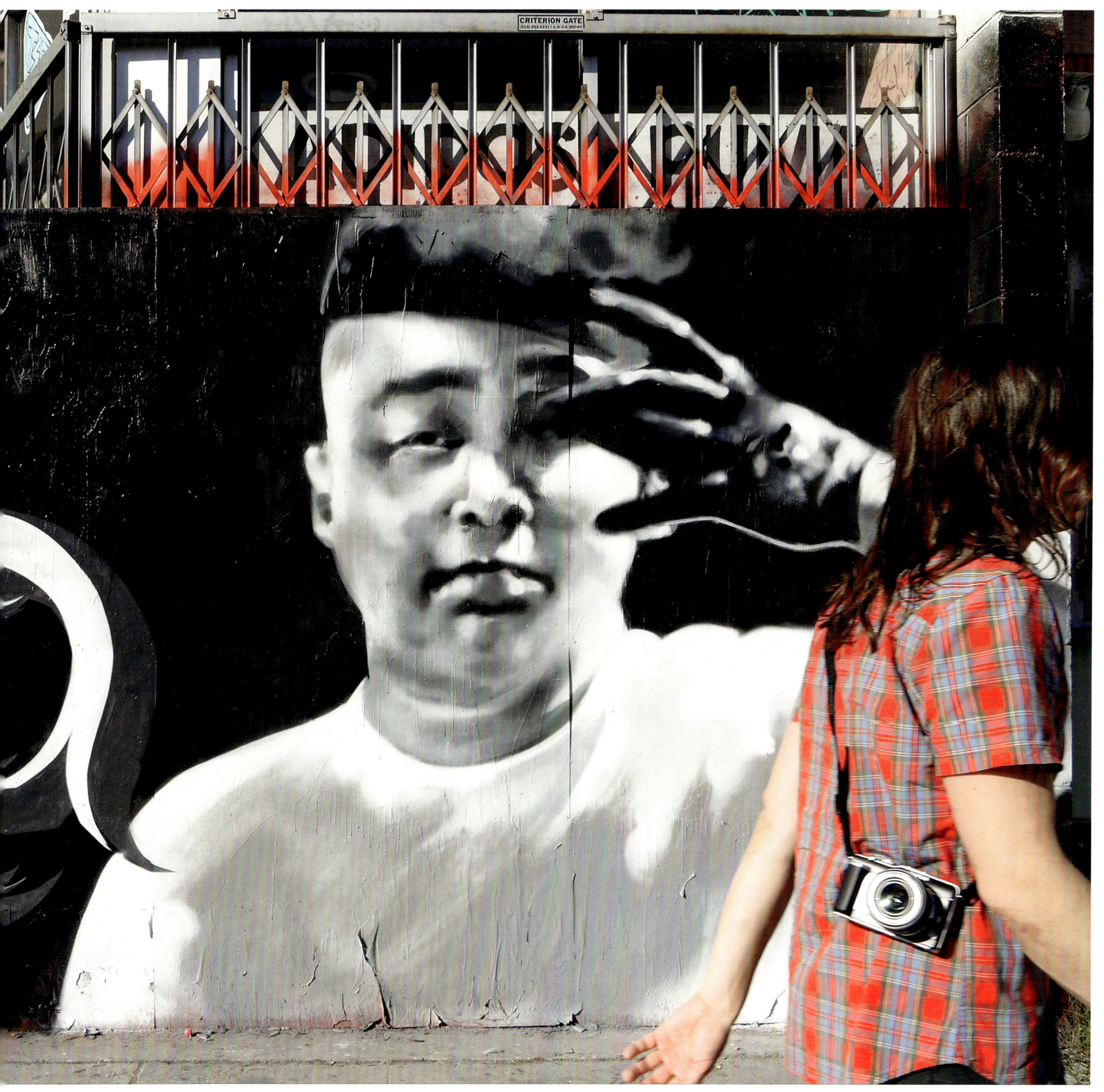
CRITERION GATE

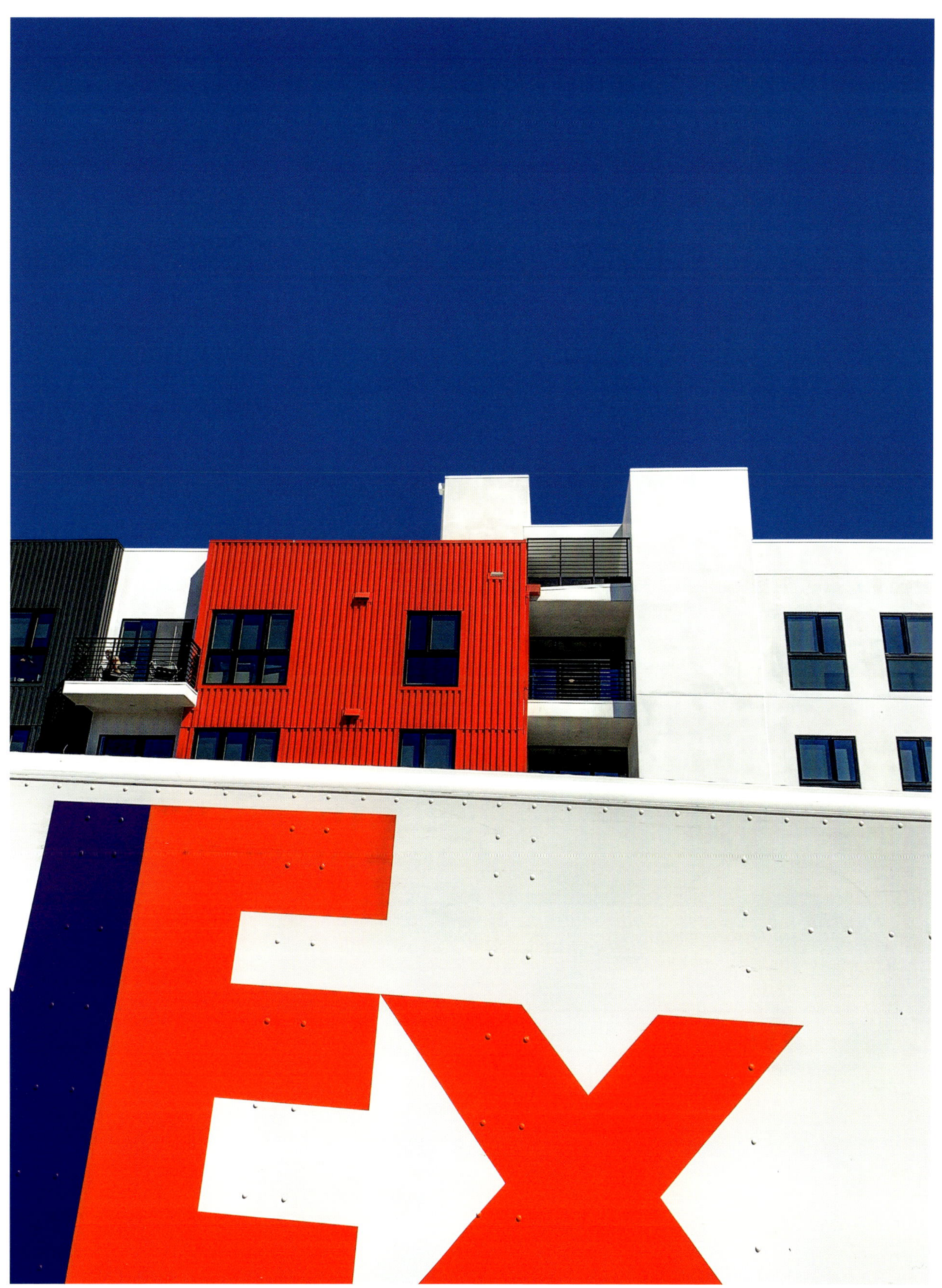

Apts. for Rent and
FedEx, West LA

Hoods

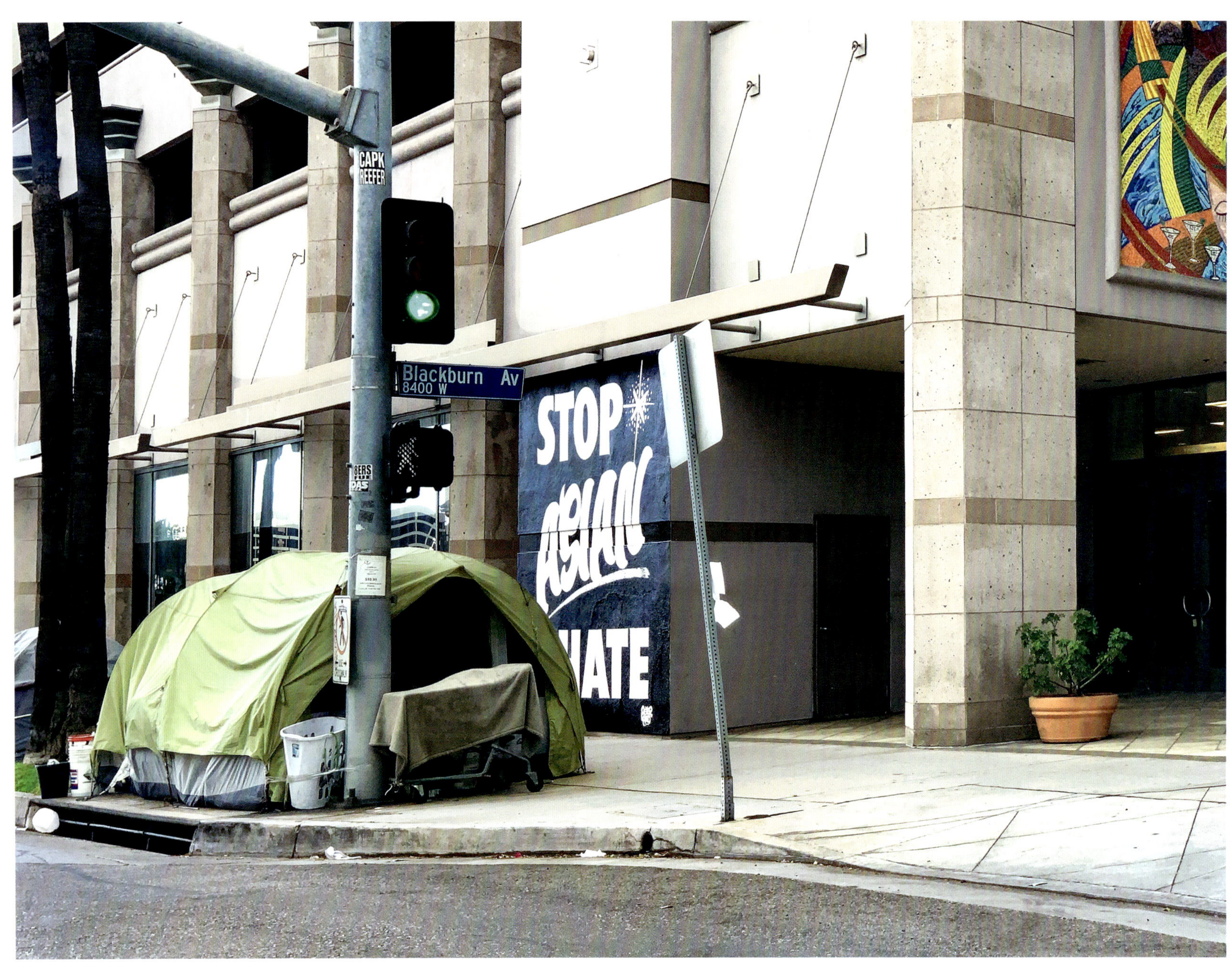

La Cienega @ Blackburn, near Hollywood

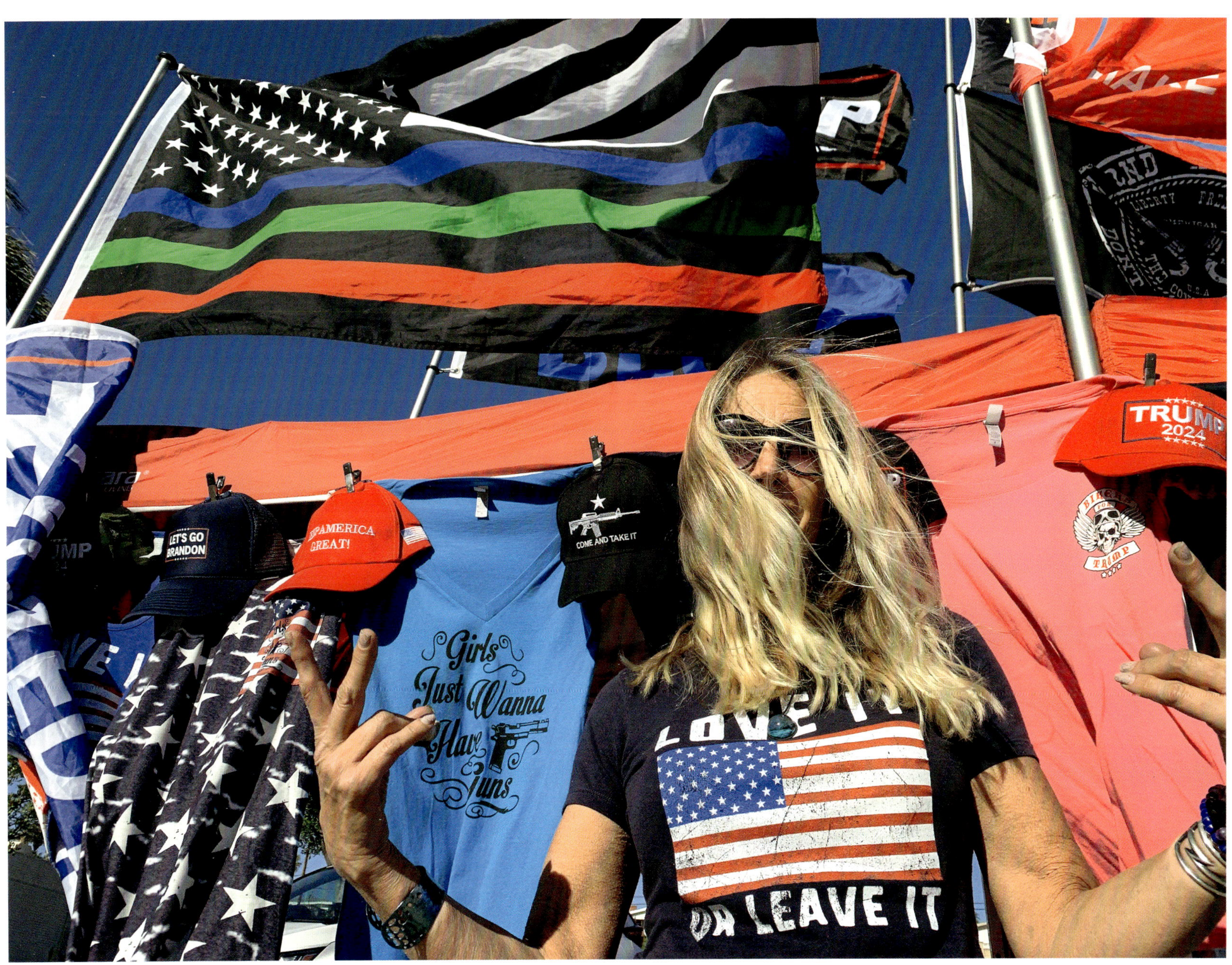

San Pedro, near Palos Verdes

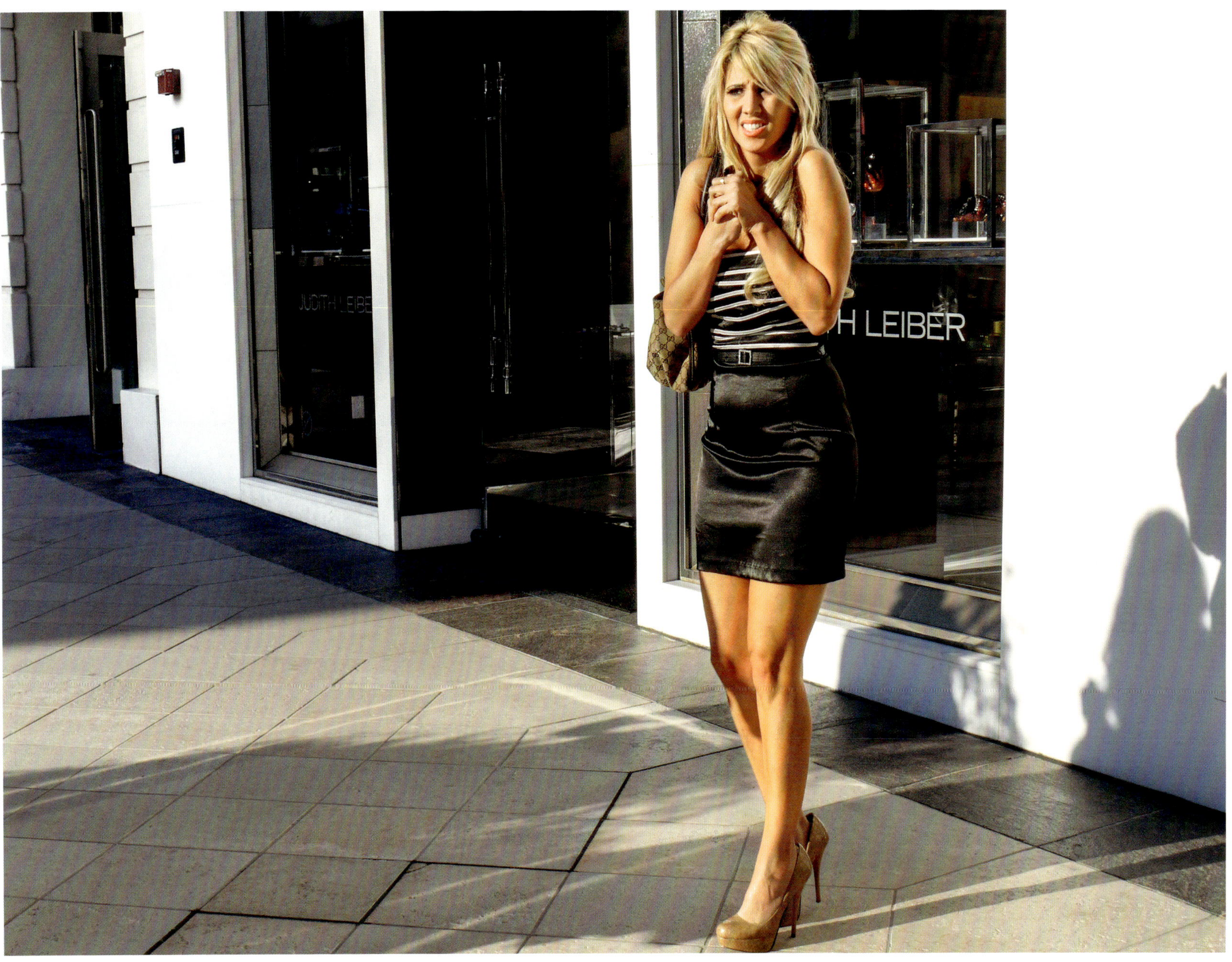

Leiber, Beverly Hills

Devon Motorworks, Beverly Hills (next pages)

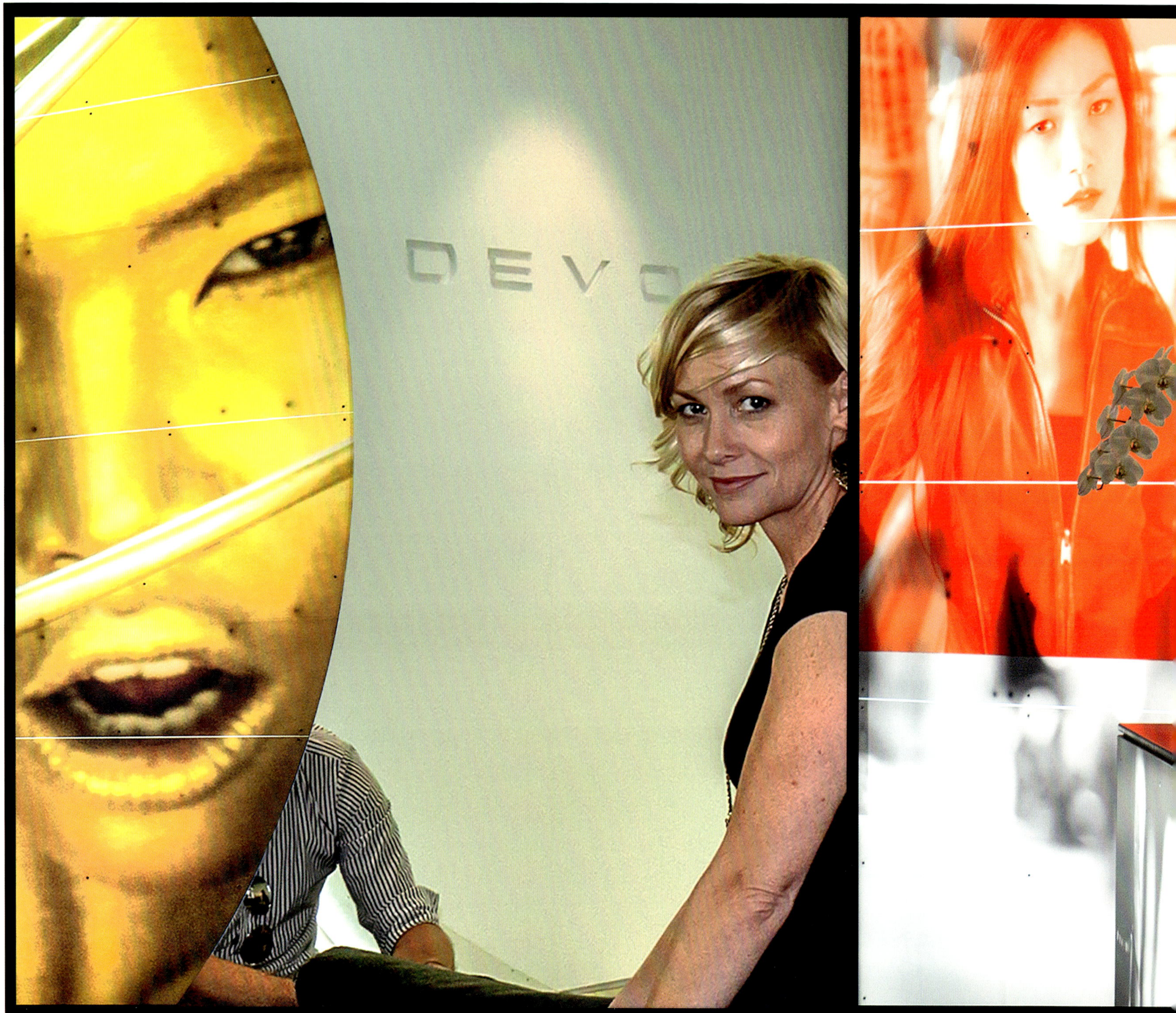
DEVO

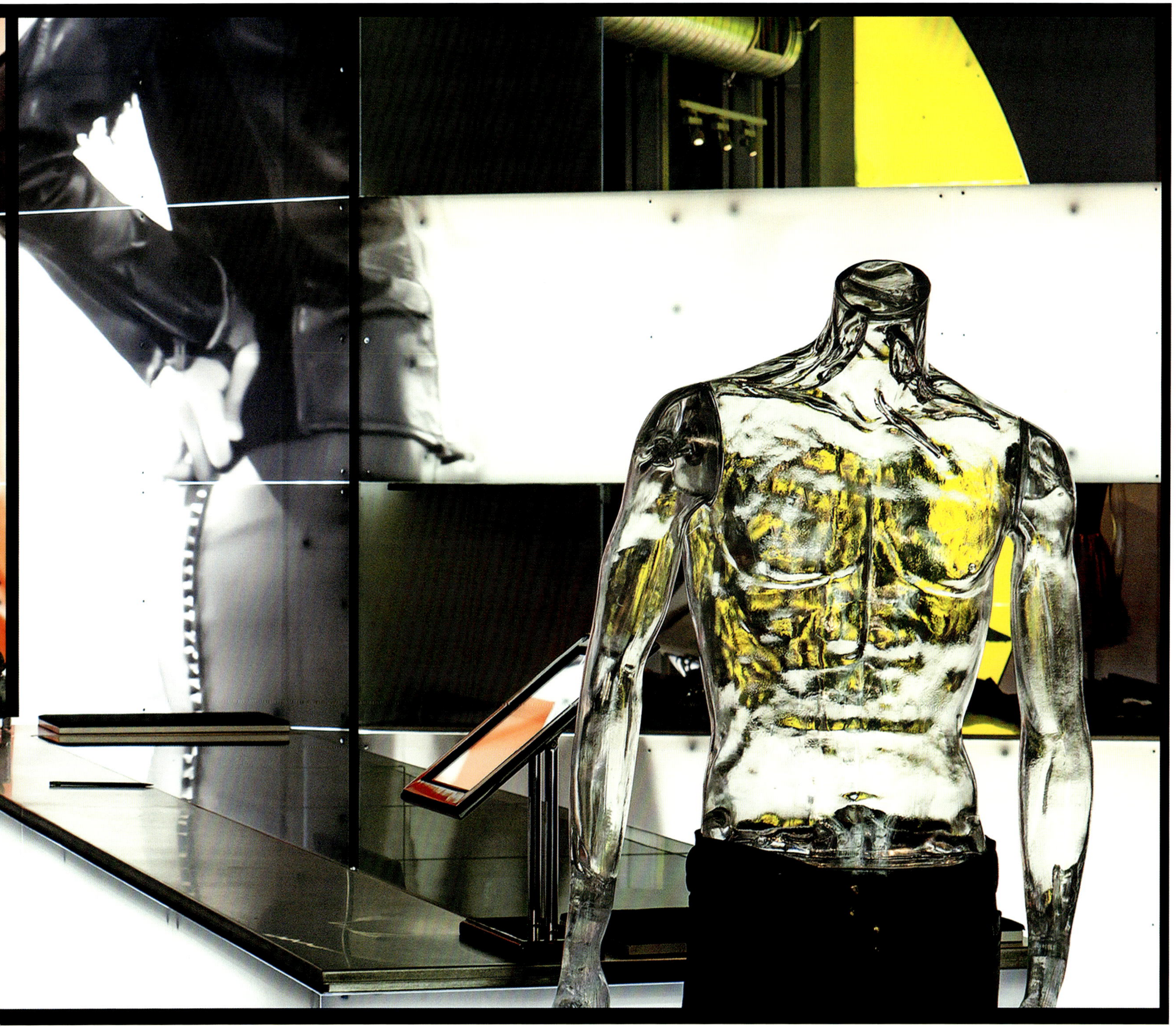

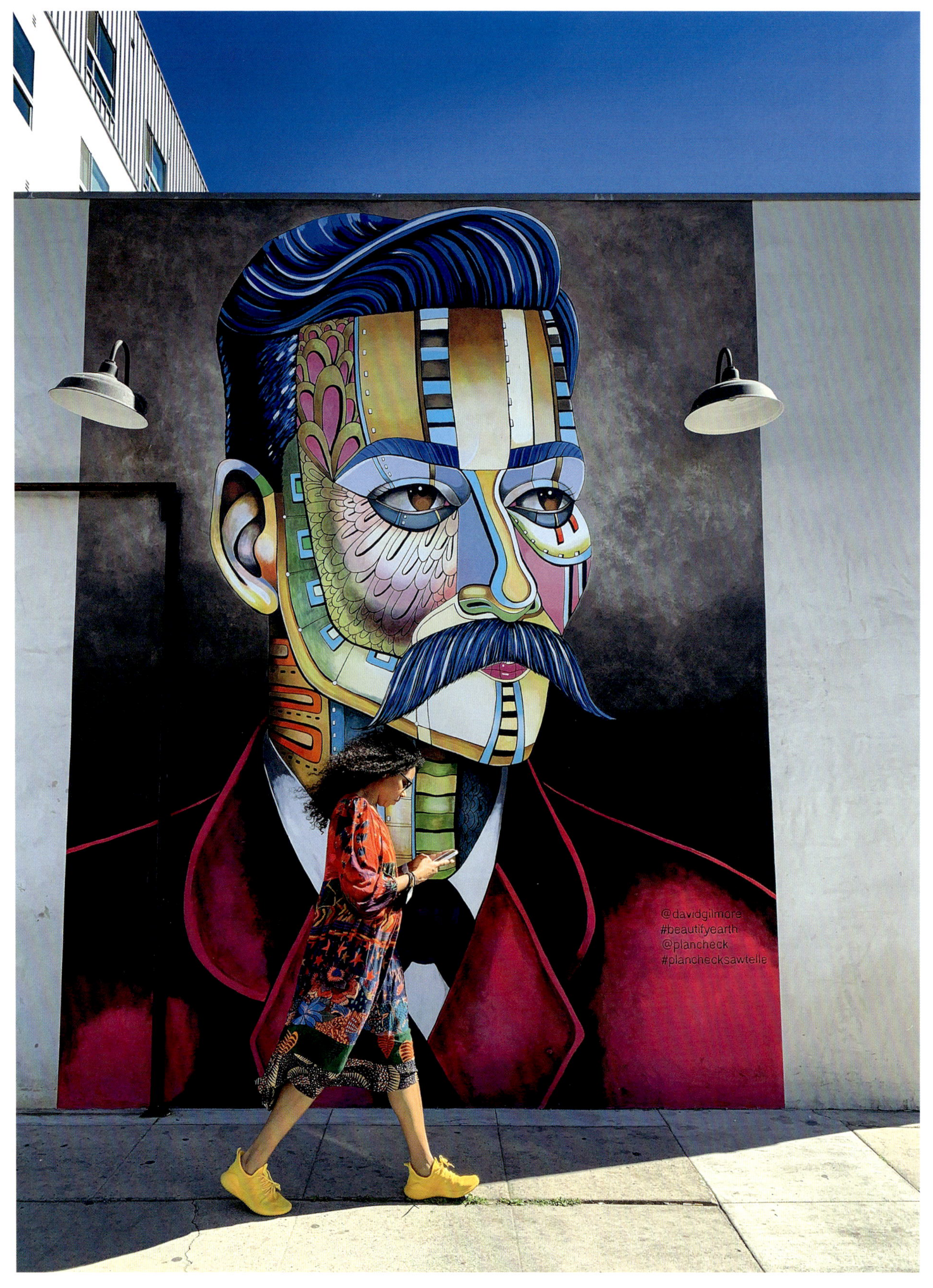

@davidgilmore
#beautifyearth
@plancheck
#planchecksawtelle

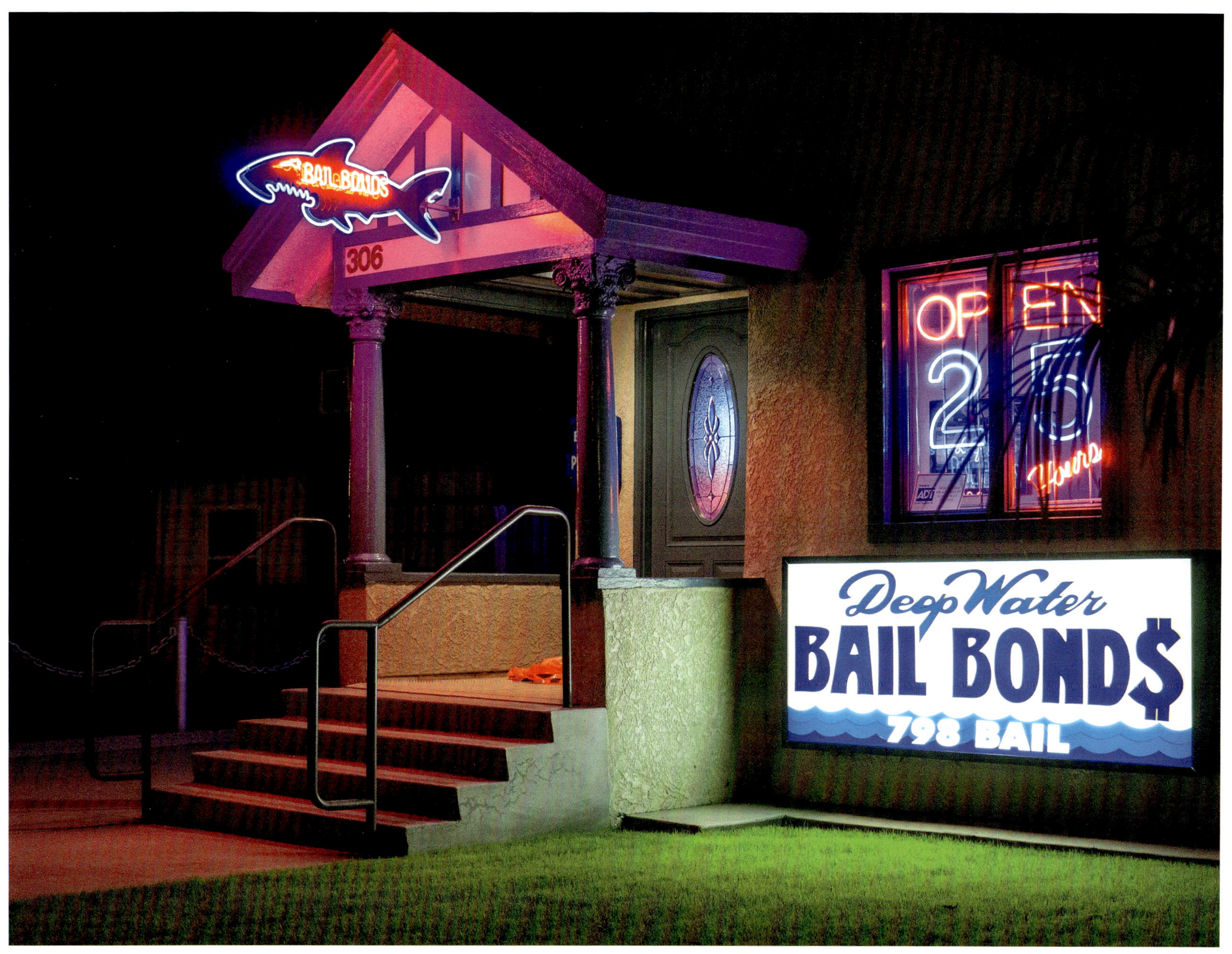

"#Beautify Earth @Plancheck," Santa Monica

"Deep Water Bail Bonds," Redondo Beach

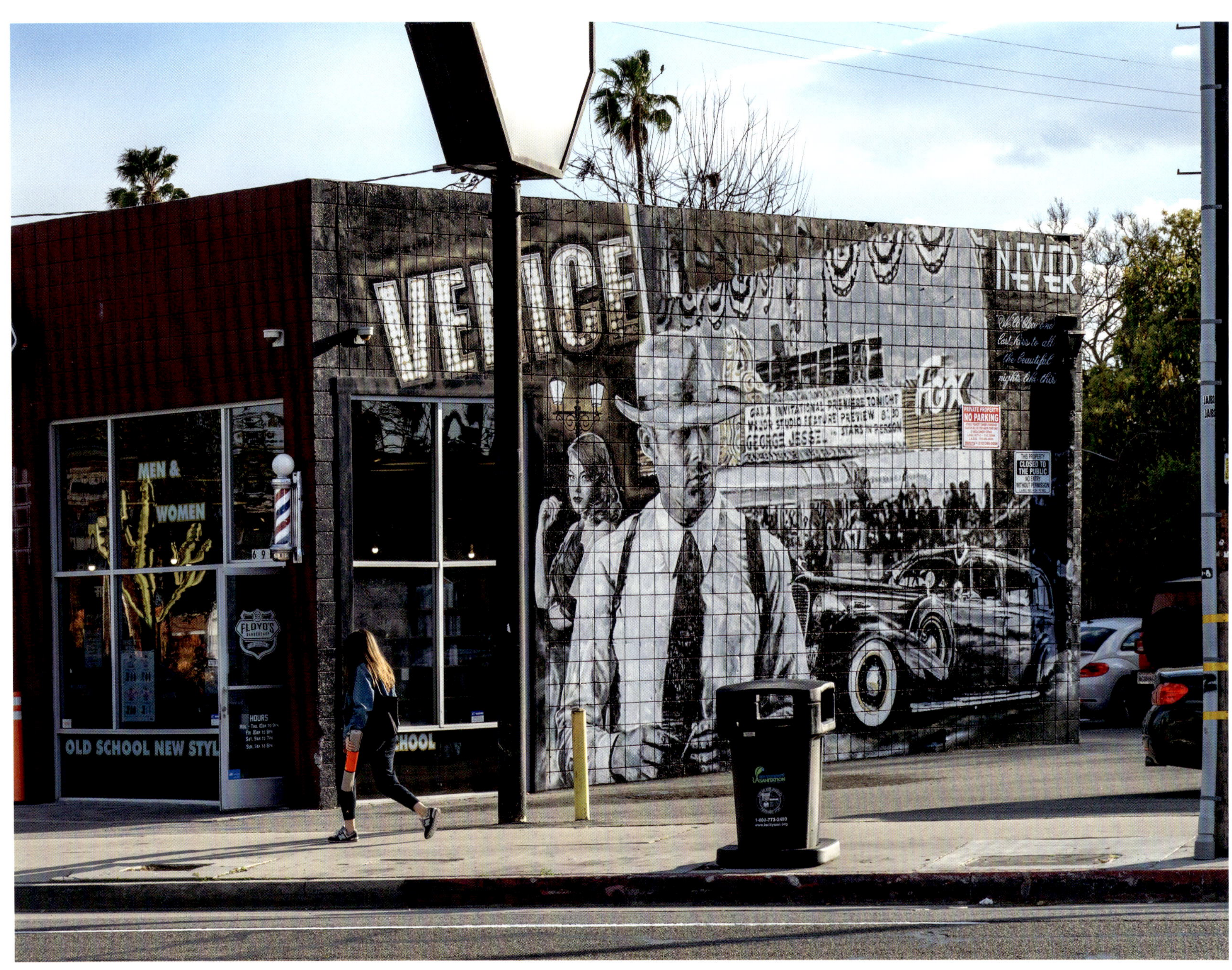

"Gala Preview" at the Fox Theater (mural), Venice

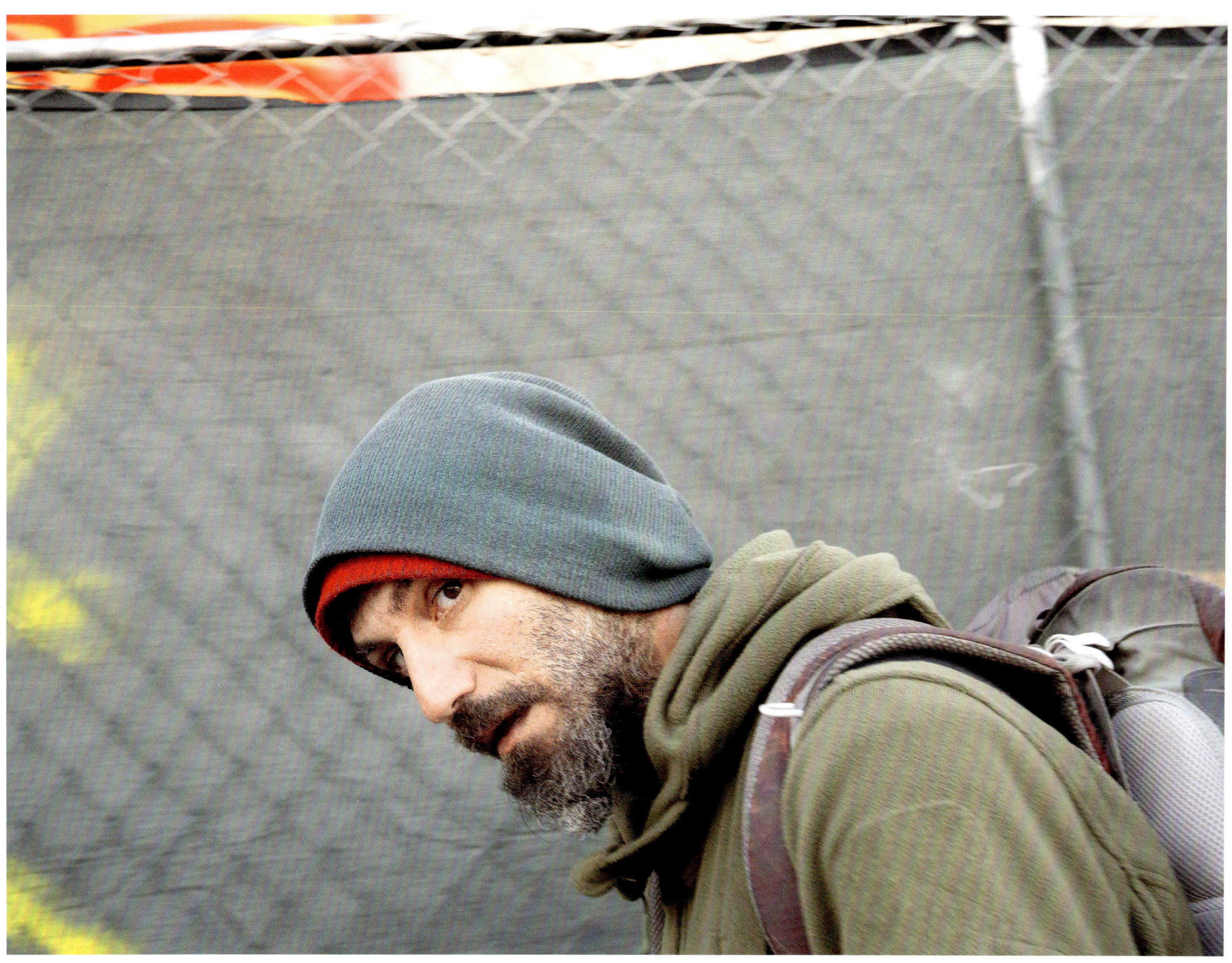

Across from the Fox Theater, Venice

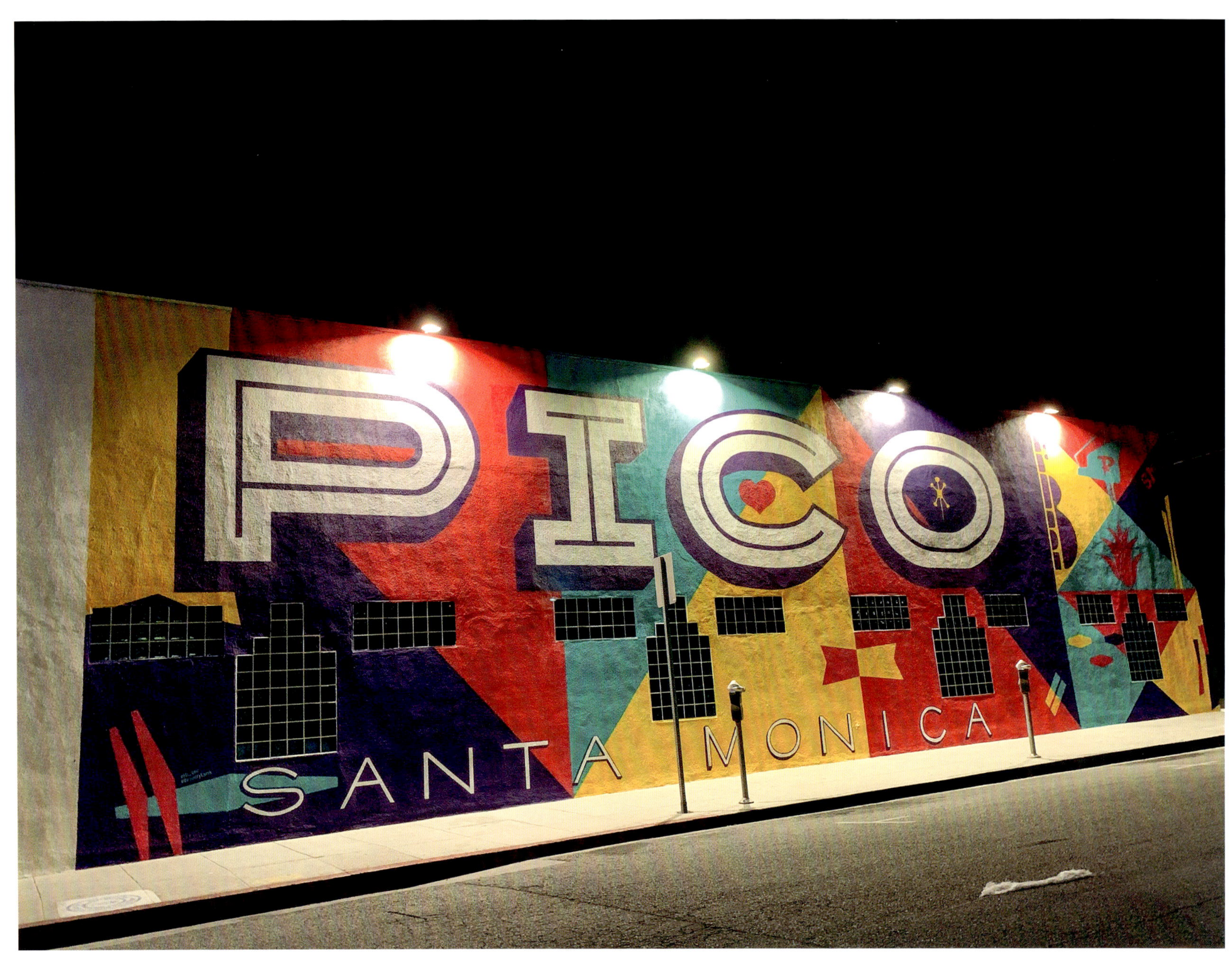

Pico District, Santa Monica

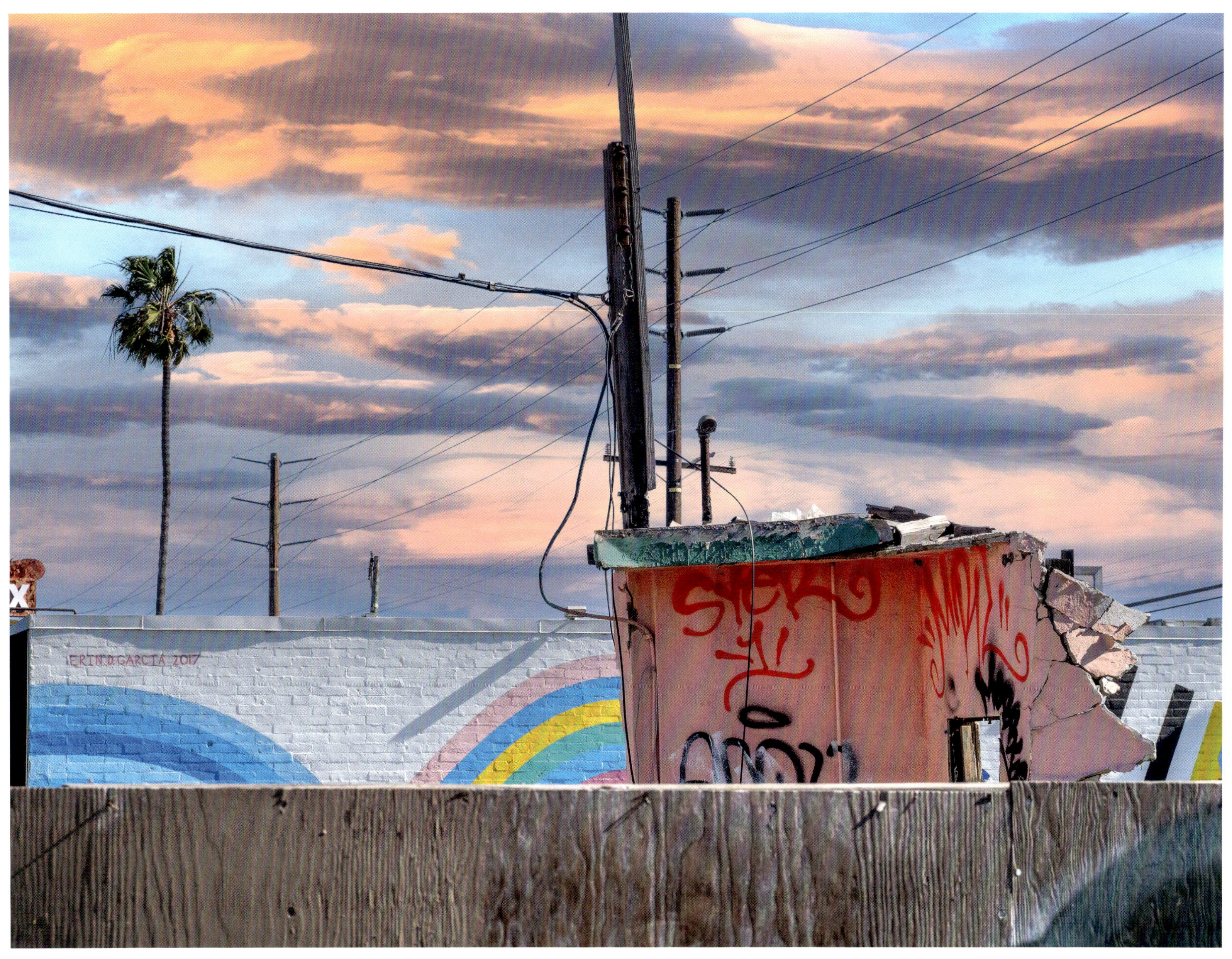

Lincoln District, Venice

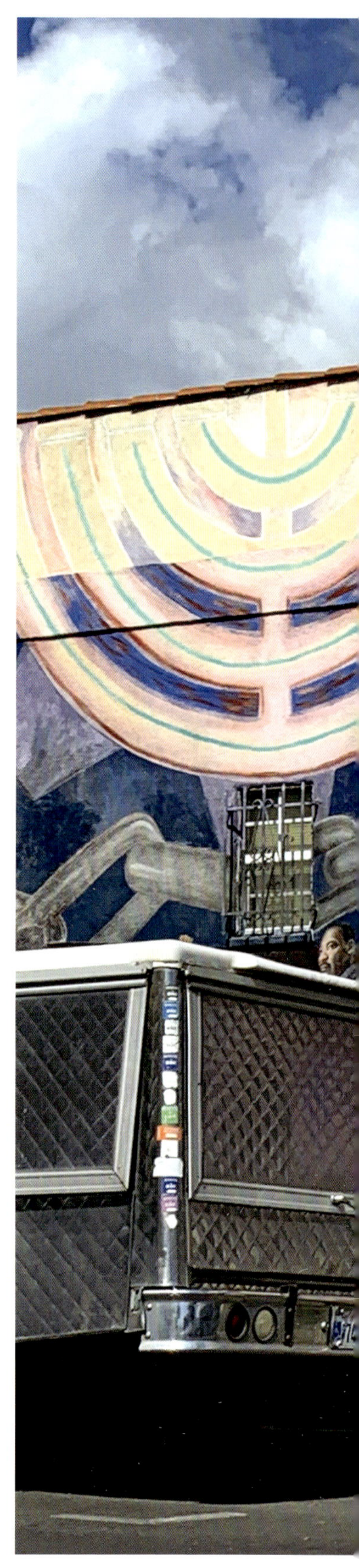

"Give us Your Tired, Your Poor…"
Defaced Mural, Fairfax District

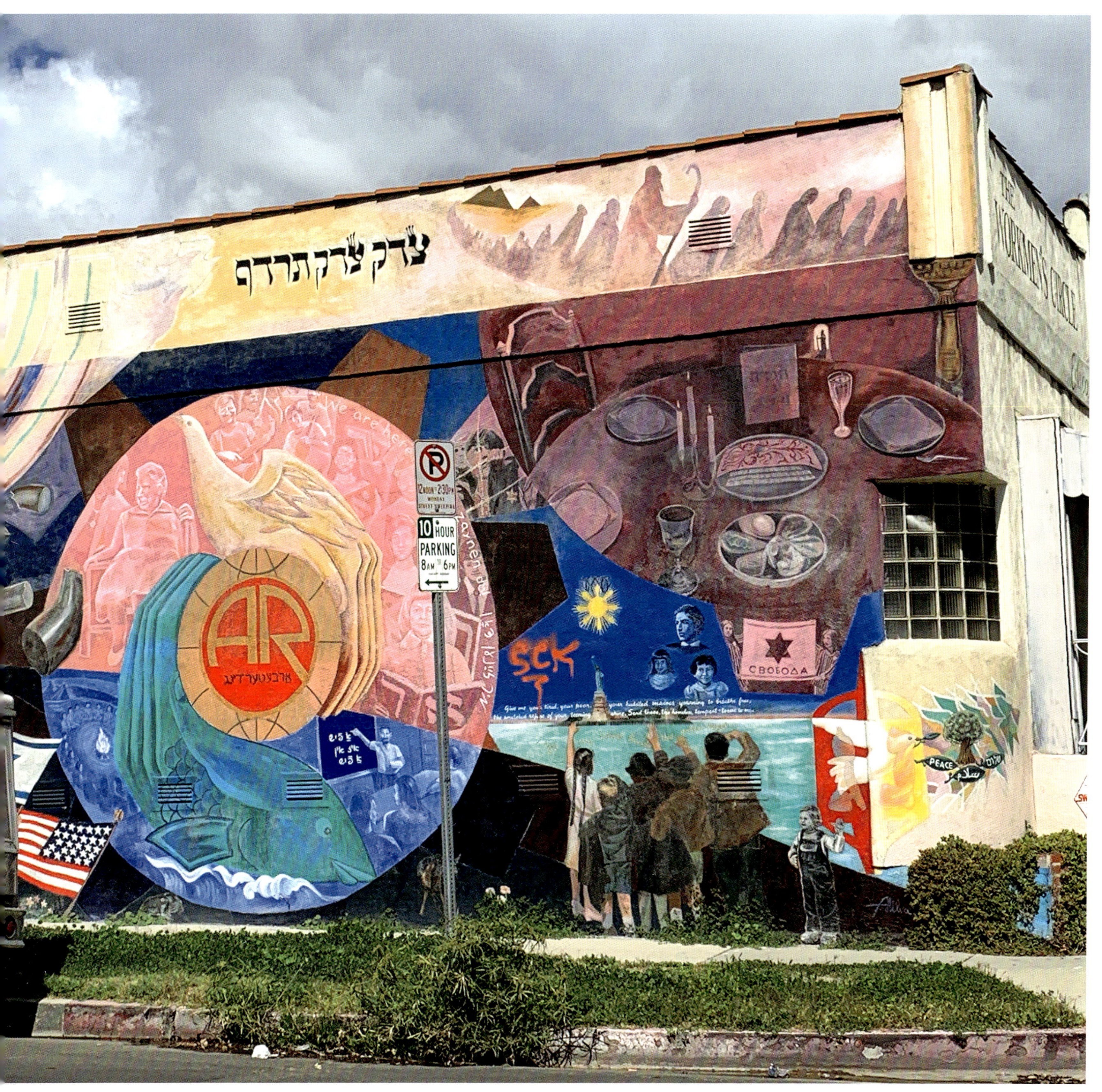

צדק צדק תרדף
THE WORKMEN'S CIRCLE
we are here
АР
ARBETER RING
СВОБОДА
SCK
Give me your tired, your poor, your huddled masses yearning to breathe free,
the wretched refuse of your teeming shore. Send these, the homeless, tempest-tossed to me.
PEACE

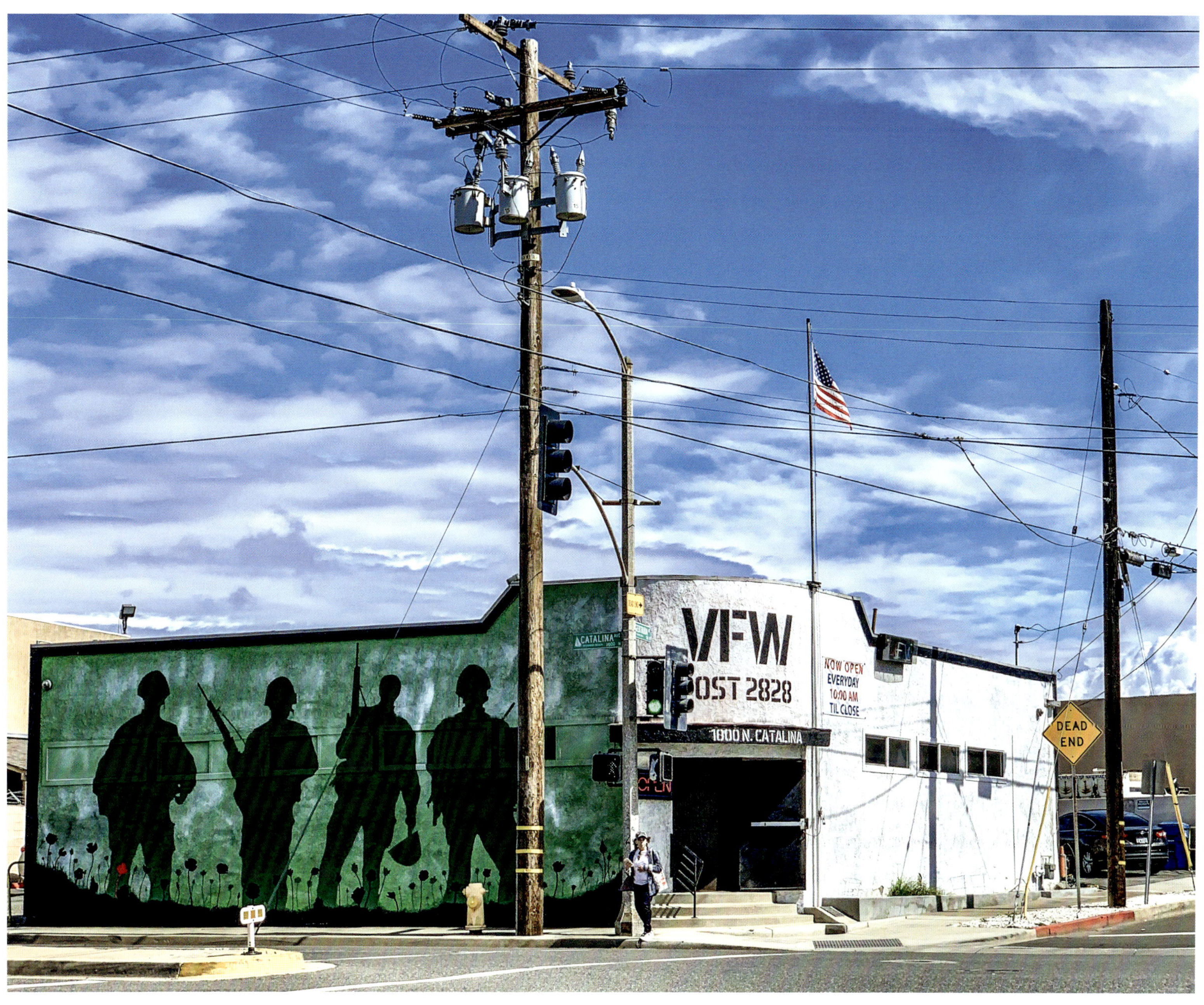

Veterans of Foreign Wars
Redondo Beach

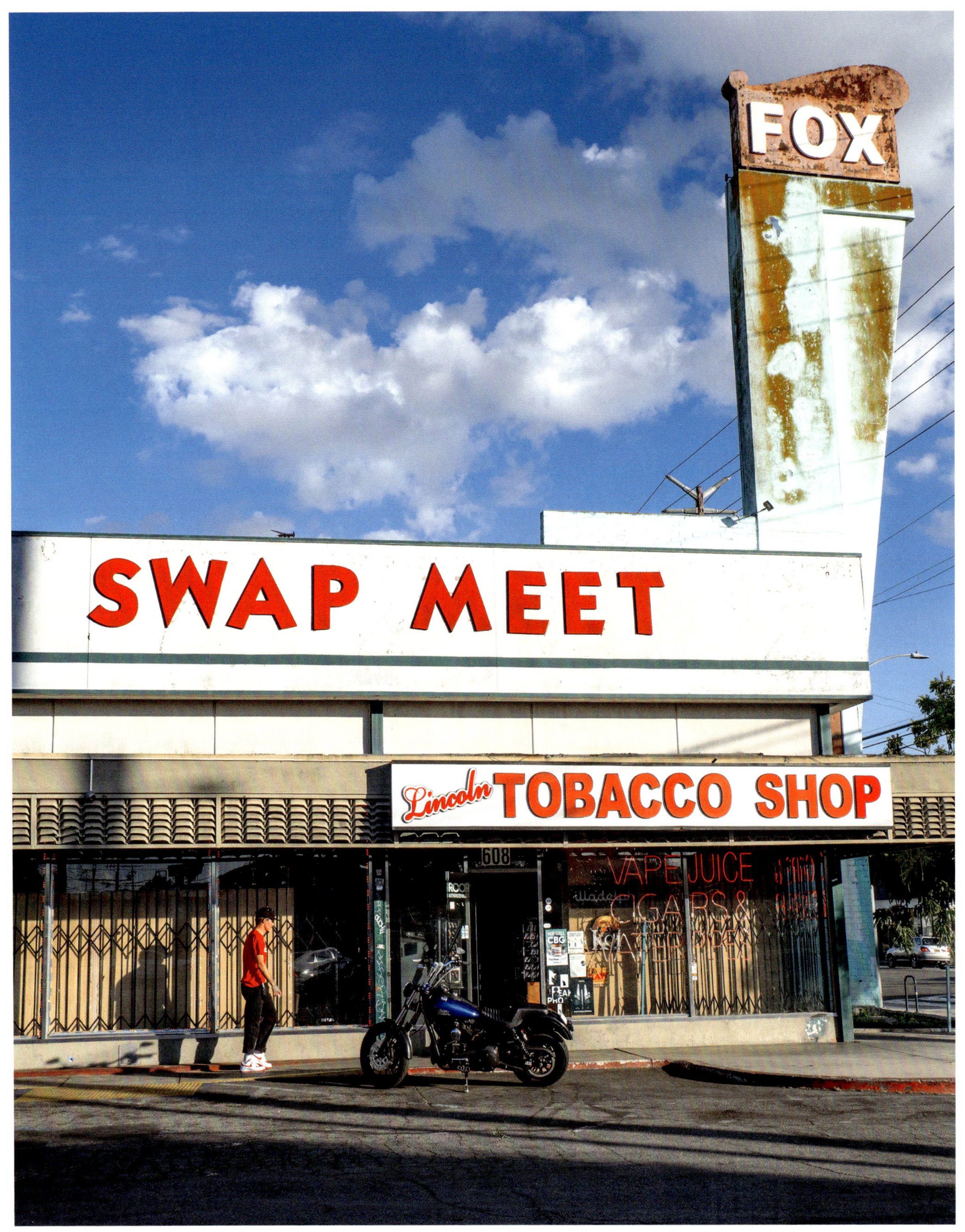

FOX
SWAP MEET
Lincoln TOBACCO SHOP
608
VAPE JUICE
CIGARS &

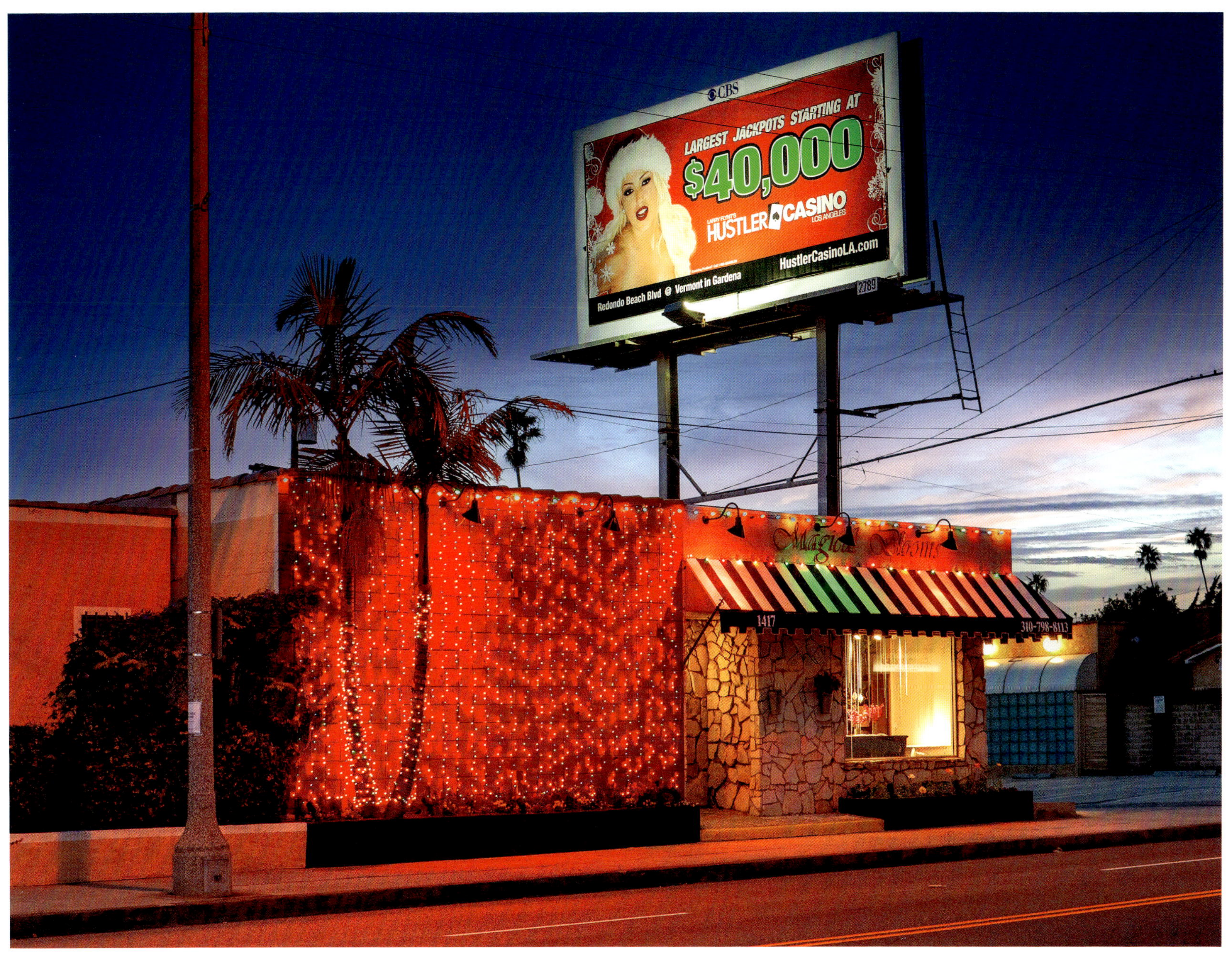

Fox Theater-cum-Swap Meet, Venice, 2022

"Hustler," Redondo Beach, 2010

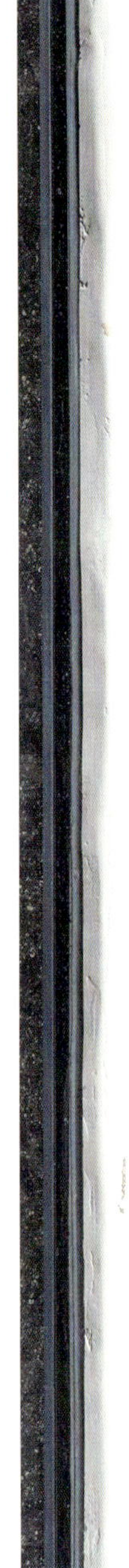
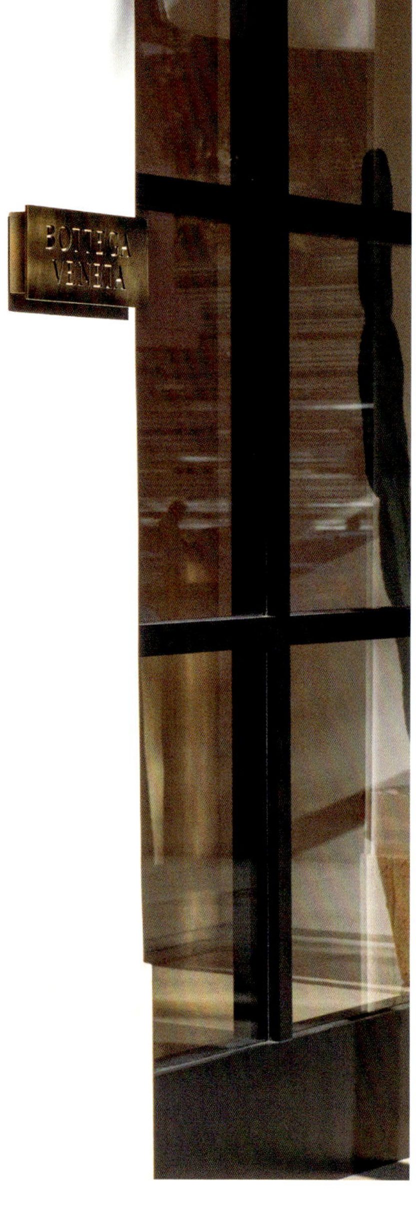

Bottega Veneta, Beverly Hills

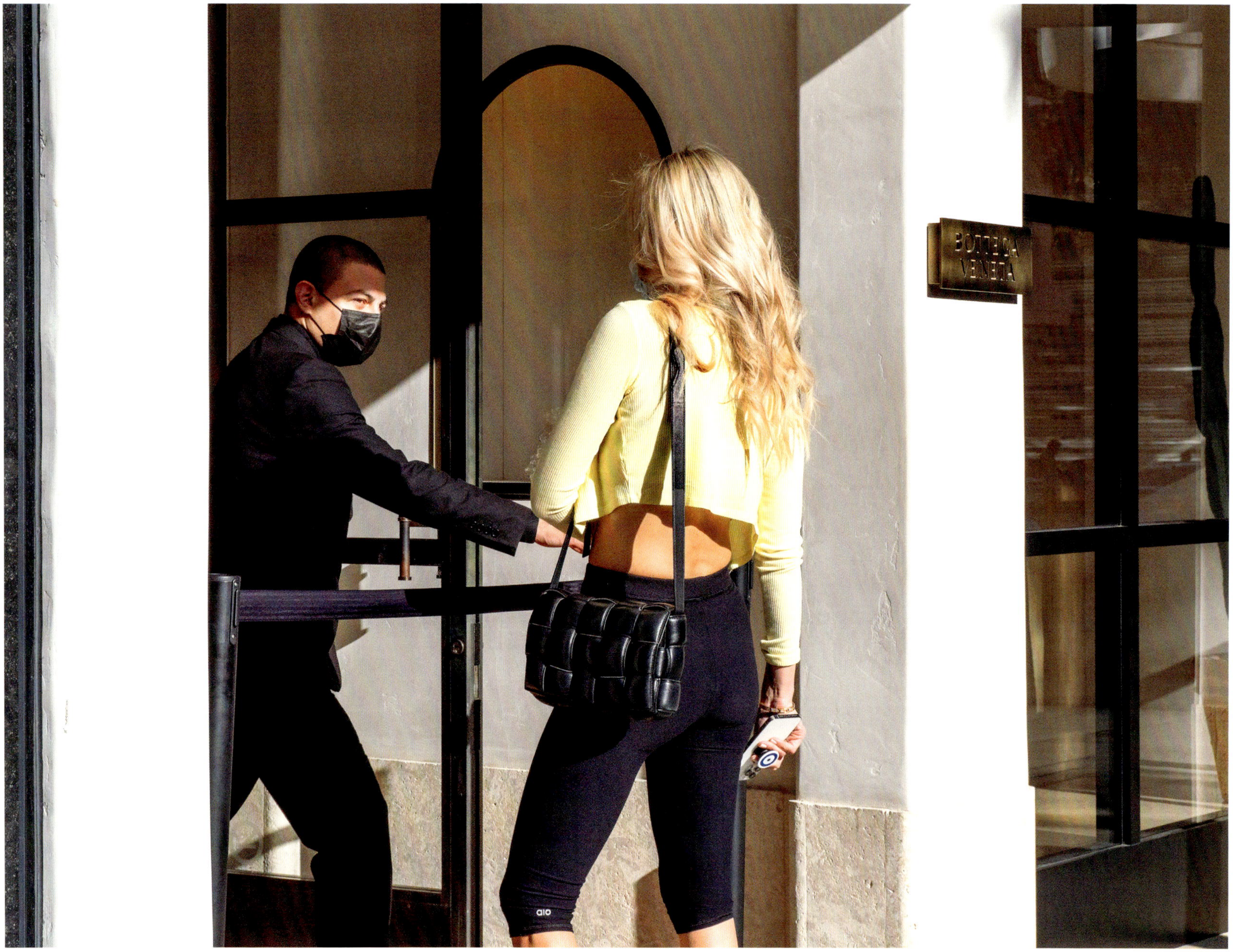

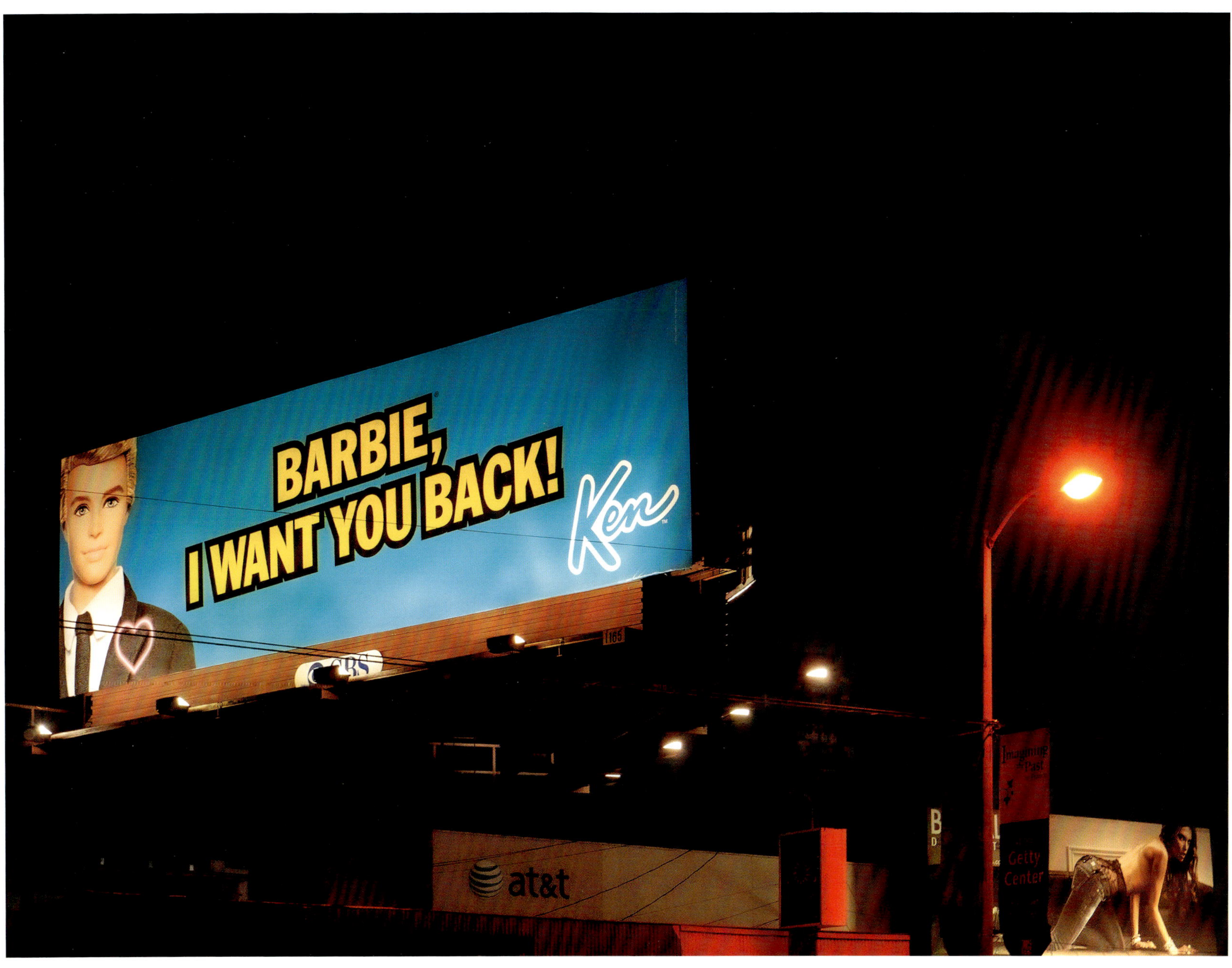

Barbie and Ken, West LA

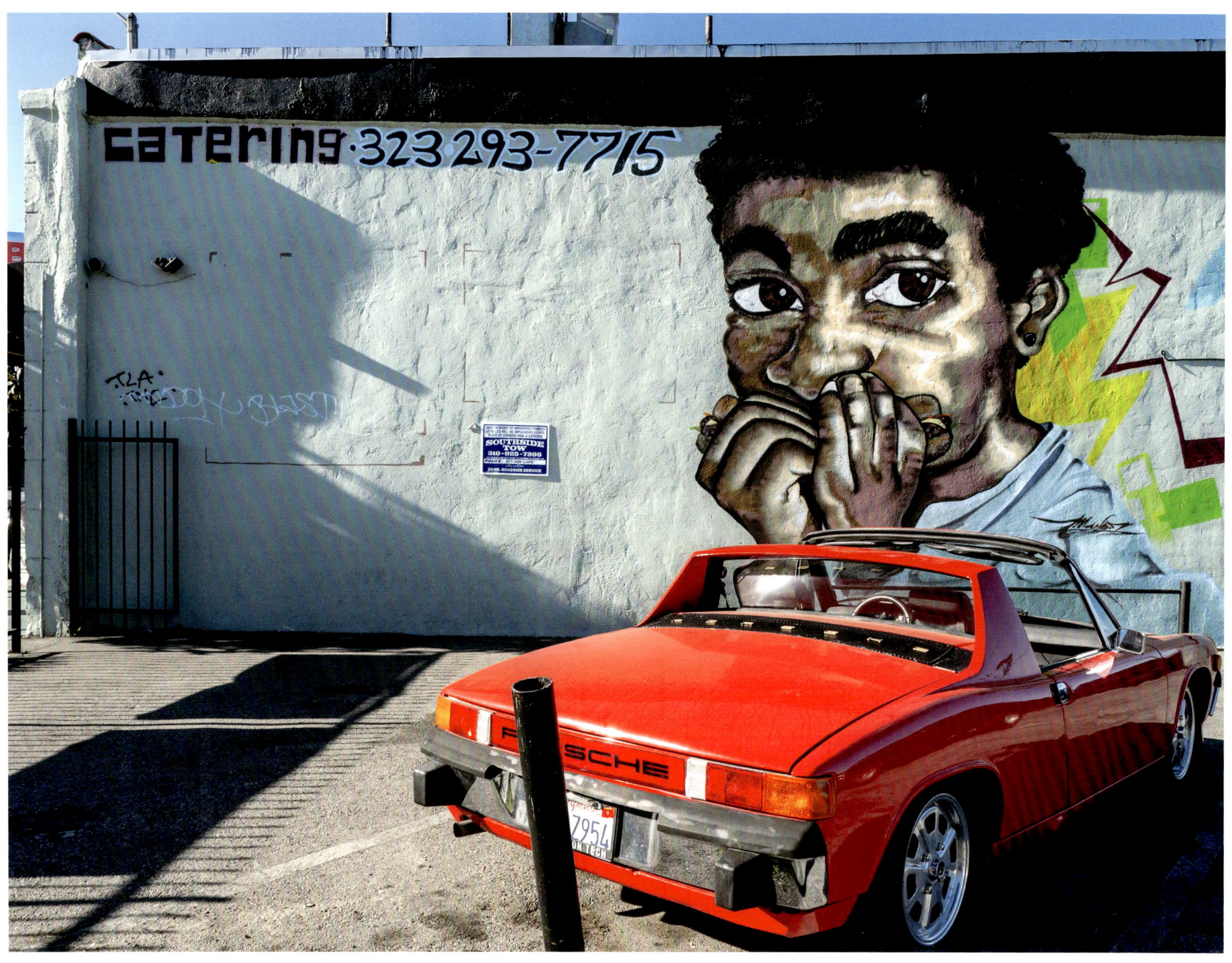

"Catering," West Hollywood

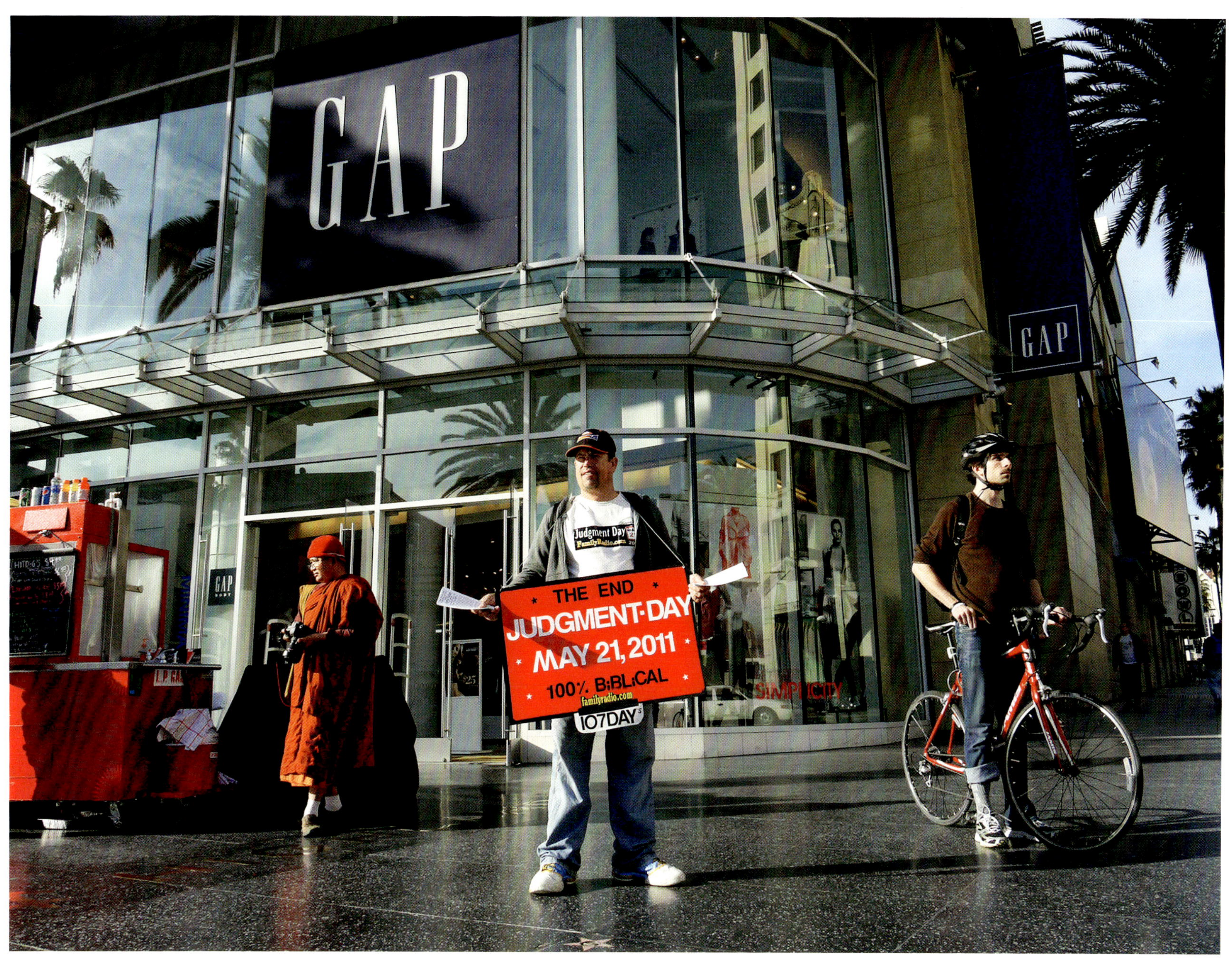

"Judgment Day," Hollywood

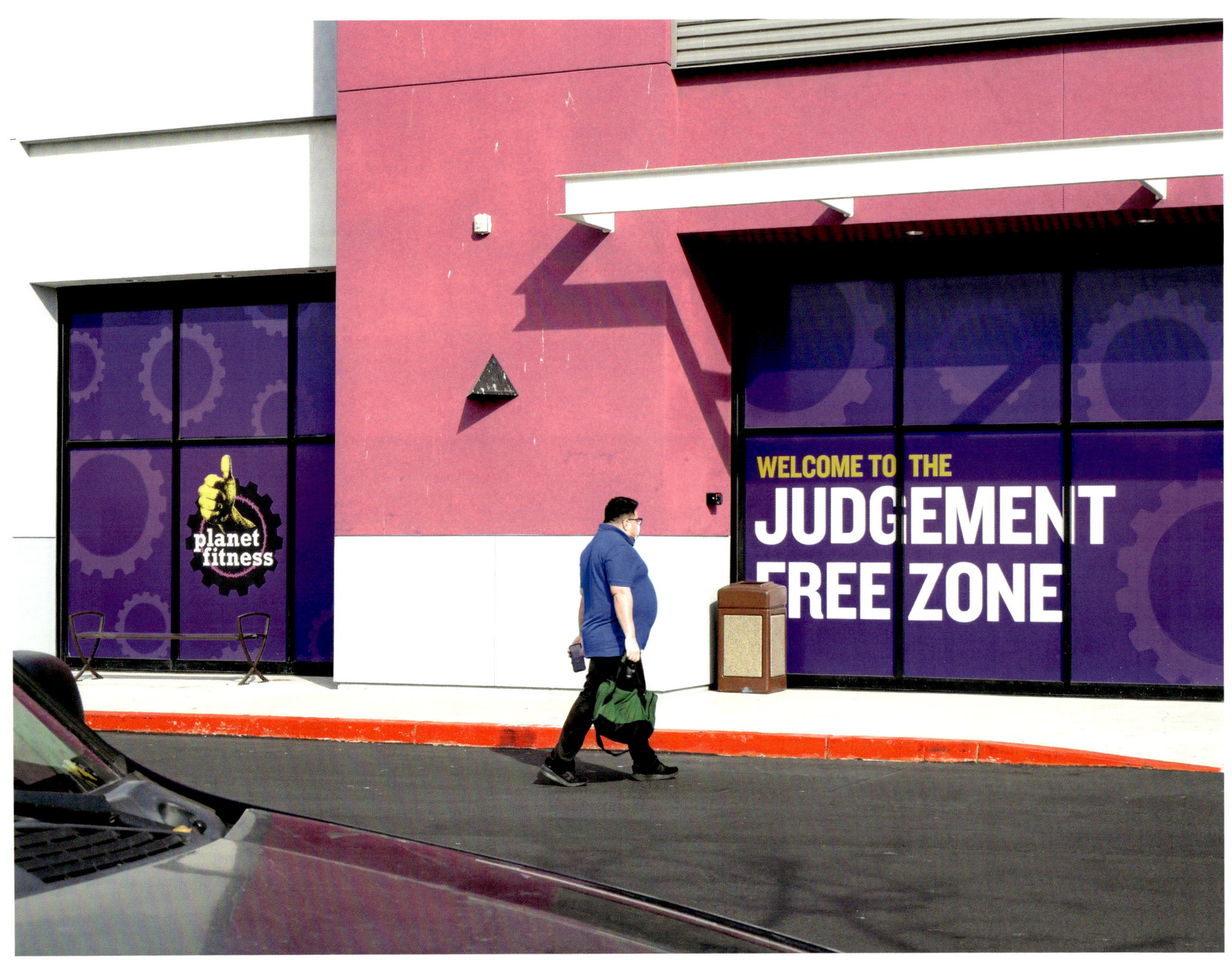

"Judgement Free," Carson

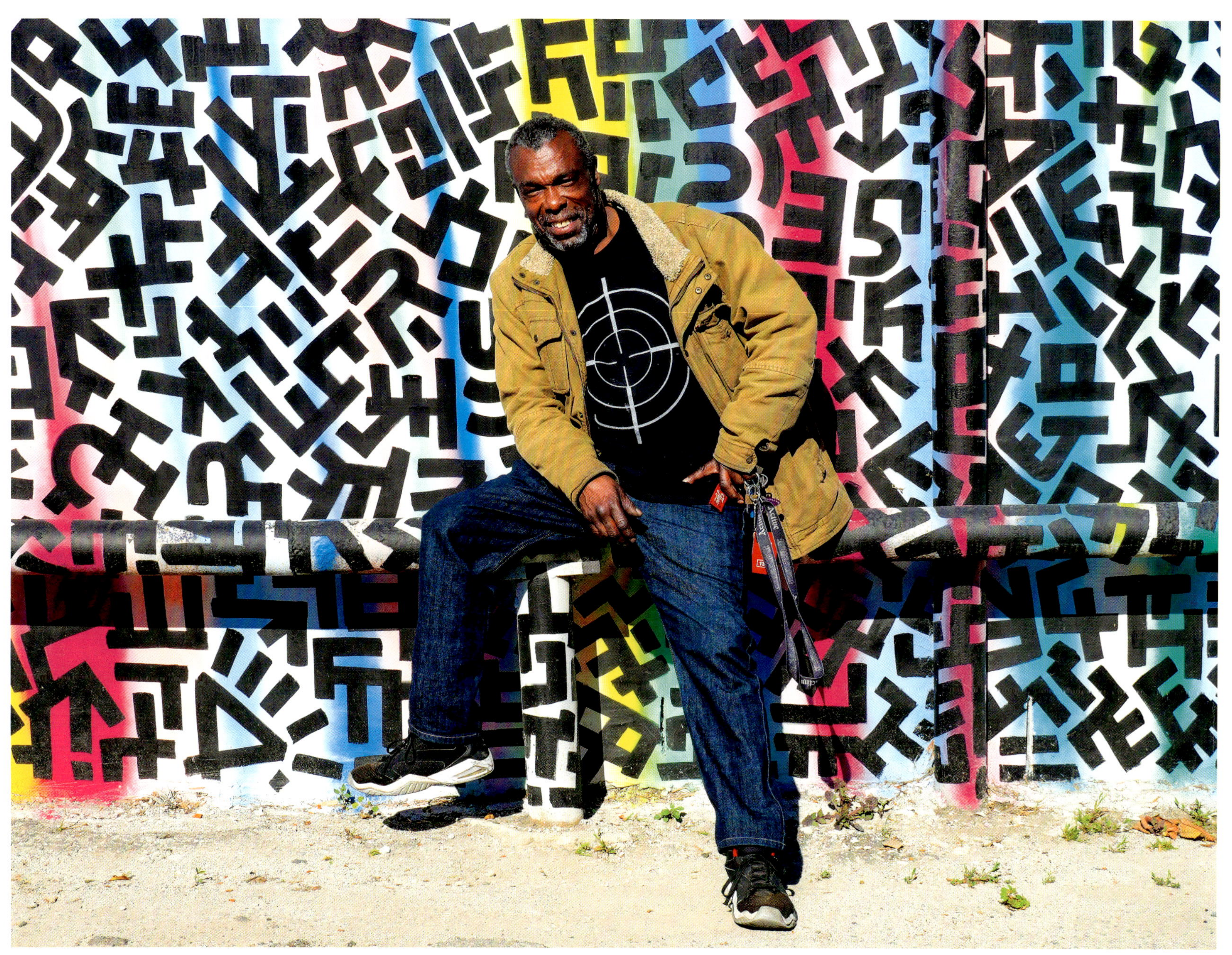

James behind Lincoln Blvd., Venice

High End   Low End   No End   In Sight

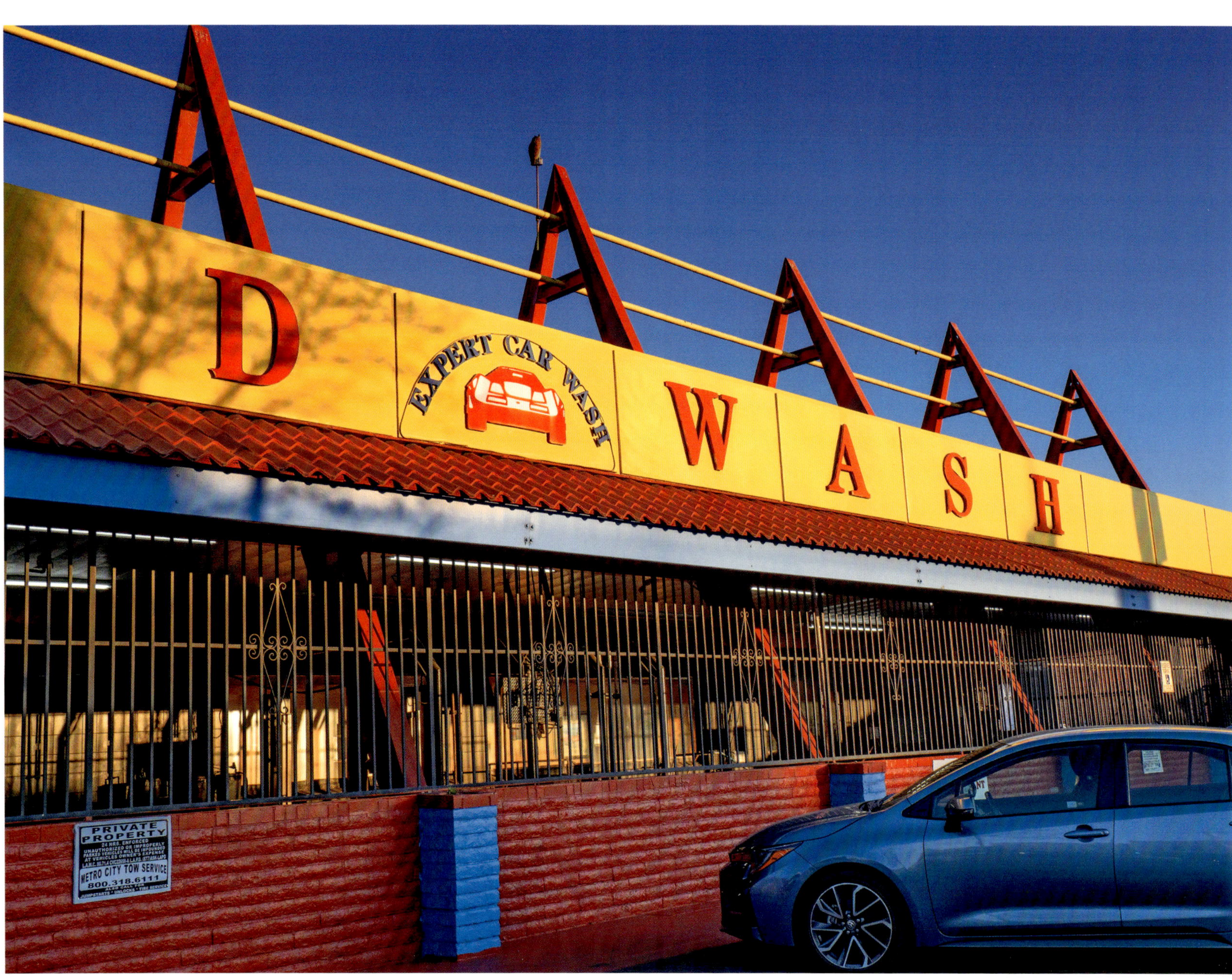

D
EXPERT CAR WASH
WASH
PRIVATE
PROPERTY
24 HRS. ENFORCED
METRO CITY TOW SERVICE
800.318.6111

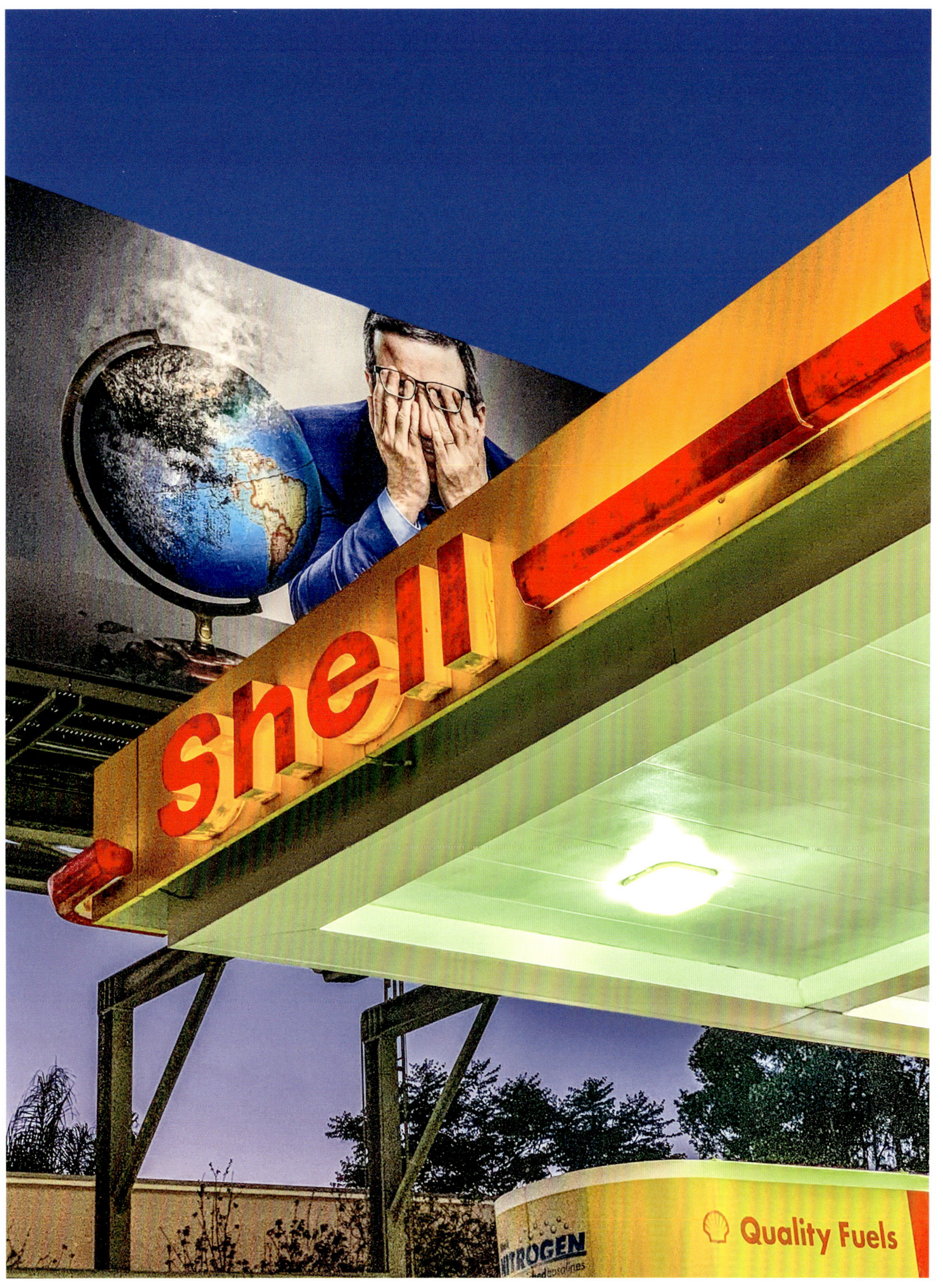

shell
Quality Fuels
NITROGEN

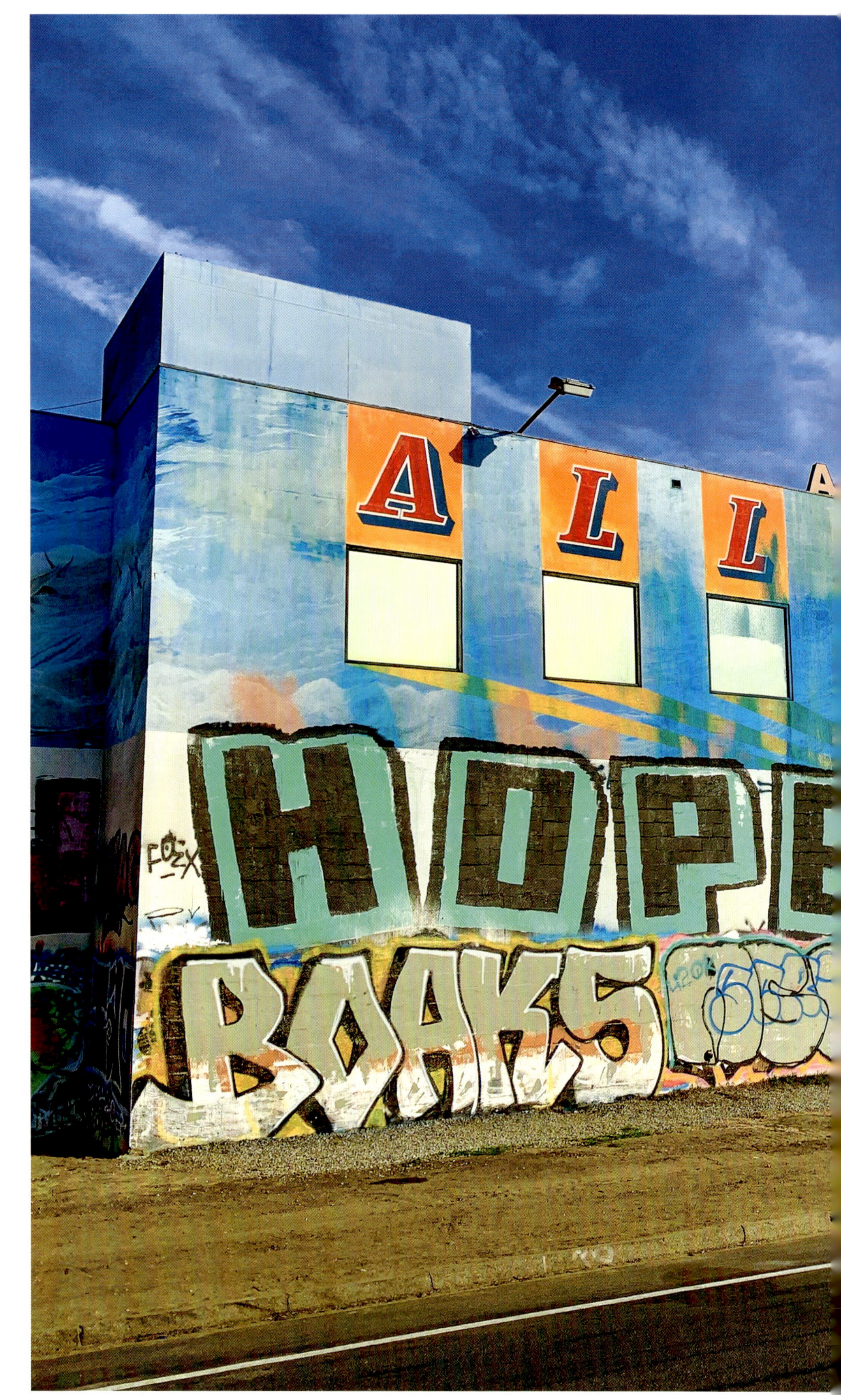

A L L A
HOPE
BOOKS

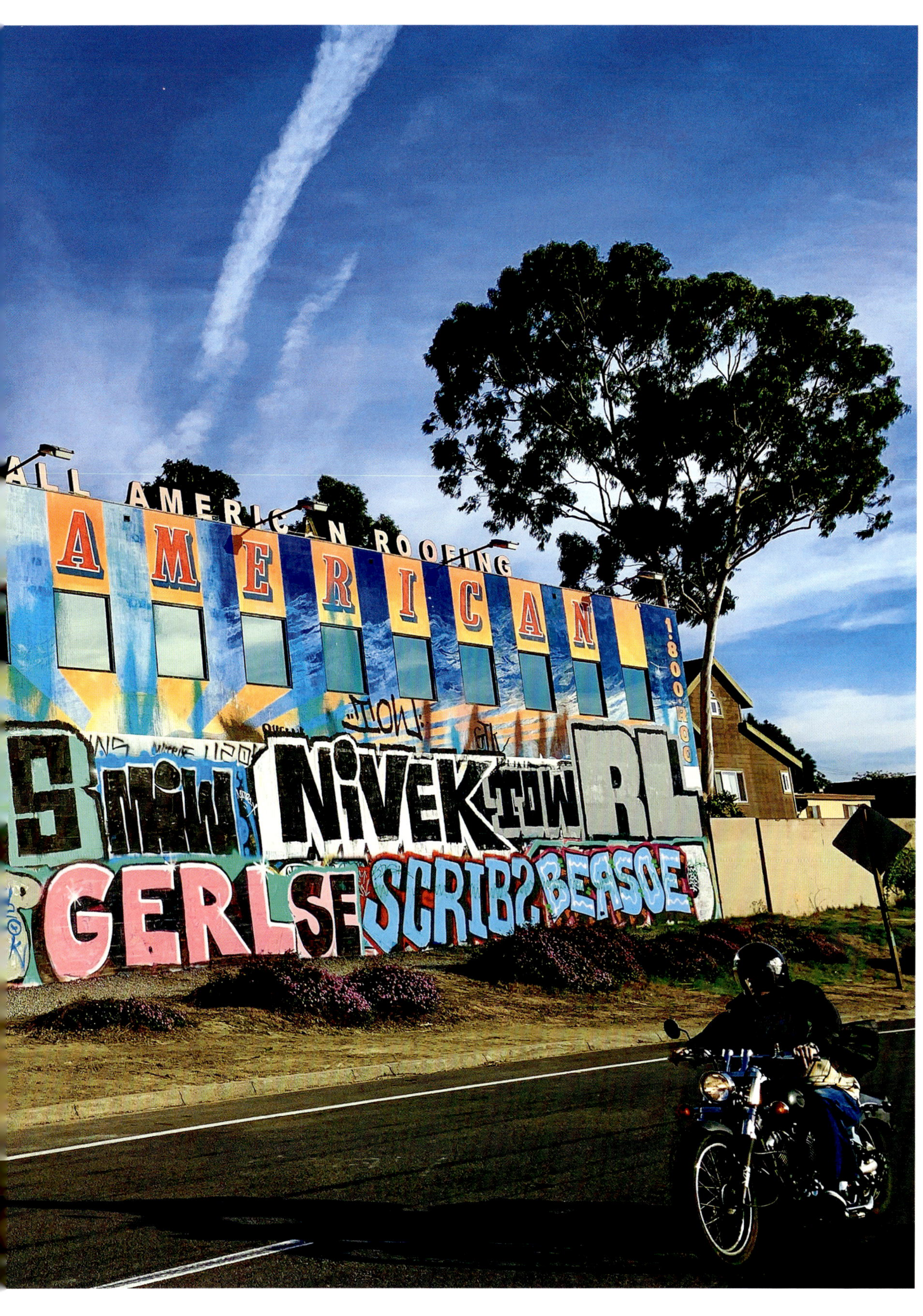
ALL AMERICAN ROOFING
AMERICAN
1 800 ROO
NIVEK-TOW
GERL
SCRIB2 BEASOE

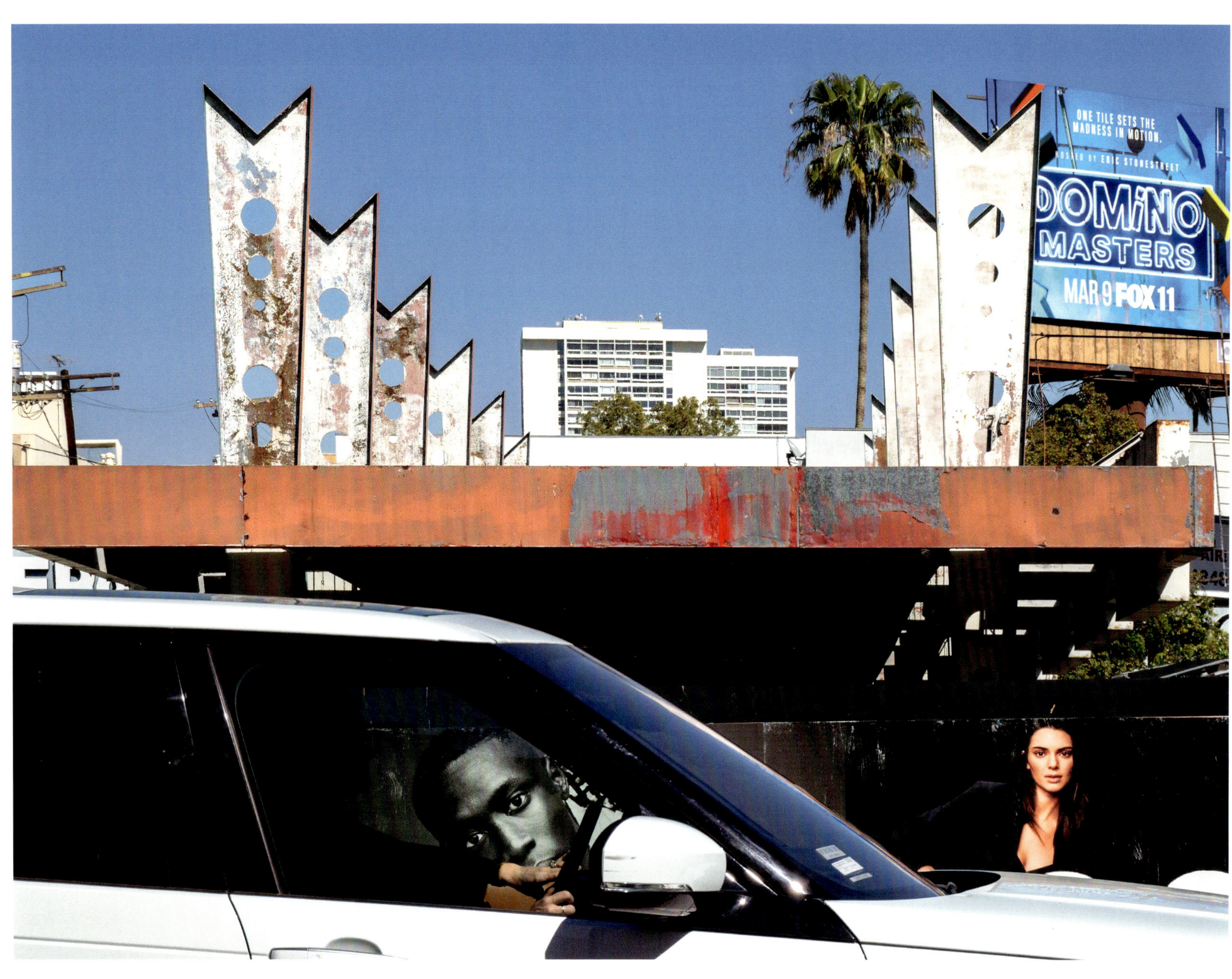

Domino Effect, West LA

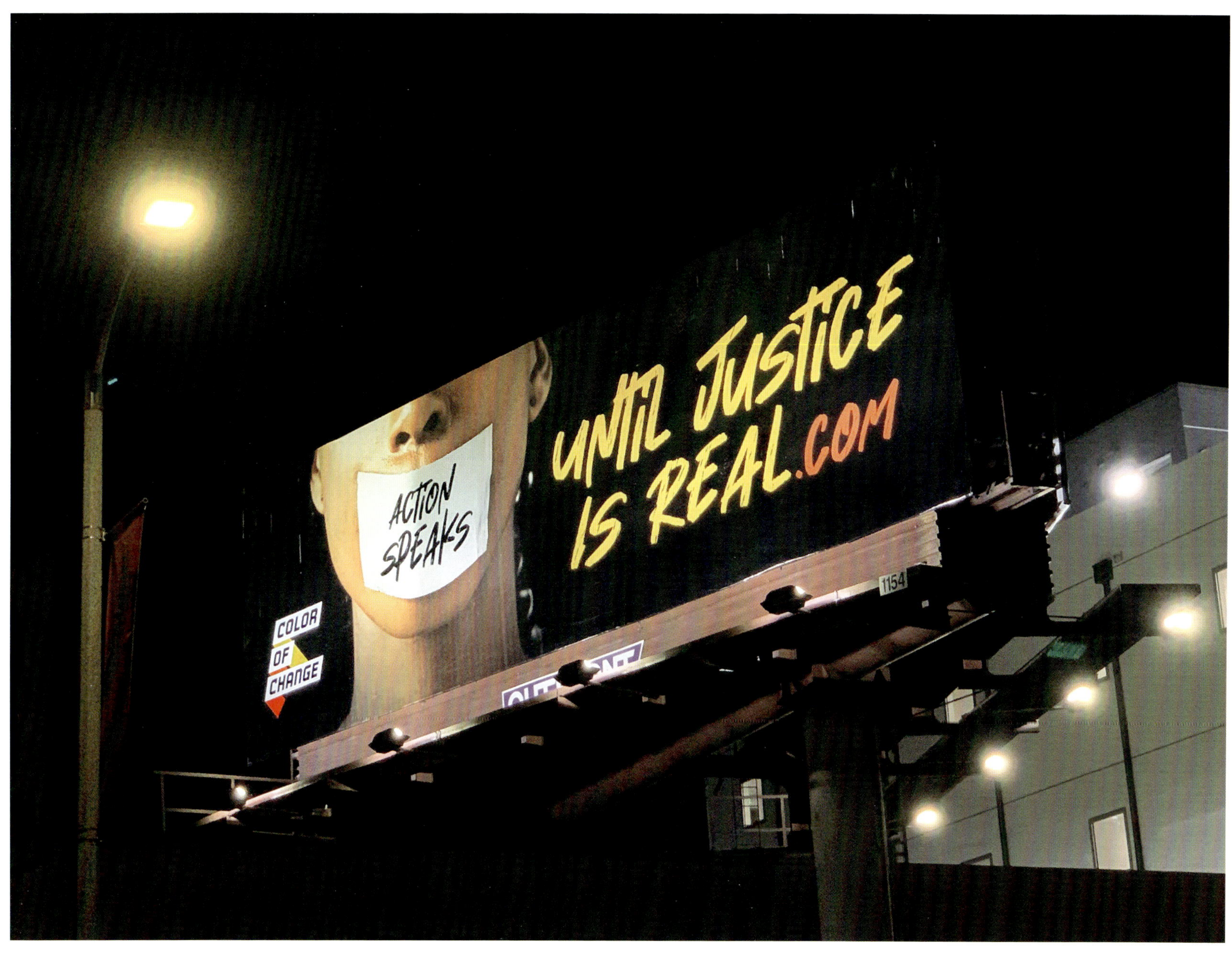

"Color of Change," West LA

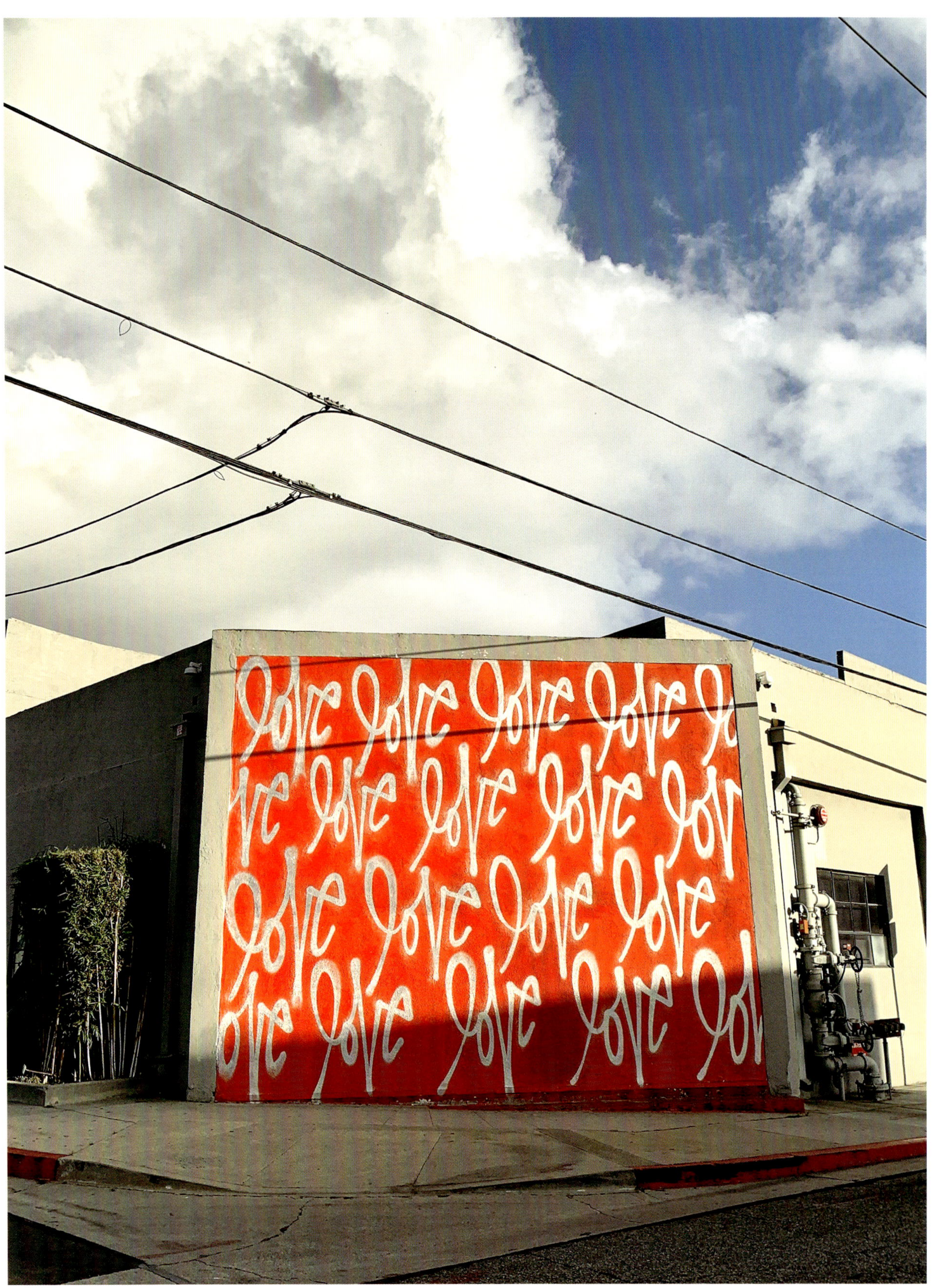

Hayden Tract
Culver City

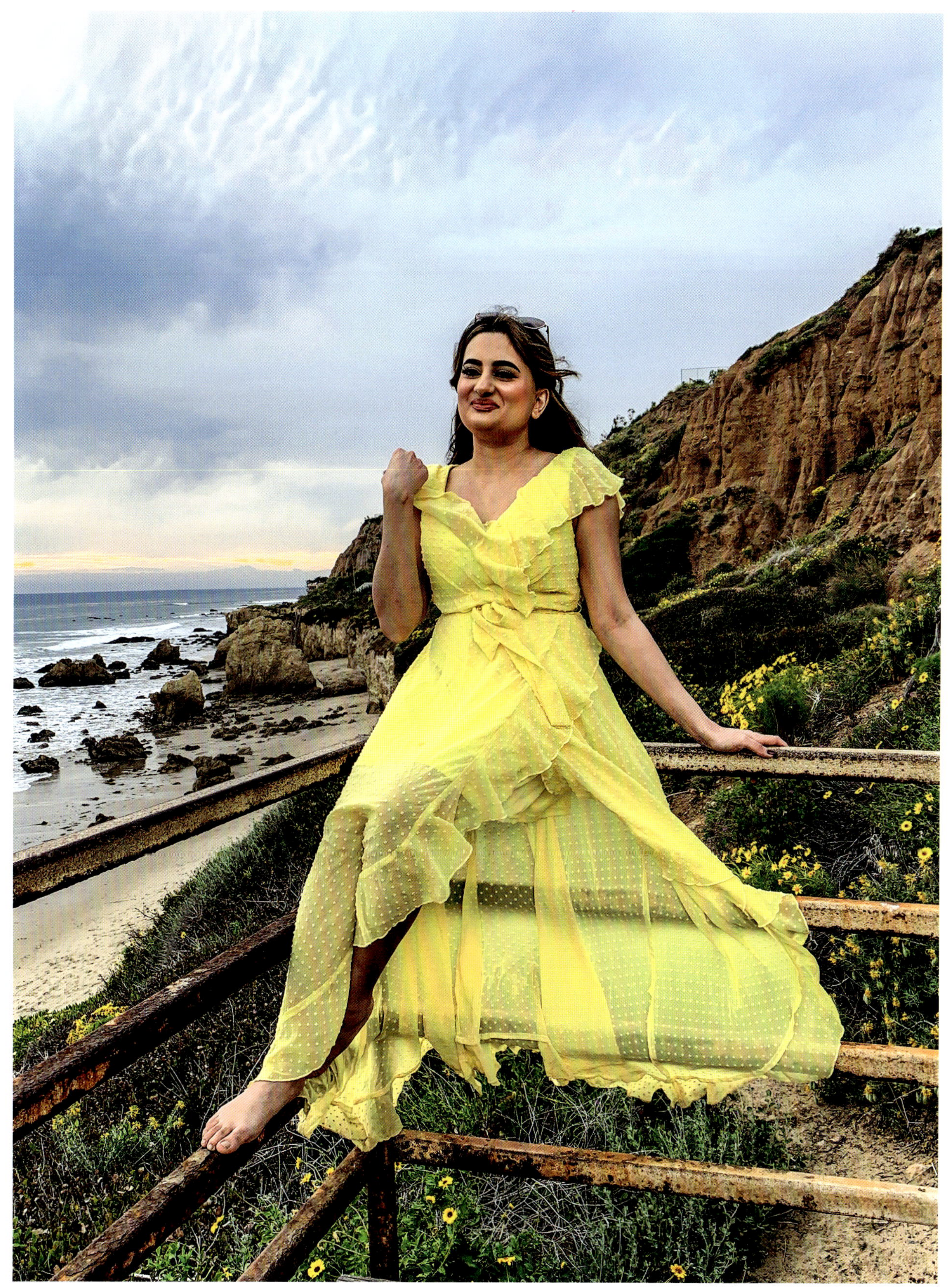

El Matador Beach
Malibu

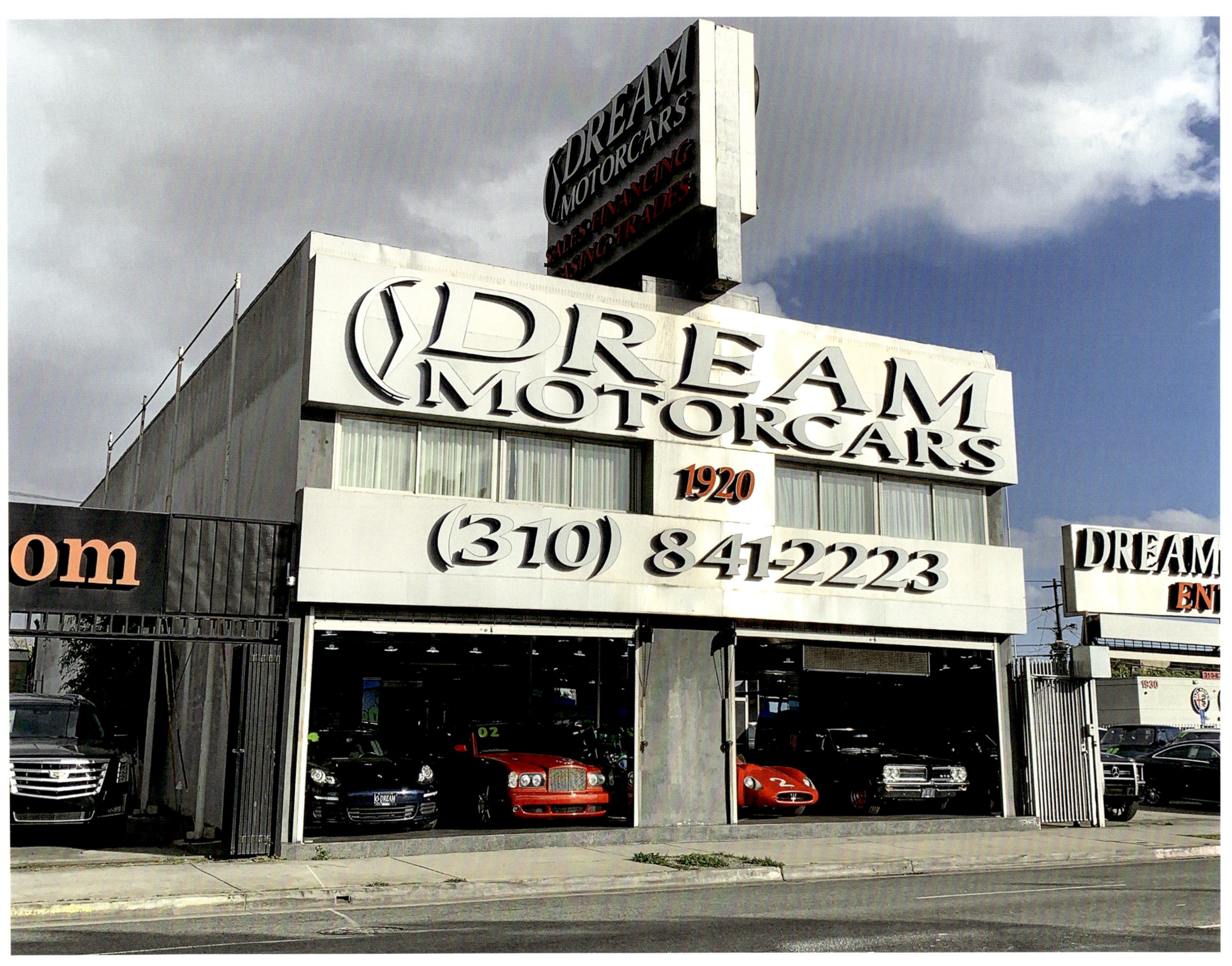

"Om Dream," Los Angeles

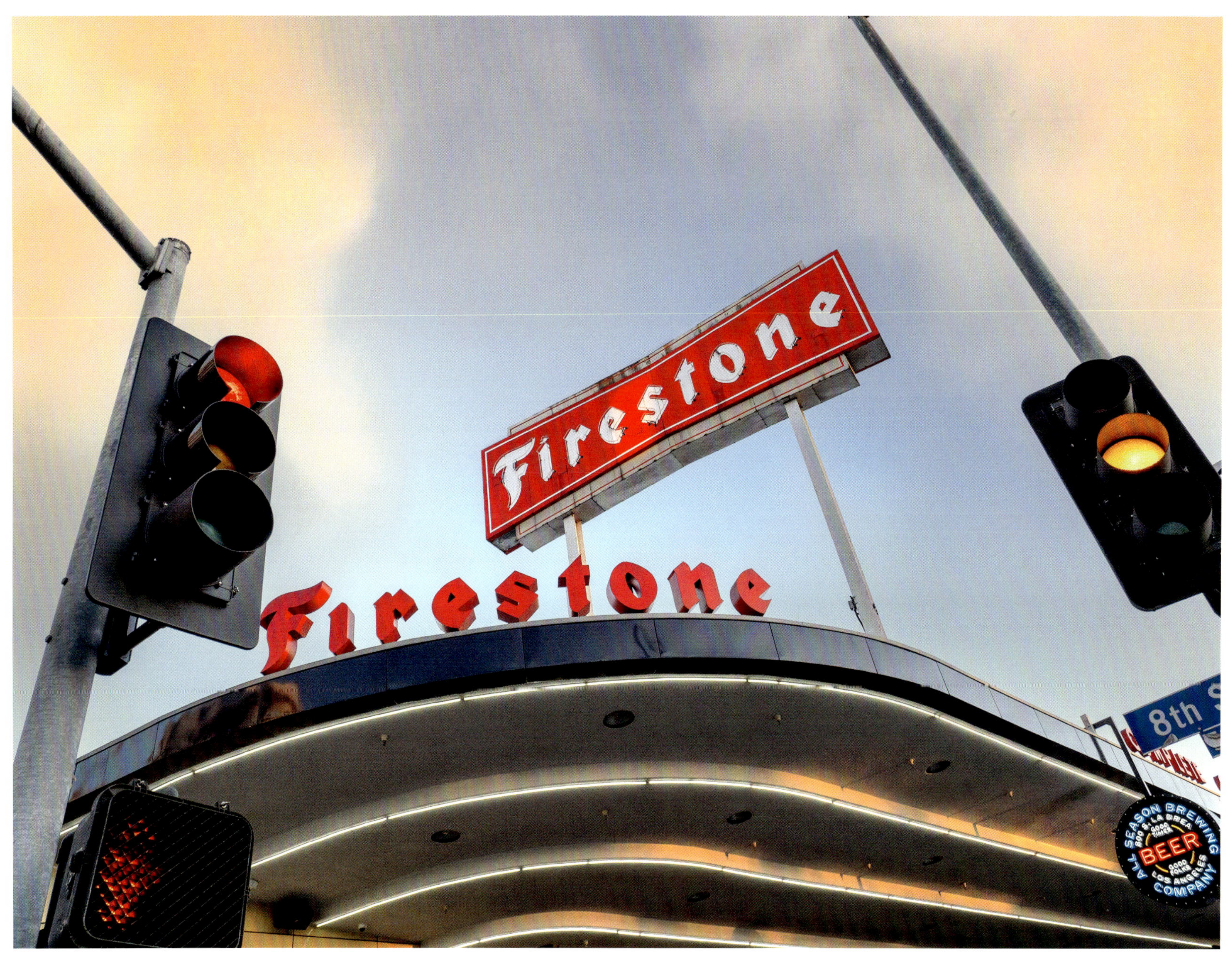

"All Season Brewing," Los Angeles

"Underworld Awakening"
"Market" at the Mall, Santa Monica

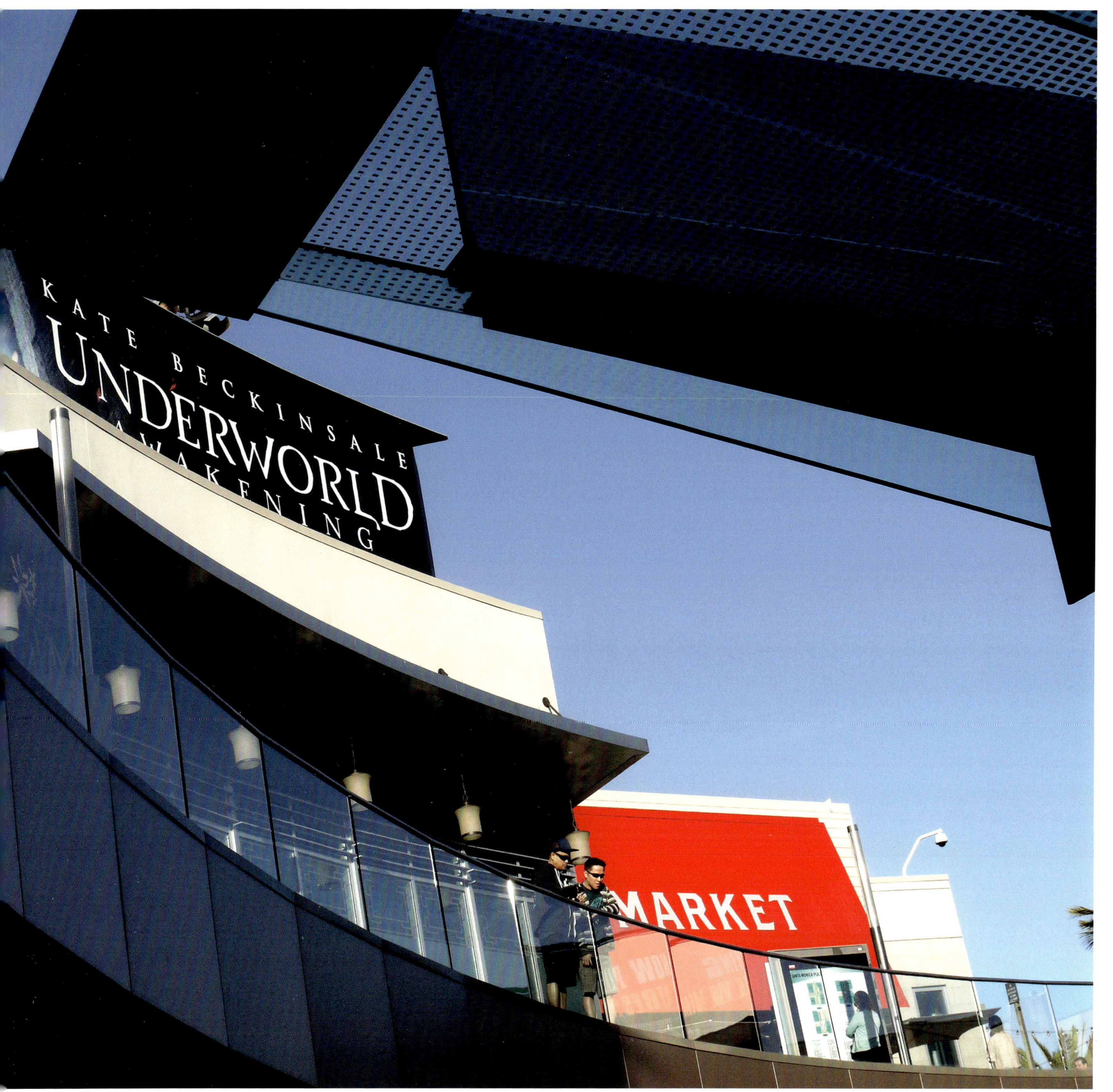
KATE BECKINSALE
UNDERWORLD
AWAKENING
MARKET

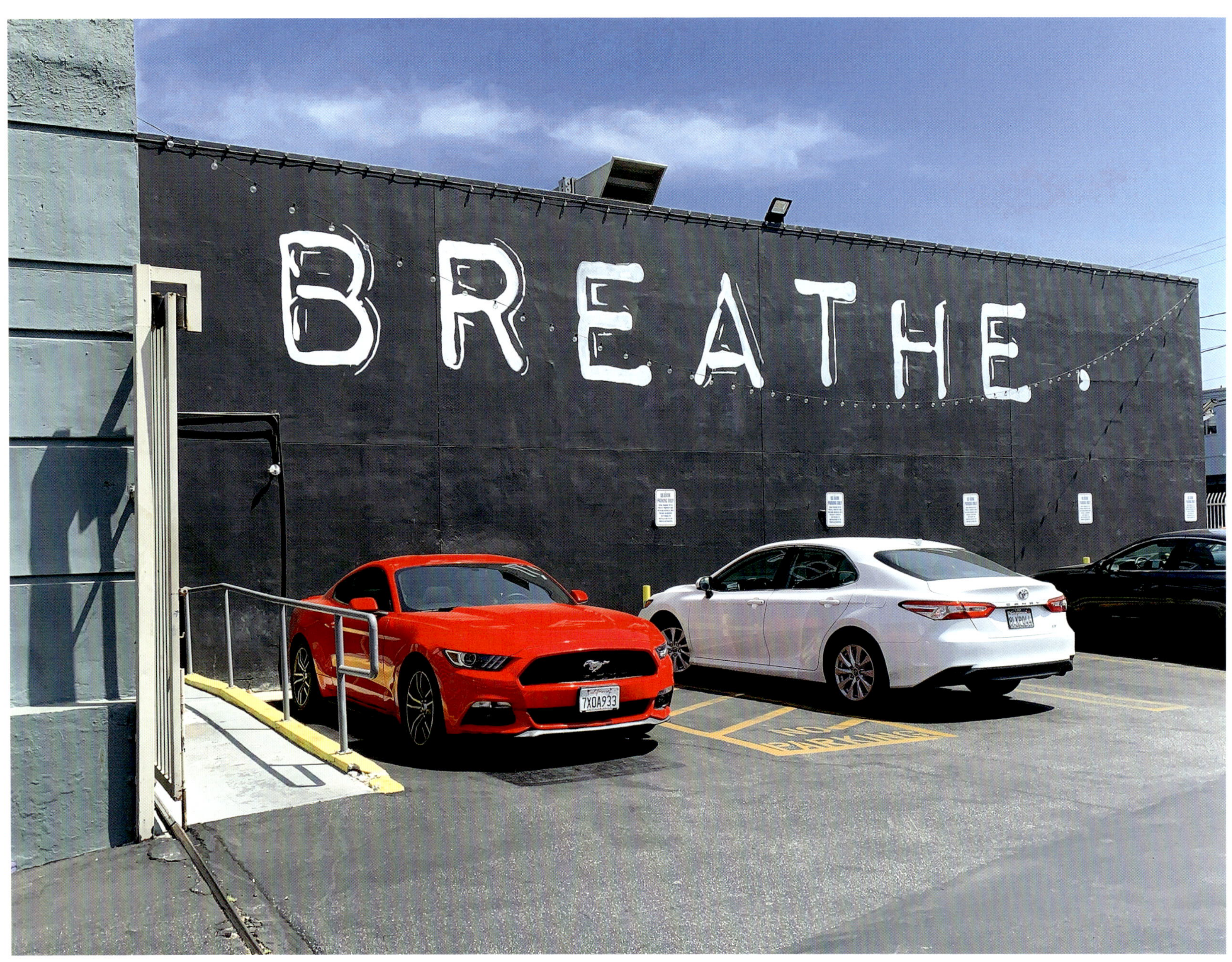

"Breathe," West Hollywood

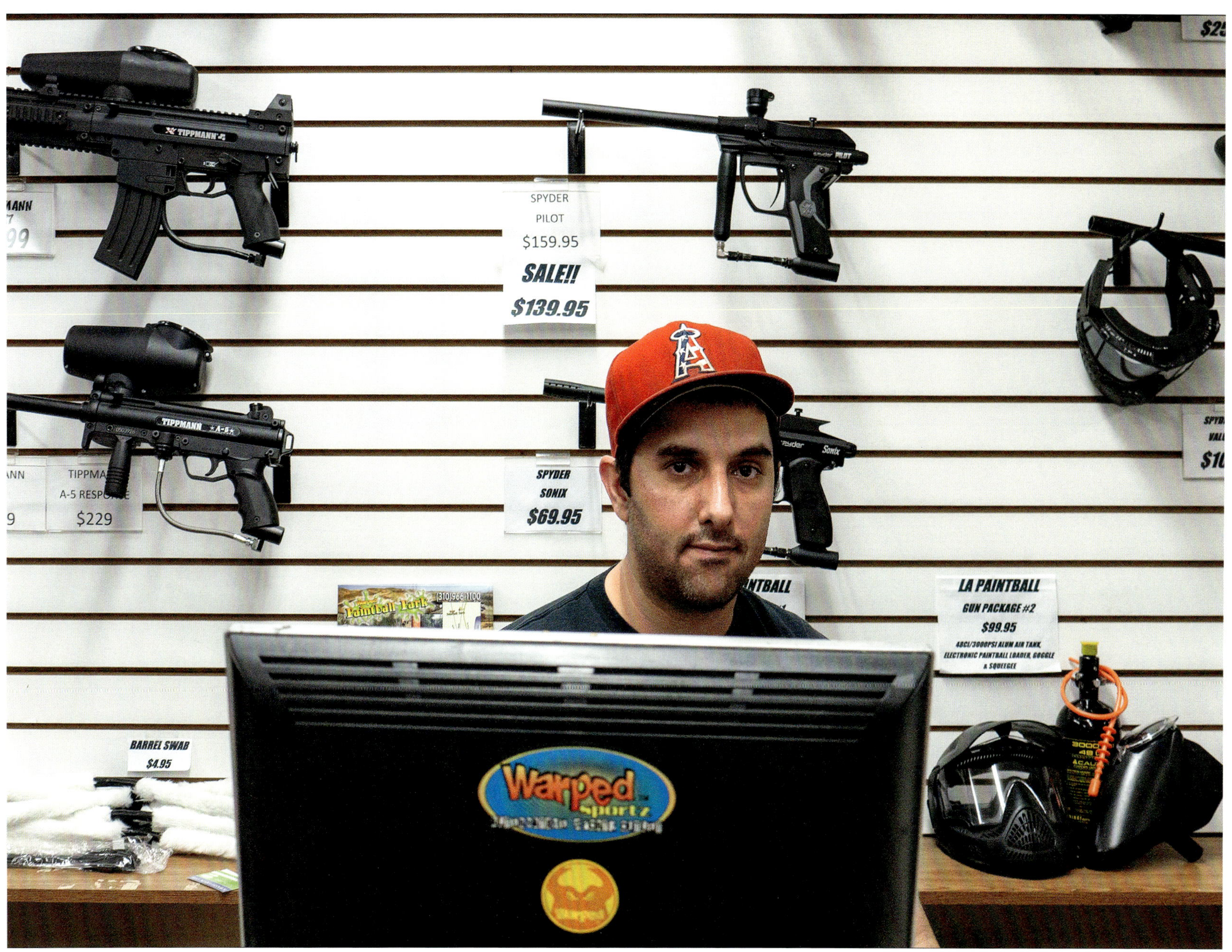

"Warped Sportz," Los Angeles

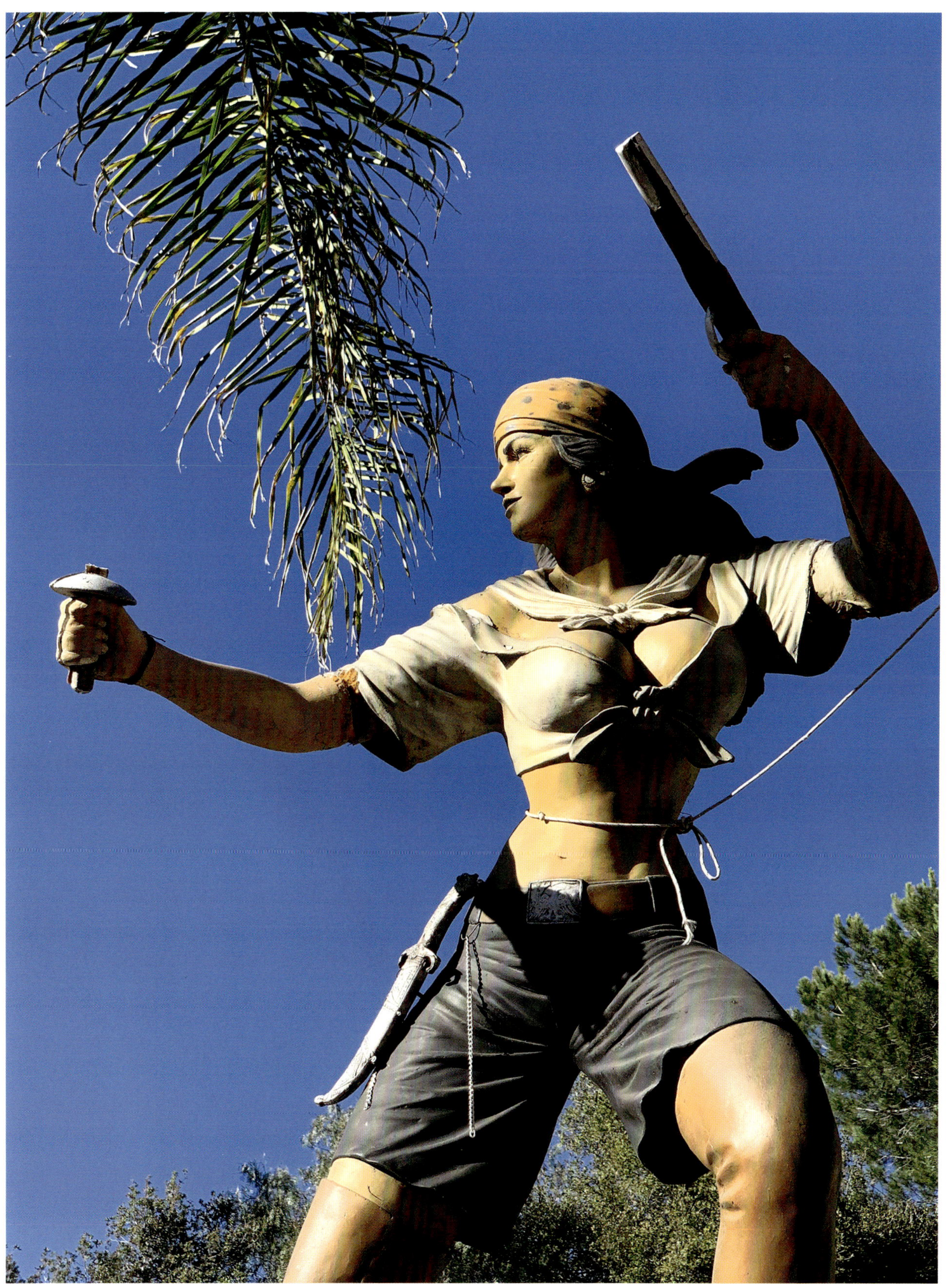

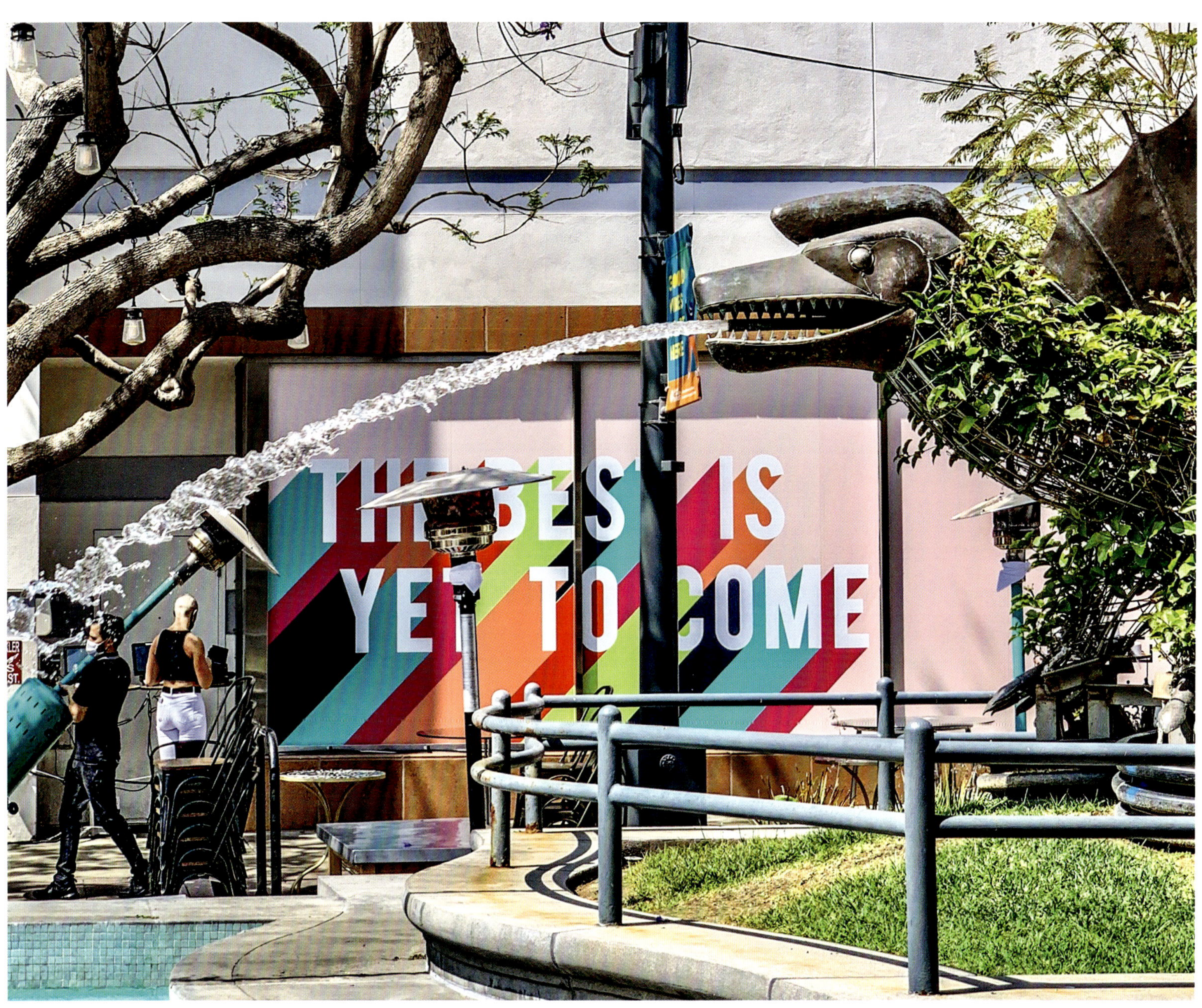

THE BEST IS
YET TO COME

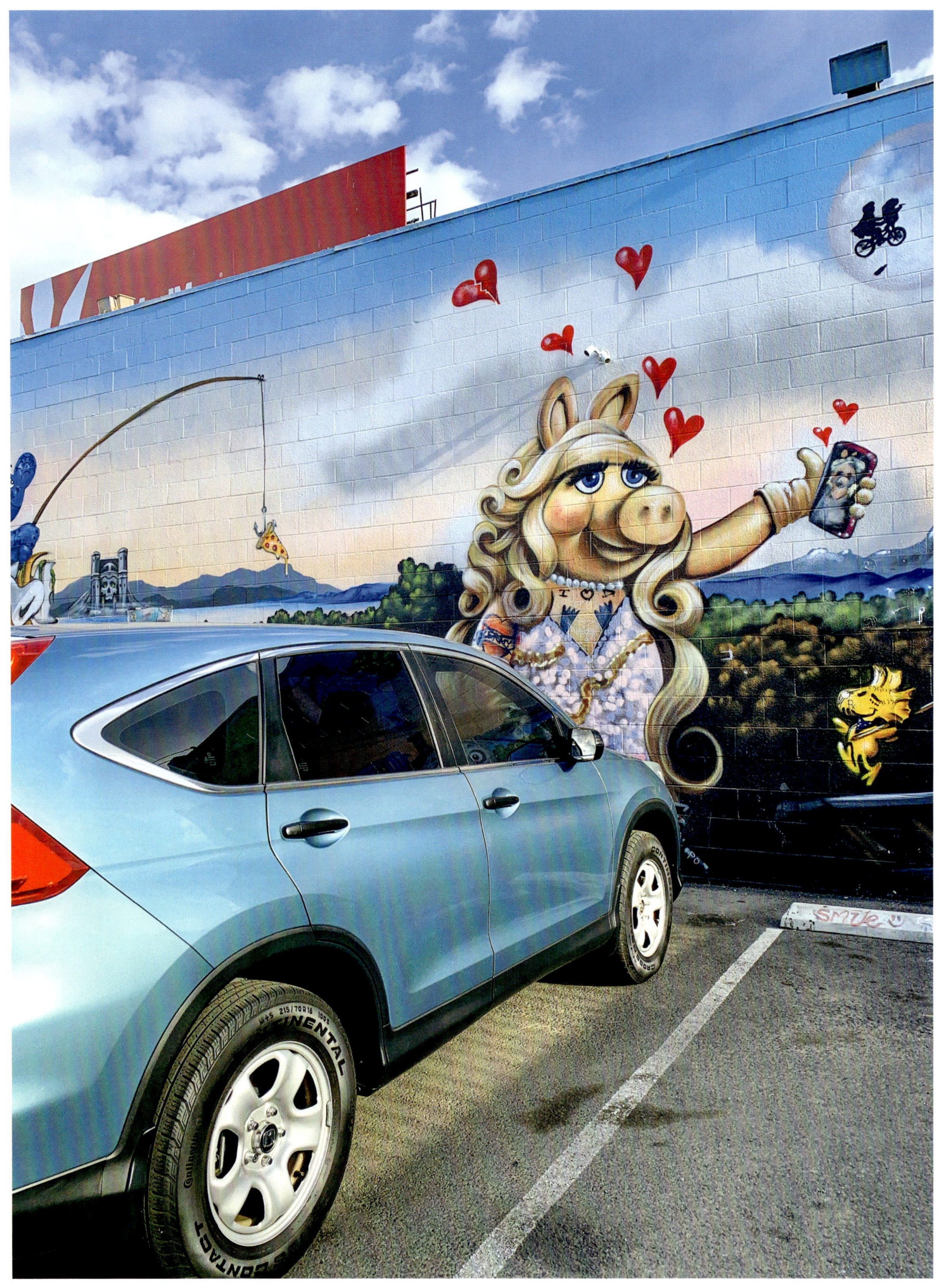

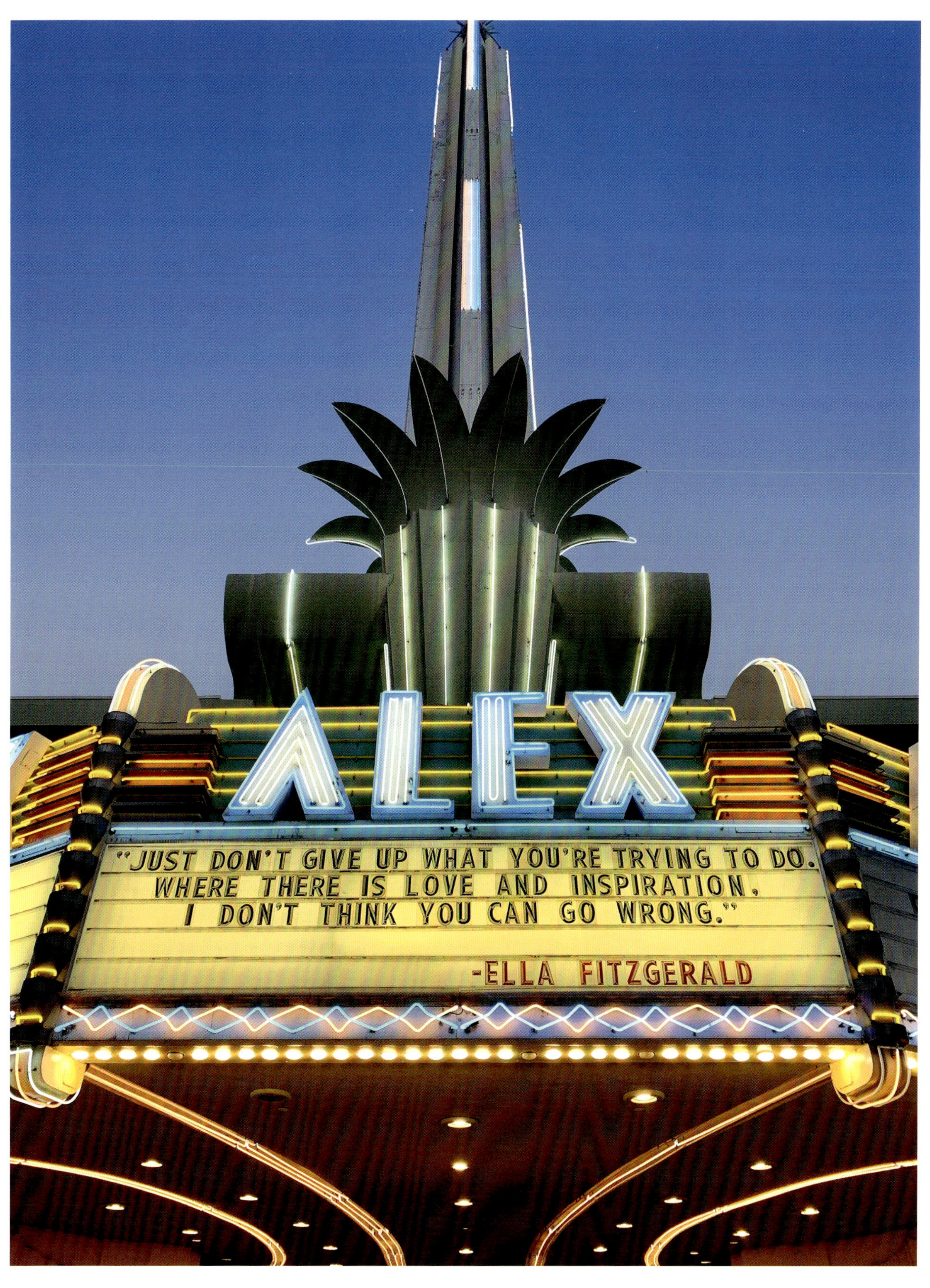

ALEX
"JUST DON'T GIVE UP WHAT YOU'RE TRYING TO DO.
WHERE THERE IS LOVE AND INSPIRATION,
I DON'T THINK YOU CAN GO WRONG."
-ELLA FITZGERALD

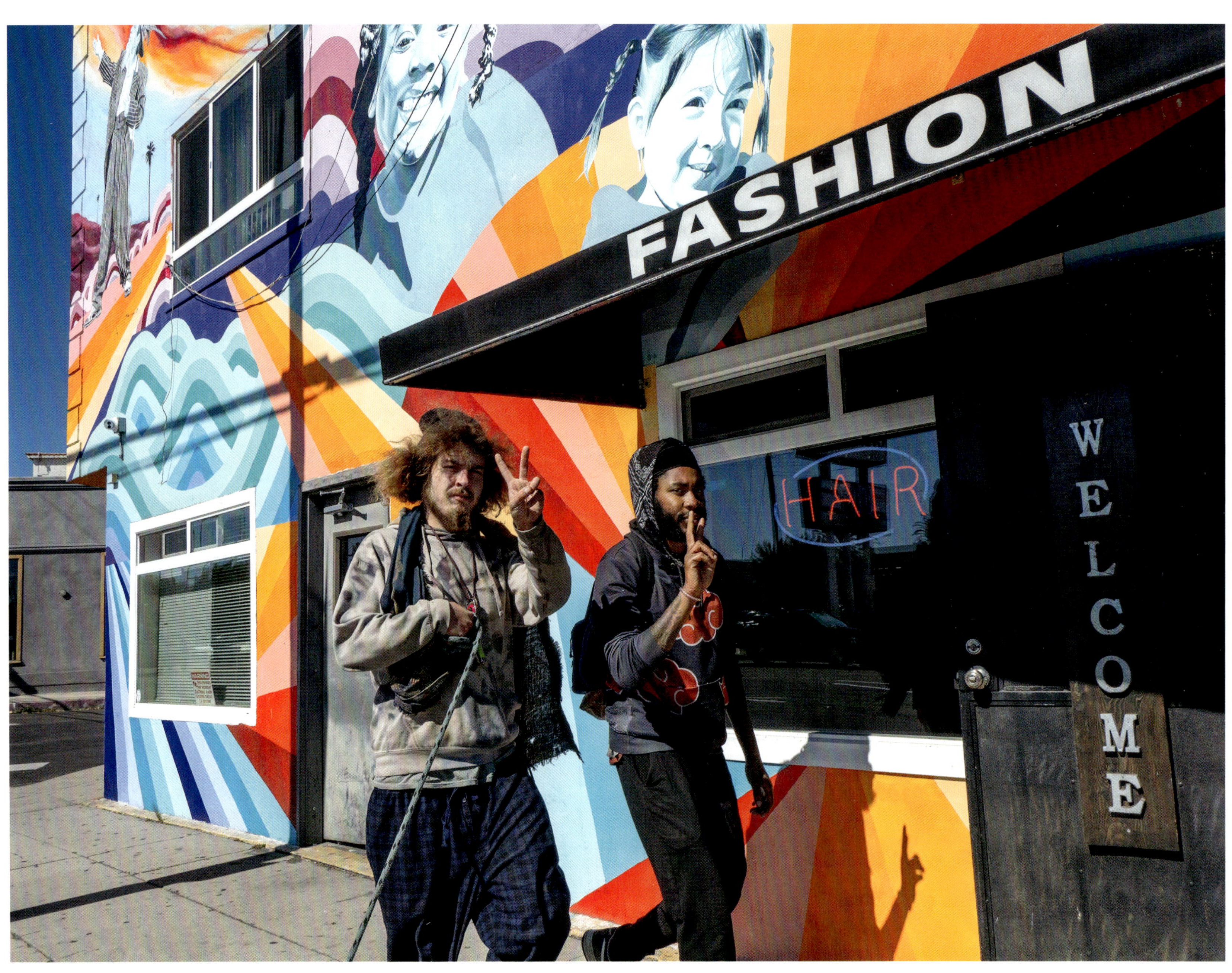

FASHION
HAIR
WELCOME

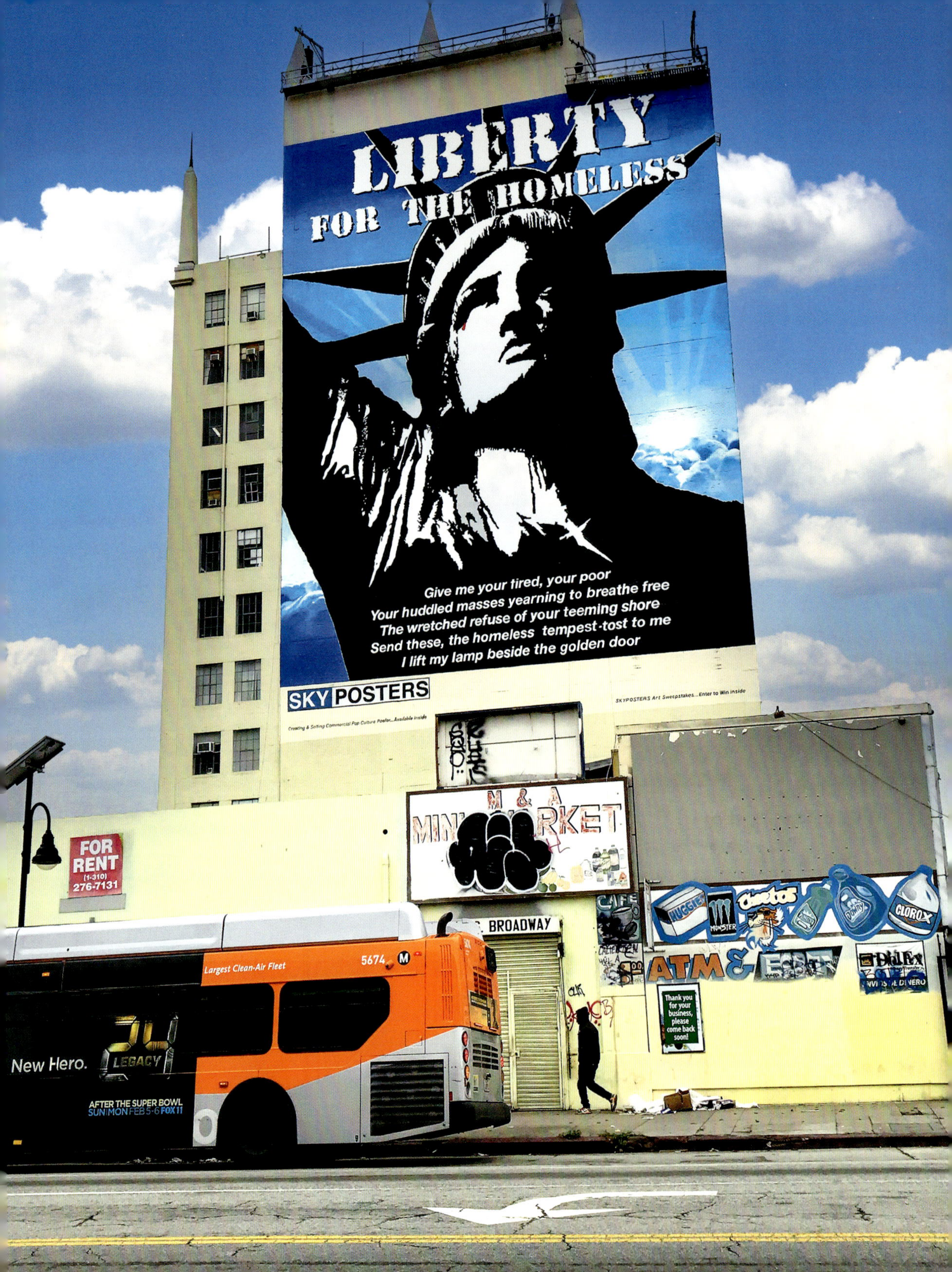

LIBERTY
FOR THE HOMELESS
Give me your tired, your poor
Your huddled masses yearning to breathe free
The wretched refuse of your teeming shore
Send these, the homeless tempest-tost to me
I lift my lamp beside the golden door
SKY POSTERS
Creating & Selling Commercial Pop Culture Poster...Available inside
SKYPOSTERS Art Sweepstakes...Enter to Win inside
FOR RENT
(1-310)
276-7131
M & A
MINI MARKET
CAFE
BROADWAY
ATM & E
Huggie
MONSTER
Cheetos
CLOROX
Thank you
for your
business,
please
come back
soon!
New Hero.
LEGACY
AFTER THE SUPER BOWL
SUN/MON FEB 5-6 FOX 11
Largest Clean-Air Fleet
5674
M

Afterword

A few years ago, when Susan Ressler invited me to write an essay for her first monograph, *Executive Order: Images of 1970s Corporate America*, I had the opportunity to revisit some truly wonderful photographs that I first became aware of about twenty years earlier while researching the National Endowment for the Arts (NEA) Photography Surveys for my book *Through the Lens of the City.* Ressler had participated in one of these surveys: the Los Angeles Documentary Project, a visual account of LA's cultural milieu made for the city's bicentennial in 1981. I enjoyed looking at her photographs again, those hip 1970s corporate office spaces that—while easy to appreciate as retro chic—at the time signaled a newly emergent postindustrial economy that would eventually lead to increasing economic inequities and the fraying of the American social contract.

Ressler's new collection of photographs may at first seem to depart from her earlier work: bright, vivid colors instead of black and white; exteriors (mostly) instead of the interiors of *Executive Order*; more spontaneous in feeling than the coolly composed shots from before. However, the two projects are linked by important underlying similarities—Ressler's keen observations of new economic realities are just as present here as they were in her earlier work, along with compositions that are more carefully crafted than they appear at first glance. Ressler's eye for detail and her steady hand are as strong now as ever, and her attention to how the American economy is inscribed on the built environment remains just as insightful.

This collection, *Dreaming California*, is—quite obviously—about California, Southern California to be more exact. But isn't Southern California what comes to mind when the word "California" is uttered? Other parts of California get more specific designations—Silicon Valley, the Bay Area, Big Sur, the Central Valley, the Sierra Nevada mountains, the redwood forests. "California" *is*, in contrast, Los Angeles and its environs—palm trees and beaches, highways and Hollywood.

So, yes, the photographs are ostensibly about California, but Ressler uses California as a metonym for the country as a whole. After all, what is California if not the epitome of the American Dream—endless sunshine, glamorous beauty, and boundless wealth? Think about how so many novels, movies, and television shows have featured young people heading west to "make it" in Hollywood; think about how much Beverly Hills and Malibu signify success in the popular imagination. It's as if the center of gravity of the United States is located in sunny Southern California—and all that it represents.

In his book *The American Dream: A Short History of an Idea that Shaped a Nation*, Jim Cullen sees in California the "apotheosis" of a particular version of the American Dream that he calls the "Dream of the Coast." This dream "does not celebrate the idea of hard work, instead enshrining effortless attainment as the

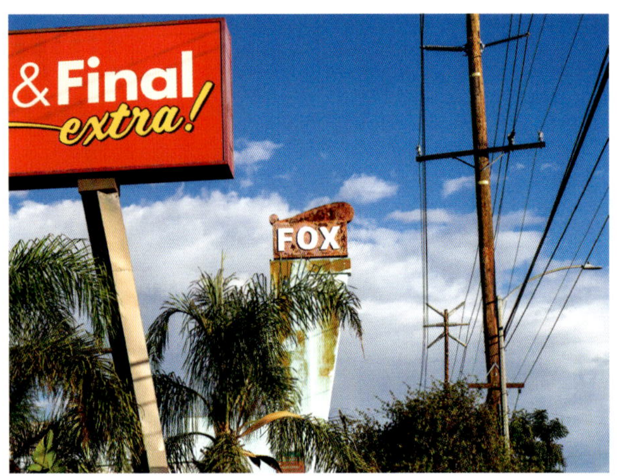

Fox Theater, Venice

essence of its appeal."[1] Cullen, an admitted fan of the decidedly un-Californian ethos of the Puritans, also admits that he "feel[s] the undertow" of the world of leisure that California represents: "I know that the culture of consumption that is finally at the heart of the Dream of the Coast preys on my worst impulses—greed, lust, gluttony. But every once in a while there is good to be seized among the goods."[2]

Look again through *Dreaming California* and you'll see Ressler's ability to see both the "goods" and the "good," with the two sometimes coexisting in a single frame. In some cases, the "good" is little more than a remnant of an older California found in the vernacular architecture that has yet to be erased from the landscape. For example, in the book's first section, "Sets, Scenes, Signs, Shops," the photograph *Fox Theater, Venice* shows the marquee of the former Fox movie theater. Rusting now, with faded peeling paint, its art deco curves and angles speak to a "golden age," not only of Hollywood movies, but of the very experience of moviegoing. It isn't hard to imagine the plush velvet chairs and polished brass fixtures of yesteryear. The marquee is placed in the center of the photograph, calling attention to itself as the most important detail, but there is another sign, a newer and brighter one that sits at the top left of the frame. Ressler has cropped out part of the sign so that all we see is "& Final *extra!*," an enigmatic message from the present. A modern marquee for a grocery store called "Smart and Final," the enthusiastic font and exclamation point portrayed in bold primary colors proclaim the shift in priorities from the older signage built for posterity. It feels impermanent, as though the store owners are freely admitting that if and when this location is no longer profitable, they'll close up shop and move on.

In addition, the words "final" and "extra" nod obliquely to the Fox Theater in its former glory when the marquee surely often read that whatever movie was being shown was in its final week, or that there was an unexpected bonus film, something extra for the audiences to enjoy. Then, too, there were the movie extras—those uncredited walk-on actors populating cocktail parties and sidewalks. Now, of course, the former movie theater has the walk-on role in the modern world, a faded movie star just barely hanging on in the industry.

Ressler's interest in juxtapositions and visual puns can be seen at the very opening of *Dreaming California*. The first photograph in the book shows a prim-faced blue-haired gorilla (is it a cartoon character that we're supposed to know?) painted on the side of a two-story building. The gorilla sits with legs crossed and

1 Jim Cullen, *The American Dream: A Short History of an Idea that Shaped a Nation* (Oxford: Oxford University Press, 2004), 160.
2 Cullen, *The American Dream*,178–179.

holds a dainty teacup in its right hand, the cup's painted saucer balanced on the fingertips of its left hand. In front, walking on a real-world sidewalk and wearing a real-world black hoodie is a thirtysomething man with facial scruff and tousled hair holding a real-world cup of coffee. The scene is immediate and ephemeral; two seconds later and the real man is gone while the prim-faced gorilla will forever be holding its teacup. (Well, at least until it is painted over or the building is torn down to make way for something newer and "better.")

The gorilla photograph is followed by two images showcasing the abundance of primary colors that Ressler employs in *Dreaming California*—and what dreamscapes these two photographs show! The first is a photograph of Legoland, taken from such an angle and position that it's difficult to get a sense of scale until one begins to notice spooled awnings and the string of outdoor café lights set against fake palm leaves and an artificial-looking (though very real) blue sky. The next photograph shows a group of people walking through the parking lot toward the "main entrance" of…what, exactly? A banner marquee tells them (and us) that they are going to "experience the incredible." We must rely on Ressler's caption to find out that this "incredible" place is nothing more than a pizza parlor.

After a few more pages of photographs, Ressler quotes from the French philosopher Jean Baudrillard. She is interested in Baudrillard's ideas of the simulacra (copies of things that have no original self) and hyperreality (the blurring of the real and the fake), and how those concepts are inscribed on California's commercial and entertainment zones. Baudrillard had a special fascination with Los Angeles and its environs. In *America,* he writes about Los Angeles: "The city was here before the freeway system, no doubt, but it now looks as though the metropolis has been actually built around this arterial network. It is the same with American reality. It was there before the screen was invented, but everything about the way it is today suggests it was invented with the screen in mind, that it is the refraction of a giant screen."[3] This is hyperreality at work.

Ressler is interested in more than simulacra and hyperreality, however, and her juxtapositions reveal more than the built environment. One of the more compelling pairs of photographs in the book is found in the "Hoods" section. In the penultimate photograph, *"Judgement Free," Carson*, a portly man is seen walking to the entrance of a Planet Fitness, gym bag in hand. A sign in the gym's window proclaims it to be a "judgement free zone," which I think is great. No one should be judged when going to the gym, even though so many other photographs in this collection show so many other people consumed with body image. As Baudrillard writes, "This omnipresent cult of the body is extraordinary. It is the only object on which everyone is made to concentrate, not as a source of pleasure, but as an object of frantic concern, in the obsessive fear of failure or substandard performance, a sign and an anticipation of death, that death to which no one can any longer give a meaning, but which everyone knows has at all times to be prevented."[4]

---

3 Jean Baudrillard, *America* (Brooklyn: Verso, 1988), 57.
4 Baudrillard, *America*, 35.

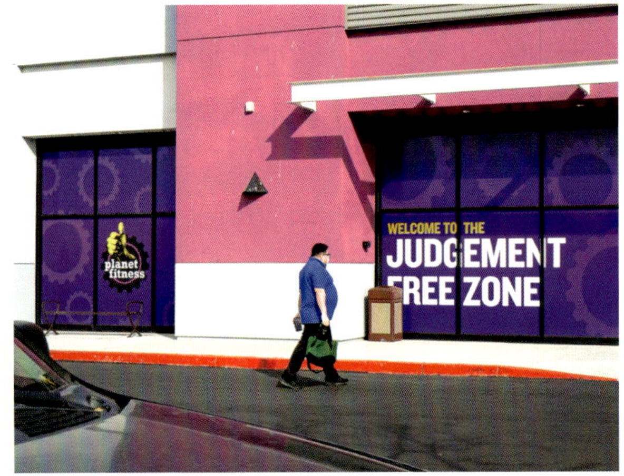

"Judgement Free," Carson

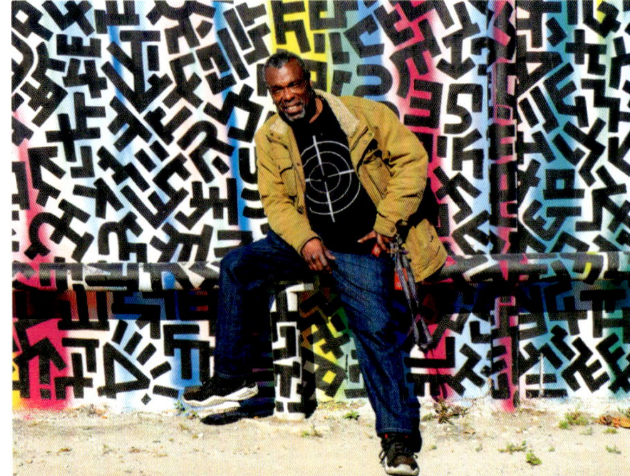

James behind Lincoln Blvd., Venice

The inevitability of death takes shape in a different way in the photograph on the facing page, *James behind Lincoln Blvd., Venice*, that shows an African American man sitting on a pipe next to a wall covered in Keith Haring–inspired public art. James wears blue jeans and an unzipped brown canvas jacket, and the T-shirt underneath shows a gun scope bullseye, dead center on his chest. Far from being in a judgement-free zone, James appears to have been judged, sentenced, and about to be executed. It is hard not to view this photograph other than in a racial context—of so many Black men being killed in the United States due largely to the fact that they are Black.

Ressler shows us that among the glitz and glamor (the "goods") of Southern California, real humans engage in real struggles that belie the California dream. The final photograph in this collection—seen on the facing page to this essay—shows a billboard featuring a close-up of the Statue of Liberty. The headline reads, "Liberty for the Homeless" in all capital letters in a stencil-like font. The billboard sits above an out-of-business minimart and debris-strewn sidewalk. This is clearly an economically distressed part of the city, and the very fact of the sign draws attention to the crisis of homelessness, not just in Los Angeles but in the United States more generally. The sign itself pulls both sides of the country together—New York to Los Angeles—a visual reminder that Ressler is interested not just in California but in the country as a whole.

It's a fitting photograph to close Ressler's book, not just because it serves as a reminder that somebody has to pay the price of the California dream, but also because it points to a different project Ressler had in mind before she started on this one. She wanted to photograph in New York City in a project that she was going to call *American Photographs*. She came to realize, however, that the American West better suits her eye and that the American West is—as Baudrillard suggests—perhaps even more American than the American east.

Calling a photography project "American Photographs" asks us to consider the first project to go by that name—Walker Evans's 1938 book and exhibition of that title at the Museum of Modern Art, the first solo exhibit of photographs ever held there. Evans remains a touchstone for anyone interested in American vernacular landscapes, his influence filtering down through the decades. One famous Evans photograph from his *American Photographs* shows part of the interior of a coal miner's house in West Virginia. Taken in 1935, the image reveals the juxtapositions between vernacular culture and a spreading mass culture that Evans was interested in. The main subject of the photograph seems to be a rocking chair that is clearly handmade, the bent and twisting branches that make up the chair's back revealing both craftsmanship and a certain jitteriness of form that would be smoothed out if machine manufactured. Hanging on the wall behind the chair is a Coca-Cola advertisement featuring a portly Santa Claus, a corporate-designed and manufactured piece of American culture that stands in stark contrast to the chair.

It would be a stretch to say that Ressler has a similar photograph in her book, but she does have one that similarly juxtaposes the local and vernacular with a Christmas-themed corporate advertisement. Titled *"Hustler," Redondo Beach*, it is one of the older photographs in the book, made in 2010. Ressler shows a flower shop called Magical Blooms, a midcentury single-story stone-clad shop set along the Pacific Coast Highway in Redondo Beach. Taken just after Christmas Eve, the exterior of the shop is festooned with holiday lights that glow red against an evening sky. The shop exudes a sense of the local; one can imagine that it has sat in this location for decades serving as a community anchor for weddings and proms, date nights and funerals. Its simplicity and sturdiness is an analog to the rocking chair in Evans's image.

The analog to the Santa Claus Coca-Cola advertisement in this photograph is a billboard that towers above the florist shop. The billboard promotes the Hustler Casino and, given the time of year that the photograph was made, it features a scantily clad woman in a Santa hat and a hint of Santa's fur collar draped over her otherwise bare upper body. It is the quintessence of ephemerality, a seasonal poster for a company whose namesake (*Hustler* magazine) was already well past its prime when the photograph was taken. Curious to know if the Hustler Casino was still in business in 2022, I did a quick Google search. It is—a slightly sleazy caricature of a caricature. I also did a search on Google Maps to see if Magical Blooms is still around, and it is, too. There is still a billboard towering above it today, but in the Google view the Hustler Casino sign has been replaced by an advertisement for Exquisite Aesthetics, an "aesthetics tattoo studio" providing "permanent cosmetics" for bodily improvements—hyperreality made flesh. (Baudrillard would understand.)

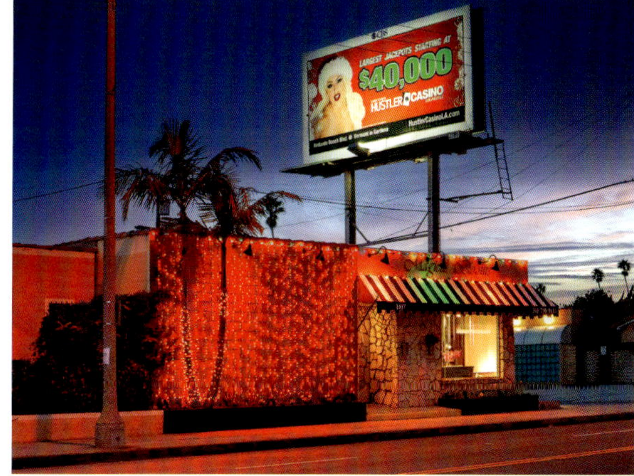

"Hustler," Redondo Beach

The billboard reminds us that Los Angeles is famously known as a city of automobiles. In *America*, Baudrillard devotes an entire section to "Los Angeles Freeways," in which he writes, "the freeways do not de-nature the city or the landscape; they simply pass through it and unravel it without altering the desert character of this particular metropolis."[5] Many photographers latch onto this perspective in their work. For example, Robbert Flick (another participant in the Los Angeles Documentary Survey Project where I first encountered Ressler's images) spent decades taking photographs from the perspective of a moving car. In a 1996 interview with Flick, the urban geographer Michael Dear, enthused about Flick's approach, exclaimed: "Robbert, the first time I saw your work, I immediately thought, 'That's it, that's Los Angeles!' That's exactly how I see this city. From the street, and at speed, it's a punctual, linear experience. . . . The city is perceived essentially as an interrupted sequence."[6]

Ressler has taken a different approach in this collection. Though fully aware of the prominence of highways and streets, these photographs feel as though she is moving at a slower pace. Ressler photographs from sidewalks and entryways, plazas and parking lots, and sometimes from inside her parked car; her photographs do not show any hectic blurring as though she was snapping pics while driving. In fact, there are surprisingly few cars to be seen in this book, and the majority of those are parked in lots or alongside curbs.

Ressler approaches California's car culture from a more oblique angle; instead of focusing on the cars themselves, she focuses on the billboards and signs that people see through their windshields, and she shows us the places where the cars take people. People have to get out of their cars at some point, and these images show us many of the places where they do so—shopping malls and pizza parlors, flea markets and flower shops, office parks and exurban homes. Ressler is interested in showing us where those freeways and streets take people, because ultimately it is people that she is interested in—the "human cost" (as she writes) of the hyperreal California dreamscape.

Ressler chose to name this collection *Dreaming California* in response to the classic counterculture song "California Dreamin'" by the Mamas and the Papas. Recorded in 1965, the song has become embedded in American popular culture and was recently used in the contemporary hit Netflix show *Stranger Things*, a science-fiction horror series set in the 1980s, the decade in which the postindustrial economy that Ressler documented in *Executive Order* consolidated itself under the banner of Reaganomics. Pulling things full circle, in the opening to *Dreaming California*, Ressler photographs inside the *Stranger Things*–themed store in the Americana at Brand mall in Glendale.

The mall itself was built to replicate an industrial-era city, with a "hodgepodge of design styles—Art Deco, Art Nouveau, Mediterranean, Classical and many more."[7] It is a simulacrum. The decades and set-

---

5 Baudrillard, *America*, 55.

6 Michael J. Dear, Eric Shockman, and Greg Hise, eds., *Rethinking Los Angeles* (Thousand Oaks: Sage Publications, 1996), 17.

7 Emili Vesilind, "Americana: The Beautiful?," *Los Angeles Times*, April 27, 2009.

tings blend and blur here—a modern construction with the facade of an early twentieth-century city center housing a store selling Netflix merchandise based on a 1980s TV show set in small-town Indiana. A store that fashions itself as an "experience" where shoppers can take photographs for their social media accounts so that they appear as if they are actors in a fictional TV fantasy. Hyperreality to the extreme.

What is one to make of all of this? How does one find their footing in this American hyperreality? What Ressler points to is the human cost of those individuals left jobless and homeless in the ongoing economic dislocations of the modern economy, the people who make their homes on the streets of Southern California because at least the weather there is better than the weather in New York or Indiana, and if homeless, they might not freeze to death.

But it is also the human cost of pursuing such a fever dream to the exclusion of more mundane realities, such as the simple pleasure of sipping a cup of coffee while walking along the sidewalk. In his book about the American Dream, Cullen points out that the Dream, though at the very core of the American experience, can and does change over time as Americans recalibrate what matters most. Perhaps what Ressler shows us in *Dreaming California* is that we are nearing the endpoint of the "Dream of the Coast," beyond which something new (dare we wish for something more humane?) might emerge.

—Mark Rice

Contributors

Larry Lytle is a noted author, artist, curator, and educator who hails from Los Angeles, California. Lytle is a contributing writer for *Black & White* magazine. During the past decade, his essays have discussed photographers Will Connell, Marcia Resnick, Robbert Flick, Thomas Barrow, Jerry McMillan, Ann Parker, and Susan Ressler, among others. He has also written about vernacular photography, collecting tintypes, and uncovering the lost photographs of the movie effects wizard Ken Strickfaden. Most notably, Lytle is known for his scholarship and writing on the life and work of American photographer William Mortensen, for whom Lytle contributed to the Center for Creative Photography's 1999 acclaimed book *William Mortensen: A Revival*. In 2014 Lytle co-edited and wrote biographical essays for *American Grotesque: The Life and Art of William Mortensen* and *The Command to Look: A Master Photographer's Method for Controlling the Human Gaze*, both published by Feral House. Lytle curated an exhibition of Mortensen's work at the Laguna Art Museum in the fall of 2022. Lytle has taught photography at the Otis Evening College of Art and Design, Los Angeles, and at California State University Channel Islands, Camarillo, where he developed the photography curriculum and has been teaching from 2003 to the present.

Mark Rice is an award-winning author and professor of American Studies at St. John Fisher University near Rochester, New York. He has published two books and contributed essays on photography and visual culture to scholarly journals such as *History of Photography, American Quarterly, Exposure,* and *Reviews in American History.* Rice's first book, *Through the Lens of the City: NEA Photography Surveys of the 1970s* (University Press of Mississippi, 2005), examined an important but previously overlooked endeavor to photograph American cities during the bicentennial era. Administered by the National Endowment for the Arts from 1976 to 1981, these surveys included the Los Angeles Documentary Project, possibly the most significant record of the Los Angeles area from that time period. Rice's second book, *Dean Worcester's Fantasy Islands: Photography, Film, and the Colonial Philippines* (University of Michigan Press, 2014, and Ateneo de Manila University Press, 2015) discussed the use of photography to promote an American imperial agenda in the Philippines in the early years of the twentieth century. It won the Gintong Aklat (Golden Book) Award for the social sciences, one of the most prestigious publishing prizes in the Philippines, and was also a finalist for the Philippine National Book Award in History. Rice contributed the afterword to Susan Ressler's first monograph, *Executive Order.*